The

WILLIAM HOWARD
TAFT
Presidency

AMERICAN PRESIDENCY SERIES

Clifford S. Griffin, Donald R. McCoy, and Homer E. Socolofsky, Founding Editors

George Washington, Forrest McDonald
John Adams, Ralph Adams Brown
Thomas Jefferson, Forrest McDonald
James Madison, Robert Allen Rutland
James Monroe, Noble E. Cunningham Jr.
John Quincy Adams, Mary W. M. Hargreaves
Andrew Jackson, Donald B. Cole
Martin Van Buren, Major L. Wilson
William Henry Harrison & John Tyler, Norma Lois Peterson
James K. Polk, Paul H. Bergeron
Zachary Taylor & Millard Fillmore, Elbert B. Smith
Franklin Pierce, Larry Gara
James Buchanan, Elbert B. Smith
Abraham Lincoln, Phillip Shaw Paludan
Andrew Johnson, Albert Castel
Rutherford B. Hayes, Ari Hoogenboom
James A. Garfield & Chester A. Arthur, Justus D. Doenecke
Grover Cleveland, Richard E. Welch Jr.
Benjamin Harrison, Homer B. Socolofsky & Allan B. Spetter
William McKinley, Lewis L. Gould
Theodore Roosevelt, Lewis L. Gould
Woodrow Wilson, Kendrick A. Clements
Warren G. Harding, Eugene P. Trani & David L. Wilson
Calvin Coolidge, Robert H. Ferrell
Herbert C. Hoover, Martin L. Fausold
Harry S. Truman, Donald R. McCoy
Dwight D. Eisenhower, Chester J. Pach Jr. & Elmo Richardson
John F. Kennedy, Second Edition, Revised, James N. Giglio
Lyndon B. Johnson, Vaughn Davis Bornet
Richard Nixon, Melvin Small
Gerald R. Ford, John Robert Greene
James Earl Carter Jr., Burton I. Kaufman
George Bush, John Robert Greene

The

WILLIAM HOWARD
TAFT

Presidency

Lewis L. Gould

UNIVERSITY PRESS OF KANSAS

Published by the University Press of Kansas (Lawrence, Kansas 66045),
which was organized by the Kansas Board of Regents and is
operated and funded by Emporia State University, Fort Hays State University,
Kansas State University, Pittsburg State University, the University of Kansas,
and Wichita State University

Library of Congress Cataloging-in-Publication Data

Gould, Lewis L.
The William Howard Taft presidency / Lewis L. Gould.
p. cm. — (American presidency series)
Includes bibliographical references and index.
ISBN 978-0-7006-1674-9 (cloth : alk. paper)
1. United States—Politics and government—1909–1913.
2. Taft, William H. (William Howard), 1857–1930. I. Title.
E761.G68 2009
973.91'2092—dc22
2009019219

British Library Cataloguing-in-Publication Data is available.

Printed in the United States of America

10 9 8 7 6 5 4 3 2 1

The paper used in this publication is recycled and contains 30 percent
postconsumer waste. It is acid free and meets the minimum requirements of the
American National Standard for Permanence of Paper for Printed Library Materials Z39.48-1992.

CONTENTS

CONTENTS

PUBLISHER'S NOTE

The founding editors—Donald R. McCoy, Clifford S. Griffin, and Homer E. Socolofsky, now all deceased—launched their American Presidency Series to present scholars and the general reading public with interesting, well-researched assessments of the various presidential administrations. They helped choose able historians to write interpretive surveys that would cover the broad ground between biographies, specialized monographs, and journalistic accounts. Each of the thirty-five series volumes published to date, therefore, is a comprehensive work that draws on both original sources and pertinent secondary literature, yet leaves room for the author's own analysis and interpretation.

The University Press of Kansas published the very first series volume, *The Presidency of William Howard Taft*, by Paolo E. Coletta, on 4 April 1973. After its thirty-six-plus years as a respected source for understanding Taft's administration, we are replacing Coletta's work with this new study by Lewis L. Gould, who has also contributed two other series volumes, *The Presidency of William McKinley* and *The Presidency of Theodore Roosevelt*. This change reflects our plan to refresh volumes in the American Presidency Series as unused source material and new interpretations come to light. Also indicative of this aim are the three revised editions that have previously appeared: *The Presidency of Dwight D. Eisenhower* (1991), *The Presidency of John F. Kennedy* (2006), and *The Presidency of James Earl Carter, Jr.* (2006).

—*May 2009*

FOREWORD

The aim of the American Presidency Series is to present historians and the general reading public with interesting, scholarly assessments of the various presidential administrations. These interpretive surveys are intended to cover the broad ground between biographies, specialized monographs, and journalistic accounts. As such, each is a comprehensive work that draws on original sources and pertinent secondary literature, yet leaves room for the author's own analysis and interpretation.

Volumes in the series present the data essential to understanding the administration under consideration. Particularly, each book treats the then-current problems facing the United States and its people and how the president and his associates felt about, thought about, and worked to cope with these problems. Attention is given to how the office developed and operated during the president's tenure. Equally important is consideration of the vital relationships among the president, his staff, the executive officers, Congress, foreign representatives, the judiciary, state officials, the public, political parties, the press, and influential private citizens. The series is also concerned with how this unique American institution—the presidency—was viewed by the presidents, and with what results.

All this is set, insofar as possible, in the context not only of contemporary politics but also of economics, international relations, law, morals, public administration, religion, and thought. Such a broad approach is necessary for understanding because a presidential administration is more than the elected and appointed officers composing it; its work so often reflects the major problems, anxieties, and glories of the nation. In short, the authors in this series strive to recount and evaluate the record of each administration and to identify its distinctiveness and relationships to the past, its own time, and the future.

The General Editors

PREFACE

In 1925, Chief Justice William Howard Taft wrote to a friend that "in my present life I don't remember that I ever was president." Historians and political scientists have followed Taft's precedent and relegated the four years that he spent in the White House to a kind of intellectual limbo. The standard biography of Taft by Henry F. Pringle, published in 1939, is now seven decades old. Two studies of his presidency by Paolo Coletta and Donald F. Anderson were published in 1973. A second interpretive biography by Judith Icke Anderson came out in 1981. An interesting volume on Taft and automobiles in the White House years published in 2003 rounds out the existing literature on this president and his administration.

Part of Taft's problem is related to his bad luck in being wedged between Theodore Roosevelt and Woodrow Wilson, two of the most written-about presidents in American history. As a one-term chief executive who did not win reelection in 1912, Taft has seemed a clear presidential failure. No major foreign policy crises marked his time in office. Old-fashioned issues such as the protective tariff added to the sense that Taft was a kind of musty leader of the nation whose conservatism seemed out of date in comparison with presidential activism.

Another problem blocking inquiry into Taft's presidency grew out of the nature of his personal papers. Available on microfilm from the Library of Congress since 1972, the Taft Papers are in one sense very easy to use. The president's letter books contain typed copies of his outgoing mail. On twenty-one reels of microfilm are readily available documents of what Taft thought and wrote. For Henry F. Pringle and the writers who followed him, surveying the letter books constituted research in the Taft Papers.

Looking at the mail the president received presented more daunting problems. The case file system that the White House adopted for storing these records meant that a researcher had to go through numerous individual reels of microfilm to get a comprehensive picture of what the president was learning from his correspondents. On the whole, that was not a course that Taft biographers have pursued. Although this book has not by any means exhausted the sources that are in the case files, I have endeavored to look into these records in shaping the narrative. I believe that the discussion of such issues as Taft's controversial speech at Winona, Minnesota, on 17 September 1909 is more complete as a result. The same is true for such topics as the Payne–Aldrich tariff of 1909, the congressional session of 1910, and Canadian reciprocity in 1911.

Although researchers have made limited review of Taft's papers, they have neglected collateral manuscript collections that are central to an evaluation of this president. This volume is the first on Taft's presidency to use the papers of Charles D. Hilles at Yale University. Hilles was Taft's secretary from 1911 to 1912, and his papers are indispensable for understanding the campaign for the Republican presidential nomination in 1912. The papers of Taft's cabinet members, such as Charles Nagel, Richard A. Ballinger, and Henry L. Stimson, are also used for the first time in a study of Taft in the White House.

Because of Taft's complex relationship with Congress, an examination of the manuscripts of his friends and enemies on Capitol Hill is crucial. Yet that simple research strategy has not been followed until this narrative was written. Accounts of the Payne–Aldrich tariff have for years relied on the outdated research of George Mowry without consulting the full range of legislators and interest groups participating in that pivotal measure. This book assembles information from such diverse sources as the records of lobbyists for the shoe and leather industry to provide a context for Taft's choices in this episode.

As leader of the Republicans, Taft encountered problems in keeping progressives and conservatives in harmony. A review of the manuscripts from both factions illustrates, as no previous treatment of Taft in this period has done, the complexity of the choices that the president dealt with as the director of Republican fortunes. Similarly, information from British diplomatic records and personal papers in the United Kingdom supply valuable transatlantic insights about Taft in office. A fuller picture of Taft as president emerges once the broader range of documentary evidence is considered.

Surveying these sources does not, of course, turn Taft into a presidential success story. His single term in office led to a sweeping election defeat at the hands of both Theodore Roosevelt and Woodrow Wilson in 1912. Taft carried only two states (Vermont and Utah) and finished last in the popular vote among the three major candidates. Such a dramatic change from his substantial victory in 1908 has led historians to view Taft's administration as a failure almost from the start of his presidency. A sense of impending political doom hangs over most accounts of Taft's years in office.

In this book, I argue that Taft, although not an outstanding chief executive, was a creditable president who confronted an unfavorable political climate for his party and the challenge of Theodore Roosevelt as an alternative leader of the Republicans. Within those important constraints, Taft was a competent chief executive who, as he argued in 1912, had kept the nation out of war, presided over a prosperous economy, and observed the constitutional limits of his office. Although these accomplishments do not enable him to rise above the middle level of all presidents, they seem more positive in light of the performance of some of his modern successors who accomplished few of the specific tangible achievements that Taft enumerated.

Yet Taft came into office with a sense of promise arising from his prepresidential career and his native talents. Although he had shown executive ability in the Philippines and the War Department from 1900 to 1908, he had done so as a subordinate for William McKinley and Theodore Roosevelt. When it came time to make presidential decisions on his own, Taft fell back on his knowledge of the law and his years as a federal appeals court judge in Ohio from 1892 to 1900. On issue after issue, whether it was the tariff, conservation, antitrust, or foreign affairs, Taft brought a judicial temperament to the Oval Office. He consulted few people, weighed his options in isolation, and rendered political judgments as he had once delivered verdicts.

At a time when Theodore Roosevelt had conditioned the American people to expect controversy and excitement from their president, Taft's reversion to a judicial model of decision making fell flat. A conservative man whom Roosevelt had pulled toward reform, Taft found himself in fundamental disagreement with his predecessor's expansive interpretation of presidential prerogatives. Instead of carrying forward the program of progressivism that Roosevelt had advocated, Taft muted the reform impulse and in time came to disagree with most of its practical applications. As the president's conservatism surfaced, Roosevelt and his allies moved away from their one-time ally. By 1912, the ideological divide in the Republican ranks and the differences between Taft and Roosevelt over regulation split the party and ensured the president's defeat.

Although he was neither successful in office nor a president who faced major crises, Taft remains an interesting chief executive. He was more systematic than Roosevelt and more organized than Woodrow Wilson. The voluminous paper trail that he left enables historians to understand in depth how the Taft presidency worked. Looking back at that calmer time in American history, a more deliberate examination of the inner workings of a one-term administration becomes feasible. More than most presidents, William Howard Taft let posterity know what he thought and why he acted as he did. In that respect, his four years in the White House are instructive and rewarding to evaluate.

The research for this book has been carried on for more than four decades. I owe special thanks to the staff of the Manuscripts Room of the Library of Congress who made my visits there between 1968 and 1990 so productive. Librarians at Yale University facilitated research in the Charles D. Hilles Papers in the 1960s and 1970s. Gene Gressley, then at the University of Wyoming, introduced me to the Francis E. Warren Papers, which proved important for understanding the Payne–Aldrich tariff and its legislative history. Don Carleton at the Dolph Briscoe Center for American History at the University of Texas at Austin facilitated an early look at the Leroy Vernon Papers. Richard Holland of the Perry-Castaneda Library at the University of Texas helped acquire many of the manuscript collections on microfilm that were used in writing this volume.

I owe thanks for research assistance over the past several years to Gregory Kupsky, Patricia Schaub, and Jeremy Young. Former students who provided research and aid in years past include Bill Childs, the late Sara Graham, John Leffler, and Craig Roell. Jason dePreaux helped me in a significant manner with gathering materials from the microfilm edition of the Taft Papers at the University of Texas at Austin. Stacy Cordery generously shared her findings from the Mabel Boardman Papers, the Alice Longworth diaries, and other collections she saw in her wide-ranging research. With characteristic kindness, Kristie Miller helped obtain important documents from the Library of Congress for me. The late Herbert F. Margulies and I corresponded for a quarter of a century about our mutual interest in Taft and the issues of his presidency. I cherish the memory of that epistolary friendship that grew out of lunches as we researched at the Massachusetts Historical Society during the summer of 1972.

Ron Yam of Amtech Computers in Austin, Texas, put his vast expertise at my disposal when a nasty virus threatened my files during December 2008. Bruce Schulman provided a very helpful reader's report for the University Press of Kansas, and Brian Balogh kindly shared with me the proof of his book *A Government Out of Sight: The Mystery of National Authority in Nineteenth-Century America* as I revised the manuscript.

Charles Calhoun of East Carolina University read the entire manuscript with close editorial attention. While catching slips and errors, he also kept my focus on the larger themes of the endeavor. John Morton Blum encouraged the writing of this book, shared with me his unparalleled knowledge of the Roosevelt–Taft era, and provided a stimulating critique of each chapter. I have learned much from him since I first sat in his seminar in the early 1960s.

Karen Gould has been listening to tales of Taft and other Progressive Era politicians for years with unwavering patience and understanding. This book could not have been written without her thoughtfulness, affection, and courageous example.

The errors of fact and interpretation that remain after all this help from so many kind and good people are my responsibility alone.

The
WILLIAM HOWARD
TAFT
Presidency

1

★ ★ ★ ★ ★

"THE MAN OF THE HOUR" IN 1908

Like many of Theodore Roosevelt's ideas, it seemed good at the time he thought of it. Since William Howard Taft would succeed him as president on 4 March 1909, Roosevelt invited the president-elect and Mrs. Taft to spend the night of 3 March at the White House before the inauguration. Roosevelt did not consult his wife before informing the Tafts. In the afternoon, with the weather in Washington turning ever colder and a blizzard in prospect, William Howard Taft and Helen Herron Taft arrived just before dinner was served.

The social event proved awkward and difficult. Roosevelt, as he usually did, dominated the conversation. Neither the incoming president nor his wife felt at ease. Edith Roosevelt and Helen Taft were not close; tensions between them had already appeared. Four years later, when Taft, defeated after one term, thought about having Woodrow Wilson and his wife stay over on 3–4 March 1913, Mrs. Taft said no. "Nellie is dead set against it because of her memory of the Roosevelt dinner to us," Taft told their friend Mabel Boardman. "You were at that funeral."[1]

That cold inauguration day, the outward appearance was that power was passing from Theodore Roosevelt to the man closest to him in friendship and politics. A happy Roosevelt believed on Election Day, 3 November 1908, that he had picked someone who shared his views and values in domestic and foreign policy. As the British ambassador noted after a chat with the outgoing president, "he dwelt, in talking a little politics, upon his confidence that Taft would be as eager as he had been to be on the most cordial terms of common understanding and cooperation with England."[2]

As the White House dinner revealed, however, the new president had a different temperament from Roosevelt. More important, Taft did not view either politics or the presidency as his predecessor did. On that cold night in March 1909, sleeping in the Blue Bedroom, which had once been the cabinet room of Abraham Lincoln where the Emancipation Proclamation had been signed, Helen Taft found it "strange to spend my first night in the White House surrounded by such ghosts." No record remains of what William Howard Taft thought as the wind howled and the ice-heavy branches snapped. Perhaps his memories turned to how he had become the president of the United States, ready to assume the duties of the office the next day at noon.[3]

He was born on 15 September 1857 in Cincinnati, Ohio, a cosmopolitan city whose relaxed ethos would shape his early life. His father, Alphonso Taft, was the last attorney general for Ulysses S. Grant and became American minister to Austria-Hungary during the administration of Chester Alan Arthur. Alphonso Taft's first wife had died after the couple had three sons. He then married Louise Torrey in 1853. William was the couple's oldest surviving child (a son had died in infancy) and had two brothers, Henry Waters Taft and Horace Dutton Taft, and a sister, Frances Louise "Fanny" Taft. Within the family, William's half-brother, Charles Phelps Taft, a wealthy newspaper publisher in Cincinnati, would have the largest impact on his life.[4]

From childhood, William Howard Taft was a large boy who became an even heavier man. He struggled with his weight all of his life. A variety of explanations have been offered for his obesity as an adult, including frustration with the sexual side of his own marriage and tension arising from his desire to please others; or perhaps there was a physiological cause. Athletic and graceful despite his bulk, William was a good dancer with a pleasing, friendly manner. His parents reared him in the Unitarian faith, and he was throughout his life tolerant of the religious values of others. Carefully kept out of public view were his doubts about the divinity of Jesus. He seemed, like his father, to be headed for a career in law.[5]

That life path took him first to Yale College with the class of 1878, where he found an emotional link to his fellow Old Blues that remained throughout his life. A talented student, he finished second in his class and was elected to the secret society of Skull and Bones. His salutatory oration, delivered in Latin, on "The Professional and Political Prospects of a College Graduate," was, according to his biographer, "not a distinguished effort." The press at the time was more kind. The Chicago *Inter Ocean* called it "a searching examination of the political errors and a condemnation of the evils in American public life."[6]

After four years in New Haven, Taft studied at the Cincinnati Law School and was admitted to the Ohio bar in 1881. During the 1880s Taft held such appointed offices as collector of internal revenue for the administration of Chester Alan Arthur and judge of the Ohio superior court, a post he received from Governor Joseph B. Foraker. He ran for an elected position only once, in 1888, for that of a sitting judge. "Like every well-trained Ohio man," Taft commented twenty years later, "I always had my plate the right side up when offices were falling."[7]

In 1886, Taft married Helen "Nellie" Herron, a woman from a prominent Cincinnati family. His new wife was ambitious and determined; she hoped one day to become first lady. She prodded and pushed her husband to excel in public life. Passionately attached to Nellie, who bore him three children, Taft wanted to please her even to the point of deferring his preference for the judiciary over other government posts. Yet an overemphasis on Mrs. Taft's role in her husband's political career is misleading. William Howard Taft had a desire to succeed on his own, a trait that he kept hidden behind a veil of disinterest in his own upward progress.[8]

Benjamin Harrison named Taft solicitor general early in 1890. In Washington he met Theodore Roosevelt, and their friendship began. After two years representing the government in court, Taft was named to the Federal Court of Appeals in the Sixth District, which covered the states of Ohio, Kentucky, Michigan, and Tennessee. He stayed there for the next eight years. In some of his most controversial decisions from the bench, he ruled against labor unions where an injunction against strikers had been sought. These rulings amid the economic protests of the 1890s gave the jurist a reputation as antilabor. Taft's dealings with organized labor would be difficult and distant from that point through his presidency. By the early months of 1900, Taft had settled into the routine of a federal judge with the hope that the administration of William McKinley, a fellow Ohioan, might elevate him to the United States Supreme Court.

His experience on the bench was crucial in forming Taft's political vision. He disliked the rough and tumble of partisanship; he much preferred the quiet of the study. The image of the dispassionate jurist weighing the competing arguments of the litigants embodied how he saw the governing process. Elections, campaigning, and pressing the flesh were to him necessary evils in a democratic society, but Taft thought that he was a gregarious creature who loved humanity. However, such traits were for the golf course or the salon or the friendly conversation. When it came time to make policy, the ethos of the jurist dominated.

An unexpected summons from President McKinley took Taft's life in a new direction. The president had talked with the judge in November 1899. McKinley concluded that Taft was "just the man for the Philippines." The administration was creating a new commission to establish civil government in the islands acquired from Spain in 1899. The new American possession had encountered a native insurrection against colonial rule. The military, led by General Arthur MacArthur, did not seem to the president to be the long-range answer to pacifying the islands.[9]

A telegram asked Taft to come to Washington. In his meeting with McKinley in January 1900, Taft protested that he had opposed the acquisition of the islands and that the president should choose someone else. McKinley answered: "We've got them. What I want you to do now is to go there and establish civil government." Persuaded by Secretary of War Elihu Root and the pleas of others close to McKinley, Taft agreed to take the post. Mrs. Taft was enthusiastic about the possibilities for advancement that the Philippines posed.[10]

The Philippine experience put Taft into the national political spotlight. He displayed impressive executive talents in bringing civil government to the islands and in treating the inhabitants with respect and dignity. He resolved through patient negotiation in the Philippines and with the Vatican the issue of lands held by Catholic friars in the archipelago. McKinley made him governor general of the Philippines in 1901. Roosevelt wanted to appoint him to the Supreme Court in 1902, but Taft declined on the grounds that his work in the islands was not yet completed. When the Filipinos protested that Taft was needed to finish his task, Roosevelt reluctantly agreed.[11]

A few months later, Elihu Root told the president that he would relinquish the cabinet post as secretary of war in the fall of 1903. Roosevelt approached Taft about taking the war portfolio and becoming "my counsellor and adviser in all the great questions that come up." In a handwritten postscript, the president said, "If only there were three of you!" Then he could have one Taft on the Supreme Court, one in the Philippines, and one as secretary of war.[12] Aware of the possibility that cabinet service might in time lead to a presidential nomination, Taft and his wife decided that they would return to the United States and accept Roosevelt's offer.

Taft's tenure as secretary of war began in early 1904. Over the next four years, he served as an all-purpose troubleshooter for Roosevelt with missions to the Far East, involvement in maintaining order in Cuba, and overseeing the construction of the Panama Canal. Taft enjoyed traveling, and his work for the president gave him ample scope to indulge that passion. When Roosevelt went on a tour of the nation during the spring of 1905, he quipped that he had left the portly Taft "sitting on the lid" to forestall trouble while the president was absent. These experiences drew the two men closer together and increased the depth of their official and personal friendship.[13]

How effective was Taft's service as secretary of war in preparation for his years in the White House? On that subject contemporary opinions diverged. By his own admission, he was not adept at handling the everyday workload of the department. "Mr. Taft has not done a great work in the War Department," wrote an informed newspaper man during the spring of 1908. "The army administration has not been improved under him, although Root did a great constructive work just before him."[14] Yet as long as Roosevelt was pleased with his performance in the cabinet, Taft was secure.

The nature of the Taft–Roosevelt relationship would be crucial for the outcome of Taft's presidency. During the period 1904–1908 the two men interacted with few visible signs of any difficulty. Later in his White House years, Taft reminisced about those occasions when he and Roosevelt had connected with long conversations about the meaning of life. They seemed in public and private to have few differences in political philosophy or personal style. "I agree heartily and earnestly in the policies which have come to be known as the Roosevelt policies," Taft said in late 1907. Roosevelt concurred. "He and I view public questions exactly alike," Roosevelt wrote in June 1908.[15]

These and other similar quotations from Roosevelt have fed the impression that from the moment of their first meeting in the early 1890s the two men were soul mates. Such an interpretation does not do justice to the ebb and flow of their friendship during these two decades. After President William McKinley was shot in September 1901, Taft predicted to his brother Horace that Roosevelt did not have "the capacity for winning people to his support that McKinley had." Nor did Roosevelt display "the same tact in dealing with his subordinates that McKinley did." After visiting Roosevelt early in 1902, Taft told his wife that "Roosevelt blurts out everything and says a good deal that he ought to keep to himself."[16]

Once he was secretary of war, Taft, like a good cabinet officer, did not offer public criticism of his chief. To family members and intimate friends, he sometimes let his frustration with Roosevelt's methods and attitude show. Roosevelt himself hinted at latent suspicion of his colleague's intentions. When Taft and Secretary of State Elihu Root favored court review of the orders of the Interstate Commerce Commission in the Hepburn Act of 1906, Roosevelt told others that "Root and Taft would backslide to the capitalists if he didn't keep them in line." To his friend Mabel Boardman, Taft said of his chief in September 1907: "I have a characteristic letter from the President. As his mind changes from time to time, he thinks it necessary to reveal to me those changes." Taft believed that Roosevelt was overemotional and sometimes prone to unnecessary excitement from the changes in the political scene.[17]

In public, both men believed that they were in accord on the ideological issues before the Republicans. What seeming divergences they had shrank in significance while Roosevelt was still in the White House. When Taft took over, their differing approaches to governing and administration became more divisive. Their most fundamental disagreement occurred over the reach of executive power. Although he shared the objectives of Roosevelt's regulatory program, Taft believed that the president should observe the strictures of the law and not rely on implied power as much as Roosevelt had done. Therefore, the task for Roosevelt's successor was to take the Roosevelt legacy and administer it in a more efficient and lawful manner. Taft also resented the way Roosevelt meddled in the affairs of government departments and bypassed cabinet officials.

The friendship of Roosevelt and Taft did not extend beyond the president himself. Taft did not like many of the men around Roosevelt, especially Gifford Pinchot, the chief forester. Nor did Taft admire the way Pinchot used Roosevelt's authority to implement conservation policies that pressed legal constraints. The secretary of war had little use for such reformers as Albert J. Beveridge, the Indiana senator, Robert M. La Follette of Wisconsin, or Albert Baird Cummins of Iowa. During the summer of 1907, Taft involved himself in Iowa politics to block the ambitions of Cummins to displace the incumbent Republican senator, William Boyd Allison. He observed of this bastion of Republican progressivism that the state was "full of gum-shoe statesmen that you can't tell anything about."[18]

Helen Taft was another source of strain for the relationship between her husband and Theodore Roosevelt. From the first, she and Theodore Roosevelt eyed each other with mutual wariness. Helen Taft also did not admire the approach that Edith Roosevelt took in her role as first lady. Mrs. Taft suspected the president of wanting another term in 1908, and she watched him for evidence to support her assumption. Within his own household, William Howard Taft did not receive positive support for his closeness to the White House. The camaraderie of Roosevelt and Taft during their joint service was genuine. When conditions changed and the rapport receded, there was no basis of solid ideological agreement or political empathy to block a deterioration of relations.

Taft's presidential hopes hinged on what Roosevelt did about a successor in 1908. Having taken a self-denying pledge on election night in 1904 not to seek another term, Theodore Roosevelt insisted that the Republican nominee in 1908 be someone who would carry on "my policies." Roosevelt would have liked for his secretary of state, Elihu Root, to run, but Root was seen as too old and too close to large corporations. None of the other potential contenders—Senator Robert M. La Follette of Wisconsin, Governor Charles Evans Hughes of New York, or Vice President Charles W. Fairbanks—suited Roosevelt either.

That left Taft. In the winter of 1906, Roosevelt offered Taft a seat on the Supreme Court as an associate justice. Taft declined in view of the work he was doing in the war department and because the opening was not for chief justice. There was also the emerging question of the presidency as 1908 neared. But Roosevelt, while encouraging Taft to run in 1905–1906, did not provide an outright endorsement. In October 1906, Roosevelt told Helen Taft that her husband was "his first choice," but mentioned that Charles Evans Hughes could be a contender if he won his gubernatorial race in New York that year. Secretary Taft saw these words as a way of goading him to be more active. An angry Helen Taft thought Roosevelt was playing with their lives. By the end of 1906, Taft issued a carefully worded statement that "in the improbable event that the opportunity to run for the great office of the Presidency were to come to me," he would not refuse. A Taft boom, fueled by funds from his half-brother, soon got under way.[19]

Yet the Roosevelt administration had not swung its full weight behind Taft. In August 1906 an outbreak of violence occurred in Brownsville, Texas. Shootings in the town were blamed on African American troops stationed at a nearby fort. Convinced that the black soldiers were guilty, Roosevelt ordered the summary dismissal from the army of three companies of African American troops three months later. Roosevelt had acted in haste and committed a miscarriage of justice against innocent men who had not shot up the town. When protests occurred against Roosevelt's peremptory action, Taft suspended the execution of the president's order. Roosevelt, who was then returning from a trip to Panama, instructed Taft to carry out his orders, and the secretary of war deferred to his superior. He thus became part of Roosevelt's unwise actions against the black soldiers—and, as it turned out, the political beneficiary in the case.

When criticism arose, Roosevelt dug in and refused to concede he had erred. The great champion of the black soldiers became Senator Joseph Benson Foraker, like Taft an Ohio Republican. Foraker, however, had opposed Roosevelt over railroad regulation earlier in the year. To have him question Roosevelt's judgment outraged the president. It was to Taft's advantage as a potential Republican candidate in 1908 for Foraker's position in Ohio and in the party generally to deteriorate.[20]

Foraker believed that he was pursuing justice for the discharged soldiers. He too had ambitions for the Republican nomination in 1908. Tensions flared in late January 1907 when he and Roosevelt clashed at a meeting of the Gridiron Club, with the two men exchanging heated epithets. In the wake of that spirited encounter, there was a definite intensification of White House support for the secretary of war. "The President is determined," wrote Taft, "that if Foraker intends to attack the administration, as he has done in the past in the Brownsville matter, and in other things, the fighting shall not be all on one side."[21]

Beginning in March 1907, Roosevelt made it clear that Taft was his choice. The cabinet officers with patronage to dole out were informed that the president had a "peculiar regard" for Taft's judgment in allocating offices "and think it wise to follow it" in making appointments. A writer in the *Kansas City Times* rendered the decision in verse:

> Says Roosevelt: "I announce no choice,
> To no man will I lend my voice,
> I have no private candidate,
> I care not whom you nominate—
> Just so it's Taft.[22]

With assurance that he could dominate patronage in Ohio, the secretary's base became more secure against inroads from Foraker.

The allocation of patronage to Taft in Ohio and other states would have long-range consequences later, when Taft was president. He would not have the offices to dispense that other presidents before him had at their disposal.

Meanwhile, Roosevelt and his private secretary, William Loeb, were "looking after the whole of the South." They made the docile delegations in Dixie fall in line behind Taft. At the same time, Taft's campaign, led by its manager, Arthur I. Vorys, moved to control the Ohio delegation and had made good progress toward that goal by the summer of 1907. Foraker sought some kind of arrangement that would divide the delegation, but Taft "wanted no compromise on my behalf with Foraker, for the reason that his views of the proper course for the Republican party to take are so widely at variance with mine." In a blow to Foraker's hopes of being competitive in Ohio, the Republican state committee endorsed Taft by a vote of 15 to 6 on 30 July 1907.[23]

It would not be quite that simple for Taft. Roosevelt had to step in during the fall of 1907 to keep the Taft campaign on course. While the secretary was carrying out an assignment for Roosevelt in Asia, the support for Taft slipped a bit after Republicans suffered election losses in Ohio and talk arose about the candidacy of the secretary of the treasury, George B. Cortelyou. To avoid a split in the administration, Roosevelt once again made his preference for Taft clear. On 12 December 1907 the White House released a statement reaffirming Roosevelt's 1904 pledge not to be a candidate in 1908. Taft wrote that the president's action "seems to have cleared the political atmosphere somewhat and given a chance to my smothered boom to rise again to respectable proportions."[24]

One more potential threat remained to Taft's chances. While the conservative candidates—Philander Knox, Foraker, House Speaker Joseph G. Cannon, and Vice President Fairbanks—all faltered, there was some life left in the prospects of Charles Evans Hughes. The Taft campaign agreed with Roosevelt that the governor should be allowed to retain control of the New York delegation. The Taft men then lined up as many second choice votes as they could. It was Roosevelt, however, who supplied the crippling blow to the Hughes candidacy. The New Yorker was set to deliver a major policy address on 31 January 1908. That same day Roosevelt sent Congress his most radical message to date. The result was presidential domination of the newspapers and Hughes relegated to the inside pages. Roosevelt chortled: "If Hughes is going to play the game, he must learn the tricks."[25]

The way was now clear for Taft to get the Republican nomination. It is impossible to tell how Taft would have fared with his party in the absence of Roosevelt's endorsement. The secretary of war had some perceived liabilities. His judicial decisions during the 1890s had left him with a reputation as an antilabor jurist. His support for Roosevelt on Brownsville had alienated the black vote in the North. His religious faith as a Unitarian was a sleeper issue that surfaced during the fall campaign. Among Republicans, however, there were serious doubts about Taft's commitment to the bedrock tenet of his party: the protective tariff.

Ever since the Civil War, the Republicans had been the champions of tariff protection. It was the doctrine that, more than any other, defined what it meant to be a member of the Grand Old Party. Its advocates believed that higher customs duties insulated American industry from foreign competition, built up the home market, and diffused the benefits of a growing economy to capital and labor alike. In the 1890s, the tariff had, under the leadership of William McKinley, carried the party to victories in the 1894 congressional elections and helped elect McKinley president in 1896. With the Republican triumph, Congress enacted the Dingley tariff in 1897, and GOP partisans credited that law with the return of prosperity at the end of the 1890s.

By 1907, however, the consensus around the Dingley Act had frayed. Divisions within the party over whether to revise rates downward festered since Roosevelt had dodged the issue during his presidency. Taft favored some reductions in the Dingley rates. He had articulated his position in a speech at Bath, Maine, during the 1906 election. He told his audience that since the enactment of the Dingley Law, "there has been a

9

change in the business conditions of the country making it wise and just to revise the schedules of the existing tariff." Taft worried that Roosevelt thought "I am a little too outspoken in respect to the revision of the tariff," but he decided to go ahead anyway. Taft's position on protection led some conservatives in the party to call him "an avowed tariff ripper." He would have to deal with that perception throughout his presidency.[26]

As a public speaker, Taft did not have a reputation for gaffes. On 30 May 1908 he appeared in New York City to honor Ulysses S. Grant. Burdened with work and prone to procrastinate, Taft had not written his speech well before the occasion, and he spoke somewhat off the cuff. During his remarks Taft observed that in the mid-1850s Grant "resigned from the Army because he had to. He had yielded to the weakness of a taste for strong drink, and rather than be court-martialed he left the Army." The aging veterans of the Grand Army of the Republic erupted in anger at this perceived slur to Grant's memory. Taft had to issue an apologetic statement to still the furor. The postmaster general, George von Lengerke Meyer, found Taft on 2 June "rather depressed today because the papers have been jumping on him for having referred to General Grant as having overcome the tendency to drink hard. I do not think it will do any harm and told him so." Meyer was right, but the problem of Taft being unprepared in public would recur.[27] In retrospect the Grant episode, small though it was, signaled that the upward arc of Taft's political career might not continue into the future.

Taft was now on the verge of the Republican nomination. The conservative "allies"—the forces of Knox, Foraker, and Fairbanks—had brought numerous challenges to Taft delegates before the Republican National Committee in early June. The panel, with Roosevelt's tacit approval, ruled in Taft's favor on 200 contests. The membership of the committee was filled with Taft and Roosevelt loyalists who would serve for the next four years. When the convention opened on 16 June, Taft had over 600 pledged delegates in his column. "I have no doubt of Taft's nomination," wrote James S. Sherman of New York on 6 June. "Of course, if it is not Taft by any slip, it will be Roosevelt."[28]

Behind the scenes, Taft managers, and especially Mrs. Taft, worried that a last-minute Roosevelt wave might sweep through the convention and deny Taft the prize. Party conservatives, in control of such events as the choice of the keynote speaker, reminded themselves that at least Taft was not Roosevelt. In this volatile situation, the president and the candidate made the puzzling decision not to speak out on the issue of Taft's running mate. They also allowed the convention to write a platform that moved the party rightward.

Taft did not exercise direct control over the choice of a vice president:

"It is a very delicate matter for me to take any position with respect to the Vice Presidency." It is not clear why the prospective nominee felt this way. As the new leader of the Republicans, his wishes, if expressed, would have carried weight with the delegates. Feelers went out to Senator Jonathan P. Dolliver of Iowa, a respected Midwestern progressive, but he declined. Charles Evans Hughes also said no. Senator Albert J. Beveridge of Indiana, believing in his own presidential hopes in the years ahead, "turned it down, flat, positively, instantly." The progressive wing of the party thus missed a chance to have a spokesman for their views within the inner circles of the Taft administration.[29]

Without guidance from the White House or Taft, the second spot on the ticket went to a New York member of the House of Representatives, James Schoolcraft "Sunny Jim" Sherman. The affable New Yorker was fifty-two at the time of the convention. He believed in tariff protection, enjoyed good relations with Speaker Cannon, and would balance the "western" candidacy of Taft with "eastern" conservatism. As one of his House colleagues put it, "Sherman's nomination will greatly help us in New York for everybody knows and likes him." Sherman did not prove to be a strong member of the Taft inner circle, and the presidential nominee had missed a chance to placate the progressives.[30]

Taft endeavored to see that the Republican platform addressed the issues that voters wanted to have tackled and which the Democrats were likely to raise. He mandated language that supported a postal savings bank system, improvement of the Sherman Antitrust Act, and more authority for the Interstate Commerce Commission to regulate interstate railroads. The major plank in the platform called "unequivocally for a revision of the tariff by a special session of Congress immediately following the inauguration of the next President." The platform language did not state the direction revision would take, but the assumption was that it would be downward.[31]

The candidate wanted to include a statement in favor of restraint in the issuing of judicial injunctions in labor disputes. As he wrote to a delegate to the convention, "it is one of the Roosevelt policies to which I have subscribed ever since he urged it upon Congress." The proposed change produced opposition from the National Association of Manufacturers and dissent from Cannon and other conservatives. As a result, the platform contained watered-down language that promised to "uphold at all times the authority and integrity of the Courts" and sought only modest improvements in the procedures when an injunction was issued. Coupled with the rejection of more progressive planks sponsored by Robert La Follette, the action of the framers of the Republican platform gave the convention a deserved stand-pat reputation.[32]

Finally, it came time for voting on the presidential race. When his name was placed in nomination, Taft received a twenty-five-minute demonstration on the floor. The duration did not equal an outpouring for Roosevelt the previous day, when Senator Henry Cabot Lodge mentioned the president's name in passing. A forty-eight-minute demonstration ensued before Lodge quieted the crowd with a disavowal of a Roosevelt candidacy. So for Helen Taft, listening in Washington as bulletins flowed in from Chicago about the proceedings, it was disappointing to hear that her husband had not achieved the same level of enthusiasm as Roosevelt. Nonetheless, the nominating and then the voting went on. When the ballots were counted, Taft had 702 votes, with the remainder scattered among his opponents. The telegraph brought the news to the candidate and his wife. That same afternoon Taft scribbled a message to Roosevelt "I hereby tender my resignation as Secretary of War to take effect June 30th next." Roosevelt accepted immediately, and as of 1 July, Taft was out of government and was the nominee of the Republican Party.[33]

Taft and Roosevelt were now in uncharted territory for presidential politics. Not since Andrew Jackson and Martin Van Buren had there been a situation where two men allied in politics had seen the presidency pass from one to the other. Van Buren and Jackson were not intimate friends in the way that Roosevelt and Taft had been for the preceding two decades. The president and his presumptive successor did not sit down and explore the ramifications of their new relationship. After four years of Roosevelt as the dominant figure in their interaction, now the authority would pass to Taft. Being a subordinate again was not a role that Roosevelt found easy to fill.

In fact, some misunderstandings stemmed from the conversations they had in these early days of the impending election. These talks would form part of a series of disputed episodes that marked the course of the ultimate break between these strong-willed individuals. Assuming that Taft would win the race against the Democratic nominee William Jennings Bryan, Roosevelt raised the question in late June, probably in a conference at Oyster Bay on 27 June, about the status of the members of his cabinet should the Republicans prevail in the fall. Would they be kept on or not? The question put Taft on the spot. If he indicated that he had plans to replace his colleagues, it would have raised immediate doubts about his loyalty to Roosevelt. According to the later accounts of this meeting, Taft remarked that he would retain Roosevelt's choice to succeed him as secretary of war, Luke E. Wright. In fact, in an expansive moment, Taft said, "I wish you would tell the boys I have been working with that I want to continue all of them. They are all fine fellows, and they have been mighty good to me. I want them all to stay just as they are." Taft left it to Roosevelt to pass the word to the cabinet members who wanted to retain their posts. The president did so, and in the process, he created expectations among his official family that persisted throughout the election. Whether Taft had spoken in haste or had not fully thought through his comments is not clear. He did not think, once he was elected, that he had made binding pledges. In the end, he kept on only two of Roosevelt's cabinet.[34]

In 1908, the custom was for the presidential nominee to be officially "notified" of his selection as a candidate sometime during the summer. A committee of distinguished party members would visit the standard-bearer, usually at his home town. Having heard that he was nominated, the presidential candidate in turn would indicate his willingness to run through a "speech of acceptance" and a "letter of acceptance." These two documents would form the basis for the campaign and would be circulated by the millions on behalf of the party. Taft went to Hot Springs, Virginia, to rest, play golf, and work on his acceptance speech. Taft recognized what was at stake. As he told Roosevelt, "the speech is so important that were I to make a break in it it might really affect seriously the whole matter."[35] The president met with Taft on 24 July to review Taft's acceptance address.

The place for the notification was Taft's home in Cincinnati, Ohio. He arrived there the day after his conference with Roosevelt about the cabinet. On 28 July the Republican faithful assembled to hear what their nominee had to say. Taft had labored over the text and told Roosevelt that it was "really a letter of acceptance rather than a speech, but it is very hard for me to go into these questions in a short way."[36] The speech was long and detailed with overtones of Taft's legal training. The underlying message of the address was evident:

> The chief function of the next Administration, in my judgment, is distinct from, and a progressive development of, that which has been performed by President Roosevelt. The chief function of the next Administration is to complete and perfect the machinery by which these standards may be maintained, by which the lawbreakers may be promptly restrained and punished, but which shall operate with sufficient accuracy and dispatch to interfere with legitimate business as little as possible.[37]

In the partisan portions of his remarks, Taft indicted Bryan and the Democrats as a menace to prosperity. He defended the Republican policy on injunctions, attacked the idea that bank deposits should be federally insured, and defended the idea of a postal savings bank against Democratic criticism. The candidate renewed his call for revision of the tariff and promised early action on the subject. He devoted one paragraph to the issue of blacks. In it he promised enforcement of the Reconstruction

13

Candidate Taft gets ready to knock the Democrats out of the park during the 1908 presidential campaign. Author's collection.

amendments to the Constitution but also praised the South for having "an influential element disposed to encourage the Negro in his hard struggle for industrial independence and assured political status."[38] Taft hoped in fact to break into the Solid South and woo away some Democrats to the Republican ticket with these conciliatory gestures toward white opinion in the region.

On a sultry Ohio summer day, Taft's speech was so long "that I had to cut it in half in the delivery, and then it was very hot work getting through, both for the audience and for me, but the audience stood it well and seemed to receive it with great approval." He spoke for seventy-one minutes, "passing over entire sheets of his manuscript at a time, saying that his hearers might read the entire speech in the newspapers." The *New York Press* said that the speech "is vibrant with the spirit of Theodore Roosevelt," while the *New York Post* predicted that "the speech seems likely to alienate still further the labor element and hot radicals of his own party, especially those in the West."[39]

It was now up to Taft to win the White House in the fall election. A campaign biography written by Oscar King Davis, a reporter friendly to Roosevelt, was coming out. It called Taft "the Man of the Hour." The manner in which the candidate handled the campaign—and, assuming a likely Republican victory, the transition from Roosevelt to a new administration—would be crucial to how Taft's presidency would develop.[40]

2

★ ★ ★ ★ ★

BEING HIS OWN KING

In the historical literature about the presidential election of 1908, sparse as it is, it sometimes seems as though William Howard Taft has only a modest supporting role. As he did so often in life, Theodore Roosevelt takes over the spotlight. The president's public letters to William Jennings Bryan and other Democrats become the basic narrative of the contest. Taft's campaign and his speaking tours recede into the background. His success in winning the White House is thus somehow diminished and he becomes almost an accidental president, thrust into a role for which he was not prepared.

A more balanced account will recognize that Taft won the 1908 election, not Theodore Roosevelt. The Republican nominee accomplished the difficult feat of building on the legacy of an incumbent of his own party, something that subsequent candidates such as Richard Nixon, Hubert Humphrey, and Albert Gore Jr. did not match. To understand the development of Taft's administration requires some comprehension of how he won the election and managed the transition from Roosevelt's presidency to his own. After securing victory at the ballot box, Taft encountered more difficulty in overseeing the shift to his style of governing. By the time he took office on 4 March 1909, many of the problems that would plague his four years in office had surfaced.

After delivering his acceptance speech on 28 July 1908, Taft faced the issue of establishing a workable organization for his presidential campaign. He and the Republicans knew that they were in for a battle against William Jennings Bryan and the Democrats. In his third race for the White

House, Bryan led a more united and cohesive party than he had available when he ran in 1896 or 1900. The Democrats believed they had a good chance to win for the first time in sixteen years. The economic downturn associated with the Panic of 1907 lessened the effectiveness of Republican claims that electing a Democrat meant hard times. Taft was not seen as the formidable candidate Roosevelt had been. Moreover, the secretary of war was not popular with blacks or labor. The Democratic platform played down such divisive topics as government ownership of interstate railroads, which Bryan had advocated in 1906. Instead, his party stressed economy in government, preserving states' rights, and combating "with unceasing vigilance the efforts of those who are striving by usurpation to seize the powers of the people or the states for exploitation by the federal government."[1]

Bryan calculated that with the Solid South in his corner he needed only to win the border states and one or two industrial states in the North or Midwest to gain the victory. He had the American Federation of Labor in his corner as well. Bryan thought about conducting a front-porch campaign for a moment, then embarked on his usual wide-ranging tour of the nation. "How can the Republicans threaten us with a panic when a panic came under the present President and is still upon us?" he asked at Lincoln, Nebraska. By early October, Bryan concluded, "things are looking well and I see no reason why they should not improve."[2]

For Taft, on the other hand, the initial portents in August were not encouraging. Because Taft endorsed a limited disclosure of campaign contributions, Republican fund-raising went slowly. "We are not receiving large sums of money," said the campaign treasurer, "and are confronted with expenditures which must be met if we are to elect our candidates." The uneasiness about labor unions and the potential for defections from the black vote also troubled GOP leaders. "The labor vote and the colored vote are both against the National Ticket," concluded an Ohio operative in early October. Taft had selected Frank H. Hitchcock to direct the presidential canvass. His deliberate methods that sought to build momentum in October displeased other party members.[3]

A notable feature of the 1908 campaign was opposition of some Christian clergymen to Taft on the grounds of his Unitarian faith. "Think of the United States with a President who does not believe that Jesus was the Son of God, but looks upon our immaculate Savior as a common bastard and low cunning imposter," wrote one evangelical editor in July 1908. Democrats hoped, said *The Nation*, on a "quiet effort to stir up orthodox church members against Mr. Taft because he is a Unitarian." At the same time, his tolerant record in the Philippines sparked charges that he was pro-Catholic. In the end, these issues do not seem to have weighed against the

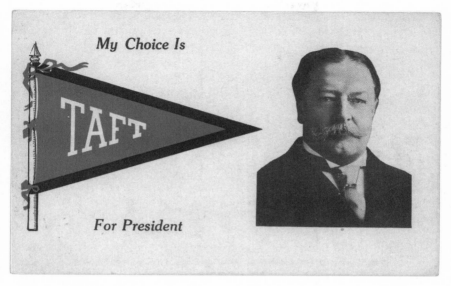

Postcard announcing the sender's choice for president were a feature of the 1908 presidential race. Author's collection.

Republican candidate in a decisive manner. He did not discuss them while the campaign was being waged.[4]

A burden on the Republicans was the growing unhappiness with the record of the House of Representatives under the leadership of Speaker Cannon. The *Chicago Tribune* reported in early September that "'Uncle Joe' Cannon seems to be the bogy man of the political campaign in the northwest." Cannon and his allies had blocked progressive legislation during the last years of Roosevelt's presidency. Accordingly, the profane and irascible Speaker had come to seem a major obstacle, especially to tariff revision. As a result, Taft told Roosevelt that "the burden I have to carry in this campaign is Cannonism, and I don't propose to be involved in a bunko game with the public" over the candidate's commitment to lowering rates. Yet Taft could not distance himself too much from Cannon and House Republicans without undermining party loyalty and morale.[5]

During the summer Taft consulted by mail on a regular basis with Roosevelt about the direction of the campaign. The two men agreed that the president would write a public letter on Taft's behalf. "Of course I shall be delighted to have your letter at any time. My impression is that possibly it would better come after my letter of acceptance, rather than after my speech of acceptance." In the meantime, the president and the candidate collaborated on persuading Charles Evans Hughes to run for a second term as governor of New York in hopes of shoring up Republican support in that key state. Except for a brief visit in mid-October, Taft and Roosevelt did not meet face to face to coordinate strategy.[6]

In the aftermath of the GOP convention, Taft's managers had contemplated a front-porch canvass on the William McKinley model without any touring on the part of the candidate himself. As September approached without much momentum from the Taft effort, Republicans urged him to take to the stump. Taft agreed. "If the candidate does not go out and work himself," Taft informed Roosevelt, "the subordinates in the ranks are not liable to tear their shirts, whereas the personal presence of the man at the head will have an encouraging and stimulating effect I believe." Therefore, the Republicans announced in early September that Taft would make a western swing. He spent time in the Middle West and even parts of the South before the election.[7]

In contrast to the impression that Taft was a mediocre campaigner, he actually did well in the 1908 race. While his speeches in September and October still echoed with judicial language, he attracted sizable and friendly crowds. Like other candidates with soft spots in their records, he stressed his affinity for working people. As he said in Ohio, "I am in favor of the organization of labor," and he denied that he was someone "who thinks and says that a dollar a day is enough for any man." As for the protective tariff, he pledged that a revision "will be made upon just and fair lines, and that the plighted faith of the party will be carried out as formulated in the platform." To counter the calls from Bryan for guarantee of bank deposits, Taft spoke out for postal savings banks that the federal government would operate.[8]

The people who flocked to hear Taft in the fall also heard him set out where he thought the next administration should go. He told a crowd at St. Louis that the pressing requirement of the country was "not to be spectacular in the enactment of great statutes laying down new codes of morals, or asserting a new standard of business integrity." What the next president needed, he said, was "the men and machinery" to carry forward the regulatory programs that Theodore Roosevelt had begun. "Taft stock is going up every day," reported one happy Republican worker in mid-October.[9]

One reason for this upturn in Republican fortunes was the intervention of Theodore Roosevelt in the race. In 1904, as the incumbent president, he had to defer to custom and not campaign. The same tradition barred him from taking to the hustings himself in 1908. He could write letters, as he and Taft had previously discussed. In September 1908 Roosevelt gave the press the first of a number of public statements in which he praised

Taft and his qualifications. The president also endorsed, in somewhat less ringing terms, the election of a Republican Congress. Roosevelt's presence overshadowed Taft to a degree, but the nominee did not seem to mind having the all-out support of his mentor.

During October 1908, the various elements of the Republican campaign came together in Taft's favor. Surrogate orators, particularly Charles Evans Hughes, undercut Bryan's position. It turned out that Hitchcock's careful construction of an organization paid off in the last weeks of the race. The Republicans had enough money to make a strong appeal in those weeks and to conduct detailed polling of individual voters to identify weak spots. Labor did not defect as much as the GOP had feared, and black voters in the North stayed with the party. Taft's ability as a campaigner and Roosevelt's timely assistance, combined with the electoral strength of the Republicans, indicated that Taft would be elected when the voters turned out.

On 3 November 1908 the Republicans won a substantial victory. Taft garnered 7,675,320 popular votes to Bryan's 6,412,294. In the electoral college, Taft prevailed by a count of 321 to 162. The number of Americans voting rose by some 1,367,000 over 1904, with the percentage of eligible voters standing at 65 percent. Taft improved on Roosevelt's showing by some 50,000 ballots. In essence, Taft had duplicated the McKinley–Bryan outcomes of 1896 and 1900. He did well in the cities, carrying New York City, Chicago, and Jersey City, and losing narrowly in Boston. Of course, Roosevelt's support helped, but Taft demonstrated against Bryan that he could campaign and win in his own right.

Beneath the surface, there were signs of trouble for the Grand Old Party. In five states—Minnesota, Ohio, Indiana, North Dakota, and Montana—the Democrats elected governors even though Taft won the electoral votes. Ticket splitting indicated voter unhappiness with the political system in general. Observers asked if Taft could hold the discordant Republicans together. "Are we to hope that he will be a bigger man than the party?" queried one columnist, "and that is the hope in which most progressive men are supporting him."[10]

Taft received the news of his victory in Cincinnati, where he told the partisans who came to serenade him that he intended to have an administration that would be "a worthy successor of that of Theodore Roosevelt." In Washington, a happy Roosevelt informed aides that "we have beaten them to a frazzle." The French ambassador noted that "The President's joy at the result of the election is overflowing." Taft returned to Hot Springs, Virginia, for some golf, relaxation, and cabinet making. It seemed as if a smooth transition from one friend to another lay ahead for the Republicans and the American people.[11]

This postcard announcing Taft's victory sounded the familiar
Republican themes of patriotism and prosperity after the
Democrats and William Jennings Bryan were defeated.
Author's collection.

In fact, things began to go wrong between Taft and Roosevelt almost at once. It started on 7 November when the president-elect sat down to write Roosevelt to thank him for what he had done in the campaign. "The first letter I wish to write is to you, because you have always been the chief agent in working out the present status of affairs, and my selection and election are chiefly your work. You and my brother Charley made that possible which in all probability would not have occurred otherwise." Taft went on to express "deep gratitude" for all Roosevelt had done for him. At the time, Roosevelt did not indicate that the letter had affected him in any way, but he bristled at the comparison of his efforts with those of Taft's millionaire half-brother. Twenty months later he would be complaining that Taft's remark was like saying that "Abraham Lincoln and the bond seller Jay Cooke saved the Union."[12]

Taft, of course, knew nothing of Roosevelt's reaction, and the two men seemed as friendly as ever. For the president-elect, the major task before him was the selection of his cabinet. That duty proved to be more difficult and complex than Taft anticipated. Because Taft and Roosevelt were from the same party, they had an identical pool of talent from which to draw. Also, because Taft was seen as a legatee of Roosevelt, it seemed logical to expect that he would retain the members of an administration with which he was himself identified. The president-elect did not share with Roosevelt his approach to cabinet making or ask for advice about how to manage the process. Of course, Roosevelt himself had not been through the making of a cabinet as a new president. He had inherited McKinley's cabinet in 1901 and made changes thereafter.

Taft had not been impressed with several of his colleagues in the Roosevelt cabinet, and he did not think they were wise choices to continue in office. His judgments in this regard had some merit. Several of Roosevelt's subordinates—Elihu Root, Taft himself, George B. Cortelyou—were first-rate talents. Others in the cabinet of the second Roosevelt term were less distinguished. Charles J. Bonaparte had been over his head as attorney general. Truman Newberry, the secretary of the navy, was seen as callow at forty-four and was not a gifted administrator. James R. Garfield, as secretary of the interior, had deferred to Gifford Pinchot and the president. The secretary of war, Luke E. Wright, had served with Taft in the Philippines. "He is not as active as he might be," Taft concluded, "and he isn't as decisive in his methods as I should like to have him."[13]

Although these were defensible conclusions, the problem for Taft was that questioning the abilities of these men implied some doubt about Roosevelt's judgment in selecting them in the first place. Then there was the conversation in June 1908 about retaining the cabinet officials. Roosevelt had taken the opportunity to tell all the men involved that they would be kept on. In the case of Oscar Straus, the secretary of commerce, Roosevelt informed him in late November: "Well, I can tell you one thing; you will be the head of the Department under the next administration." Truman Newberry received similar assurances from Roosevelt in the fall of 1908. So when Taft's family told him to "be his own king" and choose a cabinet that had few Roosevelt holdovers, there were political hazards in such a course.[14]

Taft conducted his cabinet making alone at Augusta, Georgia. He invited "leaders of public opinion" and prominent Republicans to visit him and provide "their impression from a different standpoint than the one I am likely to have." The deliberations were closely held. As one journalist noted, "Taft, Knox, and [Frank H.] Hitchcock appeared to be the only men who have any knowledge on the subject and they are as tight as an old sea salt ashore." In this atmosphere of judicial-like secrecy, rumors abounded and men close to Theodore Roosevelt fretted. "It is evident," wrote James R. Garfield, "that hostile influences are at work with Taft & are estranging him from the President."[15]

The most important cabinet choice was secretary of state. Taft offered the place to Elihu Root, but after four years in the post, Root was looking forward to being elected the next United States senator from New York. When Root declined, Taft turned next to Senator Henry Cabot Lodge of Massachusetts. "I gave my reasons," Lodge wrote, "& he understood why I did not wish to leave the Senate." That left the man who was probably Taft's first choice all along, Senator Philander C. Knox of Pennsylvania.[16]

Knox was fifty-five in 1908. He had been McKinley's attorney general briefly and then continued on into Roosevelt's first term through such major legal controversies as the Northern Securities case in 1902. Elected to the Senate in 1904 from Pennsylvania, he had displayed a conservative voting record. In the 1908 race for the nomination, he had been one of Taft's challengers among "the allies." Wealthy from a lucrative corporate law practice, Knox was a short, bald man with a taste for the good life, including a round of golf daily and a string of trotting horses. An aide recalled that "his very short but portly figure was carefully and expensively dressed." Roosevelt called him "a sawed-off cherub."[17]

The selection of Knox encountered an immediate snag that neither he nor Taft had anticipated. As a member of the Senate, Knox had voted to increase the salary of the secretary of state in 1907. That put the secretary of state designate up against the clause of the Constitution in article 1, section 6, paragraph 2, that barred a lawmaker from holding an office "the emoluments whereof shall have been increased during such time." The president-elect persuaded Congress to reduce the salary of the secretary of state back to what it was when the pay increase was voted. The Democrats grumbled about what had been done, but the way was cleared for Knox to take up the portfolio at state. Watching from his home at 1603 H Street, Henry Adams commented that "Knox did not know enough law to know that he was ineligible, and did not know enough diplomacy to organize his Department which he has thrown into confusion."[18]

Knox proved a very influential member of the cabinet who stayed with Taft through the entire administration. He was not popular with the diplomatic corps. "The trouble with the Secretary of State," wrote the British ambassador in 1910, "is that he is hopelessly ignorant of international politics and principles of policy, and is either too old or too lazy to apply his mind to the subject and try to learn."[19] The problem for James Bryce and Whitehall was that Knox and Taft did not take much interest in European affairs. They concentrated instead on Latin America and the Far East in pursuing their policy of what became known as "dollar diplomacy." The president gave Knox a free hand in organizing the State Department, and the secretary did so through his primary aide, F. M. Huntington Wilson. When the appointment of Knox was made, it was generally greeted with praise for the new secretary's abilities and knowledge of the law.[20]

The second cabinet post that most concerned Taft was the attorney general. In many respects, the new president intended to be his own attorney general when it came to selecting federal circuit and appeals court judges and justices of the Supreme Court. Given that assumption, Taft sought one of the best corporate lawyers he could find. His choice, George Woodward Wickersham, was a partner of the president's brother, Henry Waters Taft, in New York City. The mustachioed, balding Wickersham was fifty, a Republican, and a believer in the enforcement of the antitrust laws in the same spirit as the incoming chief executive. He did not have much political acumen, and his antitrust policy would contribute to the sense within the business community that the administration lacked sympathy for their situation. Taft recognized that his choice was a corporate attorney, "but why the United States should not have the benefit of as good a lawyer as the corporations, I don't know."[21]

Two posts within the cabinet went to Roosevelt holdovers. The secretary of agriculture was James "Tama Jim" Wilson of Iowa, who had first been appointed by William McKinley in 1897. Popular in the farm belt, Wilson was a pliable administrator but well protected by members of Congress. Taft would conclude in 1911 that he lacked a grasp of the affairs of his department.[22] For secretary of the navy, Taft moved Roosevelt's postmaster general, George von Lengerke Meyer of Massachusetts, over to the Navy Department. Meyer's selection would please Lodge and the

Massachusetts delegation and keep a Roosevelt appointee in the cabinet. Meyer proved an active secretary who sought to shake up the navy and its accustomed ways of carrying out its mission.[23]

From the beginning, it was clear that Frank H. Hitchcock would probably be the postmaster general in recognition of his service as Taft's campaign manager. Forty-one years old and a veteran of Republican politics, Hitchcock proved to be an effective administrator of his department, but he was not as helpful to Taft on the patronage side of his job. During Hitchcock's tenure, the first use of trucks in the mail service occurred.[24]

The problem of what to do about the Roosevelt cabinet members shaped how the rest of the official family fell into place. Taft decided that he did not want Luke E. Wright to stay on at the War Department. Instead, he chose Jacob M. Dickinson, a southern Democrat, for the post. Taft was eager to make inroads in the Democratic South. He cherished the belief that if the race question could be put aside, the natural affinity of southerners for Republican doctrine would emerge. So the new president reached out across party lines to select a southern Democrat who was loyal to the opposition party but who had not voted for William Jennings Bryan.

Dickinson met these criteria. He was from Tennessee, had served as assistant attorney general in the Cleveland administration, and was counsel for the Illinois Central Railroad. The president-elect also believed that Dickinson would provide the executive energy to bring the Panama Canal to completion. He had been president of the American Bar Association from 1907 to 1908. In that organization he fought against the admission of African American lawyers to membership. Taft became quite taken with "Mac" Dickinson in the first two years of his term. The secretary accompanied the president on his national tour in the fall of 1909 as a welcome traveling companion.[25]

The second Democrat whom Taft picked out for his cabinet was Franklin MacVeagh of Illinois for secretary of the treasury. This position presented Taft with some difficulties. He thought about offering the portfolio to Congressman Theodore E. Burton of Ohio, who was engaged in a campaign to succeed Foraker in the Senate. That move would have helped the chances of the president-elect's half-brother, Charles P. Taft, who was also making a try for the Senate. In the end, Burton preferred the Senate. There was some consideration as well about former Ohio governor, Myron T. Herrick, but that too did not work out. With his usual sarcasm, Henry Adams concluded in mid-February 1909 that "in regard to the Treasury, Taft has made a still worse muddle; he has hawked it over the country; Burton, Herrick, and I know not how many more have refused it."[26]

As time pressed Taft to make a choice of a treasury secretary, the name of Franklin MacVeagh became prominent. MacVeagh was seventy-one, a Chicago wholesale grocer with banking ties, and a Yale graduate who, like Taft, was a member of Skull and Bones. Originally a Republican, MacVeagh had become a Democrat in the 1890s but rejoined the GOP when Bryan and free silver emerged in 1896. He was a municipal reformer in Chicago. Although MacVeagh had studied law, he lacked the corporate connections of other attorneys in the Taft cabinet. As an adviser told Taft, "under all of the circumstances, I think MacVeagh best man you can get. You have lawyers enough. He is a business man of experience, wide acquaintance, excellent ability, and high character." Taft's penchant for present and former Democrats led Speaker Cannon to quip: "The trouble with Taft is that if he were Pope he would think it necessary to appoint a few Protestant Cardinals."[27]

Two places remained to be filled: Interior and Commerce. Those vacancies brought Taft right up against the problem of the Roosevelt holdovers. James R. Garfield was secretary of the interior and Oscar S. Straus held the post of secretary of commerce and labor. The president-elect was not impressed with either of his former colleagues. In the case of Garfield, who was from Ohio, Taft deemed him too close to Gifford Pinchot. There seems to have been little chance that Garfield would ever be retained. Taft was already thinking of Richard Achilles Ballinger of Washington state, who had been commissioner of the general land office under Roosevelt. The president-elect probably had his resolve strengthened when a friend conveyed to him the comment of Pinchot about Ballinger at Interior. "I couldn't work with him as I have with Jim. Jim and I think alike concerning the matters in which the Forest service and the Department of the Interior are closely related. Ballinger and I might clash."[28]

Ballinger was a graduate of Williams College and a lawyer who had made his way in the Pacific Northwest during the 1890s. In 1904, he became the mayor of Seattle. During his single term, Ballinger cleaned up the city and in the process impressed his college friend, Jim Garfield. When Theodore Roosevelt sought a commissioner of the General Land Office in early 1907, Garfield sponsored his appointment. During his months in office, Ballinger seemed to bring efficiency and drive to his post. When he left government service in 1908, Garfield said that he had "a reputation for ability, industry, and fairness." Relations with Gifford Pinchot, on the other hand, were troubled, as Pinchot's remarks on Ballinger's cabinet candidacy indicated. Ballinger had doubts about the legality of many of Pinchot's actions on land use and conservation policy. Once Taft had decided on Ballinger, he told Garfield that he would not be kept on. Garfield noted in his diary: "Taft's letter curiously weak & not sincere—evidently difficult for him to write because he was not willing to tell his real reasons for deserting the first plan to keep most of the present cabinet."[29]

The remaining cabinet post was Commerce and Labor, held by Oscar S. Straus. As the first Jewish member of the cabinet, Straus represented a constituency of growing importance, but his position became more tenuous once Taft had selected another New Yorker in George Wickersham for Justice. That choice dictated that Taft look elsewhere, which he did with Charles Nagel, a Missouri Republican who was another attorney with close ties to Adolphus Busch and the brewing industry. Finding a cabinet member from a border state such as Missouri fit in with Taft's emerging southern strategy. There was natural disappointment when another Roosevelt appointee was excluded. Straus told Roosevelt that "through influence of surroundings Taft did not wish to take those who distinguished themselves under him." Roosevelt's terse comment was, "unfortunately you have been too close to me, I fear."[30]

After the Taft cabinet was announced in late January, the president-elect started on a trip to Panama to inspect the work on the canal. In the three months since his election, his relationship with Theodore Roosevelt had encountered some difficulty even beyond the issue of selecting members of his cabinet. On the surface, matters between the two men remained amicable and friendly. Outside of public view, but amid increasing Washington gossip about a rift, the question of how the new administration would fulfill the legacy of its predecessor was much on people's minds.

One sore spot had emerged just after the election. Senator Foraker was a candidate for reelection to the Senate from Ohio. Representative Theodore E. Burton and Charles Phelps Taft were aspirants to replace him. Having his half-brother as an avowed candidate was not what Taft wanted, and he kept out of the contest. As the race developed, Charles Taft focused on securing the support of the Republican legislators in the party caucus. At that point, Foraker and Burton decided to shift the decision away from the Republican lawmakers and into the legislature at large. When that prospect arose during the last weeks of December, it appeared as if Foraker might gain enough Republican and Democratic votes to return to the Senate. Roosevelt came out strongly against Foraker on 29 December and indicated a preference for Burton over Charles P. Taft. Two days later Charles Taft withdrew as a candidate. Burton was then elected. The president-elect took the result with surface equanimity, but he wrote his brother that "I don't know what stirred the President up unless it was that you said something to him in your conversation with him, which he misunderstood."[31]

Throughout these months, people around Roosevelt looked with skepticism on Taft's actions. In the wake of the election, party conservatives asserted in subtle and overt ways that a change in approach was coming from the Roosevelt style. Roosevelt's partisans wanted Taft to hit back at these attacks on the outgoing president. Congress was in open revolt against Roosevelt, and friends of the incumbent wondered why the president-elect did not come out against such tactics. Of course, Taft had no stake in picking a fight with Congress on behalf of Roosevelt in the weeks before he took office.

Taft did have a major decision to make about his future relations with the Speaker of the House. During the days following the election, Cannon indicated that tariff revision would proceed in the manner that the House of Representatives chose. Taft bristled at these statements, which "are enough to damn the party if they are not protested against." The problem for Taft was that the irascible and imperious Cannon commanded the allegiance of a majority of the Republican House members who were going to be in the new Congress. The Republicans in the House, moreover, enjoyed only a comparatively tight forty-seven-seat majority. Taft believed that he might have defeated the Speaker had he made his preference for another candidate public. "Had I beaten Cannon, I should have had a factious and ugly Republican minority, willing and anxious to defeat all progressive measures, and with the power to defeat them, because you know as well as I that the Democrats in such a pinch are only too glad to leave the Republicans in a hole."[32]

During the transition, therefore, Taft decided that he would not encourage those who were planning to challenge the Speaker's reelection. Theodore Roosevelt thought about coming out against Cannon in a letter to Taft, but then concluded before he left the country that he should not do so because Taft was not disposed to act. The progressives in the House were disappointed with Taft's judgment, but it was difficult to argue that the president-elect at that juncture did not have a point. Still, the sense that Taft had missed an opportunity to validate his credentials as a progressive would endure within the reform wing of the party.[33]

Another source of tension during these months was the president-elect's wife, who acted in ways that irritated both the president and Edith Roosevelt. Helen Taft had been anticipating the honor and pleasure of being the first lady since her visit to the White House during the administration of Rutherford B. Hayes. She was not disposed to wait until she was a resident of the executive mansion before making her plans known. She indicated to friends in Washington that she had in mind many changes in how the president's residence would be run. Among her alterations were a new social secretary to replace Isabelle "Belle" Hagner, who had held that position with Edith Roosevelt. On a more sensitive note, the incoming first lady indicated that she would have African American servants in liveried dress instead of the white ushers who had manned the doors during the Roosevelt years. The change disappointed Mrs. Roosevelt, who told the military aide Archie Butt of her dismay. Mrs. Taft would later write "Perhaps I did make the process of adjusting the White House routine to my own conceptions a shade too strenuous, but I could not feel that I was mistress of any house if I did not take an active interest in all the details of running it."[34]

The president-elect tried to grant as many as possible of Roosevelt's wishes regarding men who had served him. There was some awkwardness regarding Roosevelt's secretary, William Loeb Jr. "Billy" Loeb sought the honor of holding a cabinet post, even for only a few months. That idea, said Taft, was "hardly dignified." Instead, Loeb was made collector of customs for the port of New York, one of the most lucrative patronage positions in the government. So the potential problem of Loeb was satisfactorily resolved.[35]

The events of the transition had frayed the bonds between Roosevelt and Taft as the inauguration approached in February 1909. Both men were aware of these developments when Roosevelt made his invitation to the Tafts to stay at the White House on 3 March 1909. "People have attempted to represent that you and I were in some way at odds during this last three months," Taft told his friend, "whereas you and I know that there has not been the slightest difference between us, and I welcome the opportunity to stay the last night of your administration under the White House roof to make as emphatic as possible the refutation of any such suggestion."[36]

When the two men and their families awoke on the morning of 4 March 1909, they discovered that Washington was in the grip of a severe ice storm. As the two men shared breakfast, Taft said, "Even the elements do protest," to which Roosevelt responded, "I knew there would be a blizzard when I went out."[37] Because of the weather, it was decided to hold the inaugural ceremonies within the Senate chamber. As they waited for the formalities to begin, Taft and Roosevelt marked time in the President's Room of the Capitol. "While they were cordial," noted a reporter, "they did not spend very much time together; for nearly ten minutes they sat by each other's side without saying a word."[38]

Once the oath of office had been administered, Taft delivered his inaugural address to the assembled political dignitaries. He began with a recognition of Roosevelt's accomplishments as president. "I should be untrue to myself, to my promises, and to the declarations of the party platform upon which I was elected to office, if I did not make the maintenance and enforcement of these reforms a most important feature of my administration."[39] He reiterated his pledge to revise the tariff in a manner that would "permit the reduction of rates in certain schedules and will require the advancement of few, if any." Changes in the tariff schedules were needed, moreover, because the government faced a deficit of $100 million in that fiscal year. The new president noted that "the scope of a modern government in what it can and ought to accomplish for its people has been widened far beyond the principles laid down by the old 'laissez faire' school of political writers, and this widening has met popular approval."[40]

Taft then called for strengthening the army and navy, and he advocated federal legislation to enforce "the treaty rights of aliens." He advocated reform of the weaknesses in a banking system that had been strained during the Panic of 1907. He also sought enactment of a postal savings bank system. In foreign policy, Taft spoke out for an increase in foreign trade in anticipation of his program of enhanced American investment in Latin America and Asia. As far as the Panama Canal was concerned, he urged that the nation move ahead to complete the construction begun under Theodore Roosevelt.[41]

A large portion of the second half of Taft's address examined the race issue in the South. He believed, he told his audience, that the Thirteenth and Fourteenth amendments were being enforced "and have secured the objects for which they are intended." As far as the voting rights embodied in the Fifteenth Amendment were concerned, he recognized that these had not been complied with, but he asserted that the South was moving in the direction of enforcement. He believed that the Fifteenth Amendment would not be repealed, but he claimed that "it is not the disposition or within the province of the Federal Government to interfere with the regulation by Southern States of their domestic affairs." Even more than William McKinley and Theodore Roosevelt, Taft was inclined to leave segregation undisturbed, with all that the decision meant for black Americans.[42]

In political terms, Taft's conclusion implied that there would be a substantial reduction of blacks appointed to patronage positions in the South. Republicans had longed used a system of "referees" in the South to decide which members of their party would receive offices in a state. Taft disliked that method. He doubted, for example, "whether, in the case of any race, an appointment of one of their number to a local office in a community in which the race feeling is so widespread and acute as to interfere with the ease and facility with which the local government business can be done by the appointee is of sufficient benefit by way of encouragement to the race to outweigh the recurrence and increase of race feeling which such an appointment is likely to engender." He would, as a result, "exercise a careful discretion" in making appointments in the South. He added

Taft and Roosevelt were still friends at the time of Taft's inauguration on 4 March
1909. Roosevelt Collection—Harvard.

that "I have not the slightest race prejudice or feeling," a conclusion that black listeners to his speech questioned almost at once. Taft had embarked on a quixotic effort to break up the Solid South and risked alienating an important Republican constituency in the North.[43]

Taft devoted the remainder of his address to the issue of labor relations. He hoped to see more legislation to protect workers on railways, but he remained adamant in defending the use of labor injunctions in strikes to curb boycotts of employers and those who did business with them. In closing, the new president invoked "the considerate sympathy and support of my fellow-citizens and the aid of Almighty God in the discharge of my responsible duties."[44]

Taft had mapped out a very ambitious agenda for his presidency. He was going to oversee revision of the tariff, push for a broad domestic agenda, reshape Republican politics in the South, treat diplomacy in a new spirit, and bring economy to government. What he did not say was that he also had plans to regulate corporations, make over Roosevelt's policy on conservation, and bring more efficiency to the operation of the federal government. The degree of Taft's self-confidence going into office was in profound contrast to his lack of experience as an elected politician and legislative leader.

When the president finished his remarks, Roosevelt shook his hand and said: "God bless you, old man. It is a great state document." With that, the former president left for the railroad station, where a crowd sang "Old Lang Syne" as he departed for his home at Oyster Bay, New York. The Tafts, meanwhile, rode together back to the White House, an innovation for a first lady. They watched the inaugural parade, received the president's Yale classmates, and attended the inaugural ball. A weary Taft went to bed, ready to begin the work of his administration the following morning.[45]

The general response in the press to Taft's inaugural address was encouraging, even among some Democratic newspapers. The *New York Times* concluded that "we are to have, it seems, during the next four years, a government of laws, of laws enforced by an Executive of a just and deliberating mind." The *Springfield Republican* sounded the same theme: "Progress under the Taft regime will evidently be more distinguished for orderliness than for jolting speed." All of which led the editors of one journal to observe that "another 'era of good feeling' seems to have dawned on the country." For the moment, the tensions between Roosevelt and Taft, progressives and conservatives within the Republican Party, and Democrats with Republicans in general, had receded. It would not be long, however, before the prospects for Taft would darken.[46]

3

★ ★ ★ ★ ★

THE NEW PRESIDENT AND
HIS COUNTRY

Although William Howard Taft's presidency soon turned sour, his first two months in office seemed positive and promising. When he had been in office seven weeks, a widely published newspaper article drew the contrast between Roosevelt's hectic approach and Taft's calmer working style. "After living in a boiler shop for seven years, it takes Washington more than seven weeks to get used to living in a sanitarium." The White House clerks went home by six in the evening, and the president did not as a rule spend long hours at his job.[1]

The nation's new leader was a man of fifty-one who stood nearly six feet tall and weighed more than 300 pounds. His weight became a source of national amusement and Taft tried hard to take off pounds. He exercised with a personal trainer, rode horseback, and played golf as often as he could. Despite these measures, his weight soared, reaching almost 340 pounds by March 1913. Students of Taft's health have associated his weight gain with the tensions of his position. They have noted that once he was out of office, Taft soon lost more than 70 pounds. He did not exceed 300 pounds again prior to his death in 1930.[2]

Taft tended to nod off at awkward moments when talking to legislators or foreign diplomats. This propensity has led researchers to conclude that the president suffered from sleep apnea. There are also indications of more serious medical problems, such as Bright's disease or neuralgia, during the presidency that raised questions about whether Taft should have resigned. The president himself seems to have had little patience with such considerations. In 1912, at the height of his struggle for reelection with Theodore Roosevelt, his brother Horace inquired about Taft's physical condition. "I don't know who is giving you the accounts of my physical condition," the president responded. "The truth is that I have been better during this active campaign than for some time, and I have come through like a thoroughbred." In a moment of unusual pique for Will Taft, he added, "You and Mabel Boardman and two or three others, constitute yourselves a self-appointed committee without my knowledge, and I don't care for your criticisms or your suspicions or fears."[3]

In the end, the president discharged his duties throughout his four years in the White House and produced a prodigious amount of letters, speeches, and veto messages during that time. Although he was a year older than Theodore Roosevelt, he outlived his friend and rival by eleven years and survived to be almost seventy-three. There is no substantial evidence showing that health problems influenced Taft's performance as chief executive.[4]

Taft, as a man who liked established routines, soon adopted a schedule of work that suited his desire for order and regularity. He rose at about seven o'clock each morning and then exercised with his personal coach, Charles Barker. After an ample breakfast, he perused some newspapers. He favored Republican papers such as the New York *Tribune* and the New York *Sun*. He had less time for the *New York Times,* which was often critical of his policies. Taft left his private quarters by 9:30 a.m. and went over to the White House executive offices. At about 10:00 a.m., he saw visitors until around 1:30 p.m. The president worked into the afternoon, and when weather and the season permitted, he was on the golf course or horseback riding in the late afternoon.[5] When the papers and issues piled up, however, Taft would work into the night. A friend noted that he had the capacity to work at a sustained pace when the occasion demanded it. Like many individuals with that talent, the president tended to procrastinate until the last minute. That trait would get him into trouble with his speechwriting commitments.[6]

For relaxation, golf was Taft's main diversion, although he approached the game more as a personal crusade. He had no patience with the notion that golf was a good walk spoiled. He played with an obsessive intent to improve his score. When he shot in the low 90s, he boasted of that accomplishment to his wife. During the early days of his term, the president played with Secretary of State Philander Knox, Senator Jonathan Bourne of Oregon, General Clarence Edwards, a longtime friend, and the White House military aide, Archibald "Archie" Butt. Unknown to Taft, Edwards leaked information to newspapers about the state of American defenses relative to Japan in 1911.[7]

Taft believed that golf took his mind from his troubles because he

Archie Butt (left), Taft's military aide, attended one of Mrs. Taft's garden parties with the first lady (seated) and the president. Library of Congress.

could concentrate only on his shots and his score. In fact, the demands of the presidency often intruded on his thoughts. He would not, for example, play with his congressional opponents because "I have better use for my time than spending it with such a blatant demagogue as either [Jonathan P.] Dolliver or [Albert B.] Cummins," two Iowa progressives. For the public at large, who still regarded golf as a game for the rich, Taft's devotion to the links came to symbolize his aloofness from ordinary individuals.[8]

The center of Taft's emotional life was his family. His wife, Nellie, was his closest confidante and most trusted adviser. She had big plans for what she hoped to do as first lady. In the first months, she signaled her desire to establish the White House as "the recognized social center of the United States" and to pursue some causes through the National Civic Federation. "The wife of the President," she told the press, "while she has no position in the strictly official sense of the word, nevertheless has obligations as the hostess of the nation which she cannot overlook or shirk. That is my idea, although it has not been that of my predecessors." One particular emphasis of Mrs. Taft was the promotion of serious music, an initiative she pursued through a series of Lenten musicales featuring such artists as pianist Josef Hofmann and violinist Fritz Kreisler. She gave special attention to showcasing female artists in these events.[9]

Then on 17 May 1909 she suffered a disabling stroke after her son, Charlie, was operated on for adenoids. Archie Butt recorded that "the President looked like a great stricken animal. I have never seen greater suffering or pain shown on a man's face." The attack impaired her ability to speak, and she became a recluse. In time she improved, but the full promise of an activist presidential wife never materialized. For her husband, Nellie's illness was a devastating personal blow. She commanded his deep reservoirs of affection, and his manner when he learned of her stroke reflected his personal distress. He followed her improvement with earnest attention and gave her personal watchful care throughout his presidency. When they were apart, he wrote her long, detailed letters, often in his own hand, detailing affairs of state. Whether her presence as an adviser would have enabled Taft to avoid some of the pitfalls of his presidency is impossible to say. Her illness represented a drain on his attention and his feelings that cannot be overstated in evaluating his administration.[10]

None of their three children was at the White House. Robert Alphonso Taft was at Yale, where he was making a distinguished academic record. His sister, Helen Taft, enrolled at Bryn Mawr in autumn 1908 and soon showed the prowess that would lead her toward a life in academe. The youngest, at thirteen, Charles Taft, was attending the Taft School that his uncle, Horace, operated. With his wife ill upstairs in the White House, the president did not have anyone close to him with whom to share the burdens of his new job.

For the most part, the Taft offspring did not achieve the celebrity status that the Roosevelt children, especially Alice Roosevelt, had occupied. The younger Helen Taft made her debut in Washington society without the hoopla that had surrounded Alice Roosevelt. The press did cover the outstanding academic record of Robert A. Taft at Yale, and they reported the 1910 traffic accident in Beverly, Massachusetts, when the younger Taft's car injured "an Italian laborer." The president's son was not found liable for the mishap. Later the president also had to deal with an impostor who pretended to be Robert Taft and duped several people while traveling in the West.[11]

The president did convey his private thoughts to his three brothers— Charles P. Taft, Henry Waters Taft, and Horace Taft—in candid letters about his personal and political situation. As a Wall Street attorney, Henry Taft did not have much political insight. Horace Taft ran a New England private school and was a free trader, so the value of his advice was limited. Charles P. Taft had some influence on the margins of the presidency but was never a close adviser.[12]

Newspapers sought to determine who were the intimate friends of the president. Among the names mentioned were General Clarence Edwards and the mining magnate John Hays Hammond. Other reporters listed the secretary of the American Red Cross, Mabel Boardman. She was the closest female influence outside of his immediate family but not an adviser in a political or policy sense. The press sometimes confused Taft's golfing partners, such as Oregon senator Jonathan Bourne, with true counselors. In fact, there really was no one with Taft to play the role he and Elihu Root had performed for Theodore Roosevelt. Taft had many friends, but few people beyond his wife whom he truly trusted for their advice and insight.[13]

During Taft's tenure as president, the White House underwent changes in its construction and design. Congress had laid aside money in March 1909 for additional offices in the Executive Office Building. With those funds, Taft himself designed an oval office that came into being during the summer of 1909. He began using the facility once he returned from his transcontinental tour in November 1909, and from that place in the center of the White House, he was more in charge of the day-to-day work of the presidency. In 1911, a primitive form of air-conditioning was introduced. "The White House refrigerating plant is just beneath his desk. The cooled air is forced into his room by fans, and statesmen who wend their perspiring way to the executive offices find Mr. Taft smiling and comfortable."[14]

Notwithstanding this modern updating, the president's residence retained some of the bucolic character it had possessed during the nineteenth century. The Tafts owned a dairy cow named Pauline Wayne, a gift of Republican senator Isaac Stephenson of Wisconsin. When milked in a stately Wayne manner, Pauline could produce sixty-four quarts of milk per day, which netted the president some $80 when the milk was sold. Her milk was also sold at an International Dairy Congress in 1911 in small souvenir bottles at 50 cents each. Pauline soon became something of a minor celebrity in her own right, with a button showing her in the stall of a business that provided such facilities for farmers.[15]

In running the White House and keeping track of the flow of paper that came to the president, the Taft years brought significant innovations. The practice had been to divide presidential correspondence into personal and official correspondence. As the amount of paper increased after 1900, that scheme became impractical as far as keeping track of specific issues was concerned. The White House filing staff developed a numerical system of case files classed either by name or by subject. Records that related to politics, for example, were given the number 300 and then grouped under that heading, subdivided by individual states. This approach allowed for a more precise classification of particular documents; it also produced an increase in case files. This method of dealing with the letters and documents that the president received endured through the administration of Dwight D. Eisenhower. In this area, Taft and his aides made a significant improvement of the workings of the modern presidency.[16]

The automobile was coming into wider use by 1909, and Taft's tenure has been correctly named the first motoring presidency. In Washington, he liked to cruise around in the evenings for relaxation. When there were speeches to be given near Washington, he would join his military aide, Archie Butt, and some cabinet members in a jaunt to the engagement. With primitive roads and unreliable cars, the president sometimes needed a push, or helped a stranded motorist with a push of his own. The ability of the chief executive to get around Washington and its environs dramatically broadened while Taft was in office.[17]

William McKinley and Theodore Roosevelt had both traveled extensively to promote their programs. Taft liked to move around even more than they did, and his propensity to visit sections of the country became a trademark of his administration. He made two national tours, one in the late summer and fall of 1909 and the second during the autumn of 1911. But he was out and about on other occasions. Democrats attacked his spending on these journeys. The annual presidential salary had been increased to $75,000 in 1909, and the opposition party contended that the president should pay for his trips out of his own pocket. In the end, Taft got the money, and his traveling went on. Republicans grumbled that he was away too much. "He hasn't the least conception of politics," wrote Republican senator Jacob Gallinger of New Hampshire in May 1910, "and is obsessed with the idea that he must be on the road, or making speeches, all the time." But the public seems to have appreciated Taft's effort to visit their states. As the Philadelphia *Public Ledger* put it, "to most of his fellow-citizens criticism of the President based on the amount of his traveling expenses is the peanut variety and not creditable to those who utter it."[18]

On the eve of Roosevelt's departure for an African safari, Taft sent him a letter that began, "My dear Theodore." The president went on to add: "If I followed my impulse, I should still say 'My dear Mr. President.' I cannot over come the habit. When I am addressed as 'Mr. President,' I turn to see whether you are not at my elbow." One of the problems that Taft faced was a shared sense among his fellow citizens that Roosevelt as president had defined how that office should work. He had been in the post seven and a half years, the longest uninterrupted tenure since Ulysses S. Grant from 1869 to 1877. Coming as it did during the first eight

The president at work in the White House. Library of Congress.

years of a new century, Roosevelt's presidency eclipsed the quieter accomplishments of William McKinley, whose time in office seemed part of a vanished age.[19]

Whether they loved or hated Roosevelt, Americans absorbed his mode of being president as the norm for chief executives. High-profile controversies, ringing messages to Congress, a preaching president in the bully pulpit—these were things the man in the White House was supposed to do over the course of an administration. When Taft failed to emulate the Roosevelt example, there was not so much disappointment as anticlimax. A judge as president seemed out of place somehow. Taft knew he could not be a Roosevelt, but he never found a way to substitute for the energy and theatrical excitement that Roosevelt had imparted to the conduct of the presidency.

Taft liked to tell people that he was not much of a politician. "Politics when I am in it makes me sick," was one of his typical comments about his adopted profession. Yet the extent to which he disliked the customs and practices of politics has often been overstated. His self-deprecation about his skills as a leader disguised a man who was as determined as McKinley and Roosevelt had been in getting his way. Taft also craved recognition of his abilities, although he was careful not to let the political world see that side of his character.[20]

His main asset was the reputation he had cultivated as a genial big man with a winning laugh. The Taft chuckle on the stump was, as a friend put it, "a form of physical enjoyment." He did not tell jokes or recount anecdotes; the moments of amusement arose from the context of his remarks. Soon the whole audience would be chuckling along with the president. As a newspaper man put it when Taft was secretary of war, "when he laughs, the surrounding furniture shakes and rumbles."[21]

There was another aspect of Taft's personality that emerged while he was in the White House. Theodore Roosevelt once called his friend "one of the best haters" he ever knew. Unlike McKinley, who kept his dislikes to himself, and Roosevelt, whose animosities came and went, President Taft nurtured his grievances. By August 1909, this propensity had made its way into the press. "The number of persons in quasipublic positions who it is said Mr. Taft does not like is notably large."[22] In his private letters, Taft was as vituperative as Roosevelt had been in describing his adversaries as "cranks," "fanatics," "liars," and "egotists." Roosevelt had often been indiscreet. Taft was even more so.

One example of Taft's ability to hold a grudge came early in his administration. Henry White was the American ambassador to France. White, a longtime member of the diplomatic service, was close to Roosevelt. For the Tafts, however, he was someone who had insulted them years before.

While honeymooning in England, where White was a member of the American ministry, Will and Nellie Taft asked for tickets to see the Houses of Parliament. The snobbish White got them admittance instead to the royal stables. So when Taft had the power, he let White go and sent Robert Bacon, another friend of Roosevelt, to the Paris embassy instead. Taft denied that he had meant any slight against White, but the damage was done. Washington insiders chalked it up as another insult to Roosevelt.[23]

Taft's verbal indiscretions were another liability for his presidency. He had a tendency to pop off about a subject without thinking through the implications of what he said. Roosevelt thought long and hard before he said something that would be published. Taft, on the other hand, tended to speak freely and without preparation in his statements to reporters and his public addresses. Whether this arose from the haste with which he wrote his speeches at the last minute or from an inability to consider the implications of his remarks, this tendency would recur during the administration, to the president's discredit.

The official staff of the White House in 1909 was still small by contemporary standards. By the end of the presidency, the total budgeted staff was eighty people, most of whom were clerks or stenographers. Taft really operated with a single secretary, one or two executive clerks, and no policy apparatus of the modern variety. Twenty-five servants attended to the personal needs of the presidential family. In many respects, the presidency was still a manageable, personalized operation, much like a large law office or medium-sized business. The staff appreciated that the president kept to a regular schedule and allowed them to work regular hours after the hectic late nights that characterized the last years of Roosevelt.

The first presidential secretary was Fred W. Carpenter, who had been with Taft in the Philippines and the War Department. Born in 1872, he grew up in California, received a law degree from the University of Minnesota, and entered Taft's employ in 1900. Carpenter was, said Taft in the fall of 1908, "just as good today as he was then, or even better, because he understands better how to control me and keep me straight." Unfortunately, Carpenter did not measure up to the demands of the presidency. According to reporters who worked with him, the secretary had a thin skin and was "diffident and easily embarrassed." Moreover, Carpenter could not deal efficiently with the press of visitors who wanted to see the president. Complaints about the slowness with which Taft did business bounced to the secretary. As the months passed, it became clear that Carpenter was just not suited to the position. In June 1910, he was named minister to Morocco, and Charles Dyer Norton replaced him.[24]

Carpenter's problems as secretary arose in large part because of the way that Taft approached the press and the public. As secretary of war,

Fred W. Carpenter came into the administration after serving as Taft's secretary at the War Department. He proved a liability and was given a diplomatic appointment in 1910. Library of Congress.

"he was always a 'good scout'" who had been accessible to reporters, who drew a comment or quotation from him on most occasions. In the White House, however, the president became more aloof. Fred Carpenter told the reporters on the day of the inauguration that "the President did not expect to see newspapermen as frequently as he had done when Secretary of War." He would send for them when he wished to see them. That change in approach did not get Taft off on the right foot with journalists, and to some extent, his relations with them never recovered.[25] Taft had always had ambivalence about the press and their treatment of him. He lacked the tough hide that other politicians developed. He found it difficult to read newspapers that attacked his policies or himself. After a year of Taft's administration, a Boston newspaper concluded that "No President since Cleveland, if, indeed that exception need be made, has exhibited so much sensitiveness to newspaper criticism as the present occupant of the White House."[26]

Taft believed that Theodore Roosevelt had spent too much time courting the press. The president thought that his good deeds in office should speak for themselves, without the need of self-promotion from the White House. Roosevelt "talked with correspondents a great deal. His heart was generally on his sleeve, and he must communicate his feelings. I find myself unable to do so," he told William Allen White. "After I have made a definite statement, I have to let it go at that, until the time for action arises, when I seek as sincerely and earnestly as I can to live up to my previous declaration." He then expected public opinion to support his policies. Taft failed to see that the presidency had changed under McKinley and Roosevelt. Now the public expected explanations and commentary from the White House. In the absence of such news, the president's political enemies soon filled the void with criticism.[27]

Taft's attitude toward the press and public relations grew out of the judgelike manner in which he viewed his official duties. He conducted cabinet meetings as though they were judicial conferences, and he viewed the decisions he had to make as if he were preparing to write an opinion. Although he wanted the Republican Party to succeed, he thought of his office as somehow above partisan considerations. "I don't want any forced or manufactured sentiment in my favor," he told a reporter in 1910. He often reminisced about the joys of his days as an appeals court judge, when he could engage "a problem with absolute indifference to the results except to solve it on its merits." Throughout his presidency, he felt most at ease when considering an issue on what he deemed to be its true qualities, without taking into account how it might play politically.[28]

These attitudes stemmed from Taft's underlying assumptions about the authority of his office and the proper role of the chief executive within the American system of government. He would articulate his views in more detail after he left the White House, but they governed his four years as president. Unlike Theodore Roosevelt, who was convinced that the president should do anything that the Constitution did not explicitly forbid, Taft was sure that the chief executive had to remain within the boundaries of the Constitution itself. He had scant tolerance for the doctrine that there were implied powers that a president might use to accomplish desired ends. Instead, the chief executive should stay within his constitutional limits and respect the legislative and judicial branches within theirs as well. "We have a government of limited power under the Constitution," Taft observed in June 1909, and "we have got to work out our problems on the basis of law. Now, if that is reactionary, then I am a reactionary."[29]

When it came to natural resources, for example, Taft had little patience with the approach of Roosevelt, Gifford Pinchot, and their zealous allies within the government. Roosevelt asserted that unless Congress had acted to prohibit his actions, the president might create forest reserves, charge for electric power on rivers on federal land, and otherwise use the bureaucracy to implement national programs. Taft found this expansive method distasteful when he was secretary of war, and he did not intend to countenance its existence within his administration. One reason he appointed Richard Ballinger as the secretary of the interior was their shared displeasure with what the president regarded as Roosevelt's freewheeling use of the executive power to circumvent the will of Congress.[30]

Taft's treatment of his cabinet stemmed from his experience with Roosevelt. He did not believe that the president should try to run the various departments. In the case of the Department of State, he told Philander Knox that the White House would not intrude into the conduct of diplomacy, and for the most part, the president kept that pledge. "I want you to know that the arrangement of the State Department is to suit you, and you can take any course you see fit," Taft told Knox in January 1909. "Whatever you do will satisfy me." Of course, in practice, things did not work out with that degree of efficiency. Taft maintained the same approach with his other cabinet officials, although in the case of the Justice Department, he did serve as his own attorney general in making judicial nominations. His loose rein on Treasury and the post office would in time prove to be political liabilities for the administration.[31]

Taft's cabinet itself was not as strong as it might have been. Knox and George Wickersham at Justice performed capably, as did George von Lengerke Meyer at the Navy Department. "Mac" Dickinson was a disappointment at the War Department, and Frank MacVeagh at Treasury did not assert himself in policy matters. Ballinger at Interior proved to be a major source of controversy for the White House in the area of conservation. James Wilson at Agriculture had been in office too long, and Charles Nagel at Commerce did not make an imprint on his post. Overall, the Taft cabinet revealed that the president ought to have exerted more control over his subordinates than he did. He would learn that lesson when he embarked on his campaign to improve the efficiency of the federal government in 1910–1911.

In many respects, William Howard Taft's growing disillusionment with Theodore Roosevelt's performance in the White House defined his presidency from 1909 to 1913. When he took office in March 1909, Taft saw himself as the direct heir of what Roosevelt had done. The new president might think that Roosevelt had been a little loose in his methods, but he believed that they were identical in their goals for the nation.

Just as Roosevelt had pushed away any possible doubts about Taft, so too had his friend quelled reservations about the former president. Yet these qualms were there, just beneath the surface. As Taft settled into the job as president, he noticed how much he had disagreed with his predecessor. Writing to his wife in October 1909 during the emerging crisis over relations between Gifford Pinchot and Ballinger, Taft told her that "the whole administration under Roosevelt was demoralized by his system of dealing directly with subordinates." Taft and Elihu Root, he said, "simply ignored the interference and went on as we chose," while other cabinet officers did not. Taft would be careful not to repeat what he regarded as Roosevelt's mistake in this regard.[32]

Doubts about method soon spilled over into questions about substance. Taft did not like what Roosevelt had done in distinguishing between good and bad trusts. He was equally skeptical of the reliance on Pinchot and other "socialists" in shaping conservation policy. As he recalled events during his service in the cabinet, Taft realized that there were many times when Roosevelt had acted in a high-handed and even unethical manner, at least in Taft's retrospective judgment. "The Colonel," as he came to call Roosevelt with more than a hint of derision, seemed less an example to be followed and more a cautionary tale to be avoided.

William Howard Taft then had profound reservations about the ways in which his predecessor had transformed the presidential office. The notion of the chief executive as a celebrity who made news through the force of his personality was anathema to Taft. He did not wish to entertain the public; he wanted to enlighten them as a jurist would a higher court. Taft struggled against the expectations for presidential behavior that Roosevelt had created. He never found a way to emerge from the huge historical shadow that Roosevelt had cast upon the institution.

Another legacy from Roosevelt limited what Taft could do in the

White House. The disposition of patronage and the allocation of federal jobs was one way that a president could discipline Congress and lead his party. For Taft, however, that time-honored weapon existed in a much-diminished form. During the prelude to the Republican National Convention in 1908, Roosevelt had doled out jobs to Taft supporters. The result was that Taft could create vacancies only by dismissing officeholders already loyal to him. "I have come into office very much as if I were Mr. Roosevelt succeeding himself," Taft told one correspondent in July 1909, with the result that "the men who fill the offices to which you refer are men who are friendly to me and appointees of Mr. Roosevelt, and were earnest and anxious to help me in my canvass."[33]

Nonetheless, there would be opportunities for Taft to wield patronage on his own behalf. The taking of the 1910 census, for example, would require the appointment of three hundred supervisors who would then name enumerators in all the states. For each congressional district, there was to be a supervisor. These circumstances created a potential for any number of political appointments for Republicans. Taft would have to grapple with those considerations during the summer of 1909. As he did so, he would confront the question of whether to give progressive Republicans in Congress a large voice in the naming of census officials within their own districts. Taft's own inclination was to keep the taking of the census out of politics, but he would discover that was easier to assert than to accomplish.[34]

In allocating patronage, Taft did implement his program of phasing out African American officeholders in the South, as he had forecast in his inaugural address. By June 1909, Booker T. Washington was writing the president about the reduction of black officials in the South, noting that "the colored people throughout the country watch very closely these little changes, and they are becoming not a little stirred up" as a result. Taft responded that "the matter of appointments and filling place is a most difficult one to carry out." African Americans observed what the White House was doing in this area with mounting apprehension. By August, Washington was reporting "the deep feeling of disappointment and sadness" among blacks regarding "the supposed attitude of President Taft." Of course, Taft did not see African Americans as his main constituency, and he blamed members of his cabinet for some of the actions taken toward blacks. His assurances by November 1909 that he "meant to carry out in letter and spirit what he had to say in his inaugural address" did not calm the resentment among African Americans at all levels.[35]

The other difficult legacy was the self-imposed requirement that Taft and Congress take up the tariff issue in a special session. By 1909, the tariff question, once a source of Republican cohesion and strength, had developed into a potential political liability for the Grand Old Party. The shift in attitudes had started after the turn of the century, when inflation worldwide produced rising prices in the United States. Consumers complained that the high duties on imports led to greater costs for the goods they purchased. Democrats linked these developments to the protectionist policy embodied in the Dingley tariff of 1897. Some Republicans, most of them from the Middle West, agreed that rates were excessive on the goods their constituents bought in the marketplace. Cries to revise the tariff appeared after 1901 and intensified during the presidency of Roosevelt.

As president, Roosevelt dodged and evaded the tariff issue. He did not understand it as a political doctrine, and his grasp of it as an economic policy was also uncertain. He knew that it had the potential to divide his party and would interfere with his plans for government regulation of railroads and other corporations. From the time he became president, he sought to keep the tariff issue off the national agenda. The upshot of his approach was to postpone discussion on a matter that went to the heart of what it meant to be a Republican.

Roosevelt's strategy allowed the tariff issue to fester. Because he had not engaged it, the next president would have to do so. Taft himself was a lower-tariff man within the Republican ranks, and he had made clear his commitment to trim duties wherever possible. At the same time, he was not a free trader, and he knew that protectionism defined the party. The expectations that had been created for resolving the tariff question thus entailed disappointing one or the other faction among Republicans. The new president hoped to get the tariff bill adopted as quickly as he could and then move on in the regular session of Congress in December 1909 to take up the key parts of his own program. He thought that he could emulate the success that William McKinley had shown in 1897 in pushing the Dingley tariff through a special session of Congress during the summer. Of course, McKinley and his party had come in after the Democratic tariff policies seemed to have failed during the depression of the 1890s. Taft would not share that advantage in timing.

When Taft took office, the American economy seemed to have recovered from the shock it received during the Panic of 1907, when banks tottered and the financial system seemed to approach collapse. For the 90,492,000 Americans, the gross domestic product had risen from nearly $47 billion in the four years from 1902 to 1906 to more than $55 billion in the period 1907 to 1911. The average worker toiled nearly fifty-seven hours a week for an average wage of 25 cents per hour. The annual earnings stood at $543, up from $516 in 1908, but were about the same as they had been in 1907, before the panic. Meanwhile, the consumer price index had risen steadily over the decade since 1901, from 28.3 in that year to 35.1

in Taft's first year. Much of the agitation for lower tariffs stemmed from the pressures of inflation, both domestic and worldwide.

For President Taft, the most urgent economic question was the state of government finances. There was no formal budget system at this time, but it was apparent that the last two years of the Roosevelt presidency had brought increased government spending. Expenditures rose some $80 million in Roosevelt's last year to $659 million and would top $693 million in 1909. A decline in government revenues from $665 million in 1907 to $601 million in 1908 helped account for a budget deficit of $57 million at the end of Roosevelt's presidency. The deficit figure would rise to $89 million in 1909 and spur the new president to look for ways to trim government spending, and in time to consider instituting a budget system for the federal government. The extent to which Taft pursued a smaller, more efficient government is one of the lesser-known elements of his presidency. Roosevelt had not worried much about government accounting. For Taft, the consideration of fiscal restraint would be a large element in his calculations.

Before the new chief executive could engage what were to him the more significant problems of society—railroad regulation, control of corporations, publicity of campaign expenses, and conservation—he had to run the gauntlet of tariff revision. There were many voices within the Republican Party warning him of the potential dangers he faced in such an approach. "It seems to me," wrote one conservative senator in April 1909, "that the new leader will have to do some effective work to keep the Republican party right side up with care."[36] Taft believed that he and the Republicans had an obligation to engage the issue and resolve it. In the early days of his administration, as the newspapers praised his inaugural address and the more relaxed atmosphere at the White House, the president found that the fractured state of the Republicans made his task even more difficult than he had imagined as a candidate for the White House. The choices that Taft made in the enactment of the Payne–Aldrich tariff of 1909 would determine the subsequent course of his administration and its place in history.

4

★ ★ ★ ★ ★

SEEKING DOWNWARD REVISION: THE PAYNE–ALDRICH TARIFF

The defining moment of William Howard Taft's presidency came early. In the congressional debate over revising the tariff during the summer of 1909, Taft revealed his approach to Congress and lawmaking. It would continue for the next four years. His decisions about how to proceed with the tariff grew out of his judgments about how best to function as the leader of the Republican Party. A case can be made that the president did as well as he could with the legislative situation that he faced in the spring of 1909. However, the perception that he had sold out to conservatives on Capitol Hill became fixed, and in some sense, his credibility never recovered.

Taft tried to learn from Roosevelt's experience with lawmakers. In these initial months, he consulted a broad range of legislators to forge a consensus about the tariff. He entertained (as Roosevelt had not done) Republicans of all ideological positions at the White House. He deferred to the advice of Republican leaders such as Joseph G. Cannon and Nelson Aldrich. To some extent, he even pressured Congress with more force than Roosevelt had utilized. When the Payne–Aldrich tariff finally passed in August 1909, however, the split among Republicans had widened. Once off his stride, Taft never really regained the initiative for the rest of his term. The battle over the Payne–Aldrich tariff turned out to be a self-inflicted wound that shaped the rest of the presidency.

Calling Congress into special session in March 1909 gave the opponents of Speaker Cannon a new chance to challenge his leadership. In turn, that provided for President Taft another occasion for him to show whether he would side with the anti-Cannon rebels or the party hierarchy in the House. The arithmetic indicated the political choices that Taft faced. Of the 218 House Republicans, Cannon commanded the allegiance of 165 to 175. The "insurgents" against Cannon numbered no more than thirty members, with another ten or fifteen waverers. These critics were articulate and vocal, but they lacked votes and a plausible alternative to Cannon as Speaker. In addition, the Speaker had some Democratic allies who would join him in defeating any attempt to alter the House rules.[1]

Taft recognized his predicament. As he wrote to Kansas editor and progressive publicist William Allen White, "I have a definite program before me as to securing certain legislation, and can not lean on a broken reed like the Democracy. I have got to regard the Republican party as the instrumentality through which to try to accomplish something." Progressives at the time and historians since have argued that Taft could have rallied the public with anti-Cannon assaults. How that strategy would have persuaded conservative Republicans in the House to abandon Cannon was not evident at the time, and it seems even less plausible decades later. When he weighed his entire legislative agenda for 1909–1910 against the single issue of the tariff, Taft concluded that he should not spend all his political capital at the outset of his term.[2]

As Congress assembled for the special session, the president had to decide where he stood on an insurgent challenge to Cannon. The Speaker and his leadership team came to the White House on 9 March 1909 to inform the president that he would not get his tariff bill through the House if he sided with the anti-Cannon forces. Taft took the advice of Roosevelt and the other party leaders to accept the hard fact of Cannon's position and move forward. The insurgents, however, regarded the president as having betrayed them and their cause. Cannon was reelected on 14 March with only some cosmetic changes in the Speaker's power. It was easier for the anti-Cannon rebels to believe that Taft's support would have beaten the Speaker than to admit that they simply did not have the votes to win. The perception that Taft had caved in to Cannon would continue to shape insurgent thinking as the tariff battle went forward.[3]

Once the special session got under way, Taft contemplated what he should do about setting the agenda for revising the tariff. That he would send a message to Capitol Hill requesting action was a given. The issue for the new president was the form his message should take. Faced with a bevy of office seekers, Taft had little time to write his message during the first ten days. At the same time, the president had ample reason to be terse. Roosevelt's practice of long, insistent messages had wearied Congress by the time he left office. An extended disquisition from Taft would have sounded the wrong note.

The president limited himself to 324 words in asking for a revision of the tariff on 16 March. He noted that the government faced an impending deficit in its receipts of $100 million and argued that the "new bill should be agreed upon and passed with as much speed as possible consistent with its due and thorough consideration."[4] He cited his inaugural address for thoughts about the direction of such revision and urged that few other subjects should be discussed in the special session. The president and the Republicans did not want the tariff revision process to drag on into the heat of the Washington summer. Worse yet would be a failure to pass a bill and have the problem spill over into the regular session in December. Taft, who hoped for some vacation time with his wife in August, also had in mind the planned transcontinental speaking tour scheduled for September and October.

Progressives in the House and Senate later asserted that the tariff message provoked disappointment and fell flat. They wanted the president to pronounce a crusade for a lower tariff. Contemporary newspapers, however, recorded that "this message was a delight to every member of Congress, regardless of party affiliation."[5] Whether that was true or not, Taft had decided to work within the strategy of courting the GOP leadership to achieve results on the tariff. That course would be seen as a blunder when the Payne–Aldrich tariff became a liability.

In shaping his course on tariff revision, Taft knew, as did other Washington insiders, that the process of voting in the House and Senate was largely designed to set the stage for the real legislative drama: the work of the conference committee. The Republicans would exclude Democrats from that panel as the final bill took shape. Then, working within the limits of the schedules that the House and Senate had adopted, the conferees would decide on the ultimate bill. Everything hinged on the capacity of the Republican leader in the upper house, Nelson Aldrich, to control events for the Senate Republicans and the Taft administration.

At sixty-seven in 1909, Aldrich had a reputation in Washington as the undisputed master of "an organization in the Senate that is effective and efficient."[6] Like Cannon in the House, Aldrich seemed to rule the Senate, but that impression was inaccurate. The Republicans held a thirty-seat majority over the Democrats, at sixty-one to thirty-one. That apparent dominance concealed Aldrich's real problem. There were among Republicans significant defectors from Aldrich's majority. Robert M. La Follette of Wisconsin, Jonathan P. Dolliver of Iowa, Albert Baird Cummins of Iowa, and Albert J. Beveridge of Indiana had all quarreled with Aldrich in the past over other issues. Disposed to regard tariff rates as too high on the products their constituents purchased, these men and those who followed them could well defect if rates were set too high. Four or five other

Republicans were ready to line up with this core group of insurgents once the Senate bill was revealed. If that happened, Aldrich would have lost ten votes from his majority. Even more important, with the Republican majority reduced to about a dozen votes, protectionist senators saw a chance to gain more concessions for the products of their states. A lobbyist for the boot and shoe manufacturers reported in late April, for example, that Aldrich was "four votes short of a majority in the Senate for his Bill." The fragile margin of the Republican coalition in the upper house was a central element in how the tariff writing turned out in 1909.[7]

At first, the tariff bill seemed to go the way the president and his allies hoped. The Ways and Means Committee in the House, chaired by Sereno E. Payne of New York, had been holding hearings and writing a bill since the last months of 1908. Payne introduced the committee bill on 17 March. The measure set rates lower on steel products, lumber, printing paper, and pig iron. It placed wood pulp and hides on the free list without duties. The fate of hides would soon become a major source of contention among Republicans. One interested Republican in the House called the Payne bill "much better than we expected" but also "better than we can hope to pass." President Taft agreed. "I am hopeful that we shall get through the tariff bill not very different from the bill as proposed to the House," he wrote on 21 March.[8]

The House spent two and half weeks debating the Payne measure. For the most part, the speeches were designed for consumption at home and did not advance any new arguments. With the Republicans in secure control of the proceedings, the members discussed amendments to the lumber schedule, the placing of hides on the free list, and reductions in the rates on barley and barley malt. Then the House beat back a motion on 9 April to recommit the legislation to the Ways and Means Committee and passed the bill by a party-line vote of 217 to 161. "We have had a tough struggle here over the tariff with the realization that after all the bill would be made mainly in the Senate," wrote one House Republican. For the White House, what Payne and the House had done was "a genuine effort in the right direction."[9]

Newspapers warned, however, that matters would be different in the Senate. There, insurgent lawmakers were expected to provide "more or less resistance" to "ultra protectionist ideas, which are expected to be advanced by the Republican leaders of the finance committee."[10] This prediction proved to be correct when the Senate took up the bill that Nelson Aldrich and the Finance Committee had framed on 21 April. The Midwestern progressive senators were outraged at the way Aldrich and his allies had reshaped the Payne bill. To construct a majority, the Republican leader had moved many of the most controversial schedules back in the direction of the rates in the Dingley tariff of 1897. Of the 800 amendments that Aldrich sponsored, more than half raised rates to what they had been in the Dingley law. The hide schedule was returned to the 15 percent rate that existed, much to the delight of the western range senators from such states as Colorado and Wyoming.[11]

The three leading progressives—La Follette, Beveridge, and Dolliver—had different motives for their position. La Follette and Beveridge had ambitions for the White House. Dolliver and Aldrich detested each other over events going back almost ten years. With their allies, such as Joseph L. Bristow of Kansas, the progressives divided up key schedules such as wool, cotton, and sugar, and launched an intensive study of how these products had gained their favored status. Then they opened a sustained offensive against the Aldrich version of the bill. "The American people expect us, if it can be done, to reduce the schedules of the Dingley tariff act somewhat," said Dolliver on 22 April. The public airing of the differences with the party leadership revealed fault lines within the Grand Old Party and complicated the task that Aldrich and the president confronted.[12]

Taft and Aldrich had agreed that the White House should stay out of the tariff-writing process until the conference committee went about its work. As the president wrote in late June, "I don't think there is any trouble about their knowing in the Senate what I am likely to do should occasion arise for my saying so in conference. But I am quite disposed not to use a threat until it seems fair and necessary."[13] The insurgents wanted Taft to come out in the open and endorse their position. They resented that, as Joseph L. Bristow put it, they had "received no support whatever in this tremendous fight we have made from the White House."[14] From Taft's point of view, it made no sense to assail the party leadership to support men such as Beveridge and La Follette.

The major newspapers chimed in with heavy criticism of Taft's position on their editorial pages. Self-interest motivated much of this public outrage. The publishers hoped to have the tariff duties on print paper from Canada and wood pulp either eliminated or reduced to lower their production costs. The House had set the duty for print paper at $2 per ton, down from the $6 in the Dingley law. The Senate bill pushed the duty up to $4 a ton. Editors attacked the Senate version and sought to increase public pressure for lower duties across the board. These considerations intensified the tensions between the White House and the press.[15]

In mid-June, Taft and Aldrich launched another move to forestall progressive pressure on the Senate tariff bill. Because the anticipated reductions in customs duties from downward revision would worsen the deficit in government finances, insurgents and Democrats were ready to propose an income tax to make up for lost revenue. As early as April, Senator Joseph Weldon Bailey of Texas and Albert B. Cummins had introduced bills to impose an income tax. Taft told his correspondents, "I do favor the imposition of an income tax."[16]

The problem from the perspective of the president was the Supreme Court's decision in the 1890s to declare an income tax unconstitutional. Accordingly, he opposed the use of a statute to secure an income tax.[17] The president needed a means to stop the Democrats and progressive Republicans from adopting an income tax and including it in the tariff bill.

In a message to Congress on 16 June, Taft proposed a corporation tax instead. An income tax should be adopted only after passage of an amendment to the Constitution establishing the power of Congress to do so. "It is much wiser policy to accept the decision and remedy the defect by amendment in due and regular course." Instead, he recommended an excise tax on corporations and joint stock companies of 2 percent of their net income annually. The tax would also provide information about corporate organization and represent "a long step toward that supervisory control of corporations which may prevent a further abuse of power."[18]

Taft's initiative was adopted because the conservative Republicans in the Senate realized that if they did not do so, the alliance of progressive Republicans and low-tariff Democrats would include an income tax in the tariff bill. Senator Aldrich agreed that if that were not the case, "I should never have come to make the proposition which I did for a message and the submission of an amendment."[19] To give the progressive Republicans some cover, the president also supported a joint resolution of Congress to amend the Constitution to allow for an income tax. On 2 July, the corporation tax was adopted by a vote of 45 to 31, and the amendment for the income tax received unanimous approval three days later.[20]

Taft's interplay with the Senate conservatives over the corporation tax intensified bitter feelings among the insurgents. They believed that the president had encouraged them to push for the income tax with promises of support, and then had undercut them with Aldrich and his corporation tax. His course, wrote Senator Bristow, "has developed here a very intense and bitter feeling." Taft denied that he had ever told the supporters of the income tax of his implicit endorsement of their plan. The main gripe of the insurgents was the president's willingness to talk with Aldrich at all. Taft saw these sessions as necessary to accomplish his legislative goals. In the public mind, Aldrich had become the living embodiment of corporate power. As a Missouri Republican wrote, "The feeling pervades the entire west that anything that originates with Senator Aldrich is the child of the trusts, and this intensifies the feeling among the masses of the people."[21]

Taft was locked in to his strategy of working with Aldrich and

Cannon. By the time the tariff bill neared passage in the Senate, the president had identified himself with some of the administrative features of the proposed law. The language of the bill created a maximum and minimum clause that allowed the chief executive to raise tariff duties on countries that engaged in discriminatory tactics against the United States. In the case of the Philippines, a subject close to Taft's sympathies, the bill liberalized trade overall while limiting imports from the islands of sugar, tobacco, and cigars. There was also a provision for a tariff commission to supply the president with greater information on how specific schedules operated. When the corporation tax was added to the provisions of the tariff legislation, the president saw even more reason to hope that the final version would be a bill he could sign. A veto remained unlikely, but as the president wrote on 13 July, "Nevertheless, as the main promise was that the revision was to be a downward revision, I shall feel justified if there is no substantial step in that direction in resorting to my Constitutional [veto] power."[22]

The Aldrich version of the tariff passed late in the evening on 8 July by a vote of 45 to 34. Ten Republicans joined twenty-four Democrats in voting against the Senate leadership. Although Aldrich probably had votes in reserve if needed, the outcome emphasized how fragile was the coalition that the Republican leader had assembled. If western senators should join the progressives, the bill could fail—a point that Republican lawmakers well understood when it came time to do the work of the conference committee.

The insurgent senators saw their chance to pressure Taft and make their case to the public as well. Albert Beveridge, one of the defectors, remarked, "I am for protection, I believe the American people are for it, but to be a protectionist does not mean that we are to be extortionists."[23] In a memorandum to the president as the conference committee started its work, Robert La Follette wrote that "unless the rates are very greatly reduced, the bill should be vetoed." The president, the Wisconsin senator went on, was "in a position to insist upon a reduction in rates below the lowest rates adopted by either house."[24]

The pleas of the insurgent senators left Taft unmoved. He intended to cooperate with Aldrich if possible. "I am hopeful that Mr. Aldrich will look at the matter largely from my standpoint, and that he will not hold out to the uttermost," the president wrote his wife on 11 July. In the two weeks that followed, the president devoted most of his time to negotiations with the conferees. He was aggrieved that Speaker Cannon had stacked the conference panel with conservatives.[25]

To get the bill through the Senate, Aldrich had to pacify the western range senators who were unhappy with having cattle hides on the free list. The strong-arm tactics of Senator Francis E. Warren of Wyoming and other members from the Rocky Mountain West resulted in the return of the 15 percent duty on hides. Lined up in favor of free hides were the boot and shoe manufacturers of the East, who sought to lower the price of their raw materials. Lobbyists for the National Boot and Shoe Manufacturers Association and the National Association of Tanners worked on their side of the question to bring over eastern Republicans to the free hide position. The question of hides soon emerged as the key schedule in the work of the conference committee.[26]

From Taft's perspective, during the middle two weeks of July, he pushed hard against his fellow Republicans to obtain reductions on wood pulp, oil, gloves, and especially cattle hides. The insurgents, for their part, argued that the president should also seek lower rates on cotton, wool, and industrial products.

The most controversial of these schedules was wool, designated as the infamous Schedule K in tariff bills. The coalition behind wool was the most powerful of all the tariff lobbies, uniting western wool growers with eastern clothing makers and retailers. Years before, these two economic interests had worked out an arrangement of schedules about wool that linked them together. Had Taft endeavored to obtain serious reductions in rates on wool products, he would have imperiled the entire bill. Critics of the tariff thought that the president could do almost anything with strong executive leadership. In fact, his room for bargaining was very constricted. As one western senator informed his wife, "We are all right on the wool schedule but in jeopardy on hides."[27]

On 16 July, a delegation of Republican House members (and one protectionist Democrat) came to the White House to argue against free hides and what was known in tariff parlance as "free raw materials." Proponents of free raw materials contended that duties should be placed only on finished products from foreign competitors. Taft listened to what his GOP colleagues had to say.

Then, in what was "not a premeditated pronunciamento on my part," the president said that "he was not committed to the principle of free raw material, but that he was committed to the principle of a downward revision of the tariff, which he had promised." If hides and other products did not need protection, then these articles "should go on the free list."[28]

This assertion of presidential authority produced positive press coverage and an outpouring of letters of support to the White House. If Taft had not taken such a stand, and were he to cave in to the conservatives, "the call for the man in the jungles would be louder than the roar of Niagara, and no power on earth could stop it." The president's action, however, did not suit the western range lawmakers, and they seemed even more intent on holding out for a duty on hides at the risk of blocking the bill. Warren and Reed Smoot of Utah saw the president. The Wyoming senator told Taft "that he would vote against the bill if free hides were included in the bill and 5 or 6 other senators would." As a way out of the dilemma, the westerners argued that they would be willing to accept free hides if reductions were made in duties on leather goods.[29]

Meanwhile, other products threatened to upset the conference committee deliberations. Speaker Cannon endeavored to raise duties on gloves to help out a fellow Republican, Lucius N. Littauer of New York. "The Speaker is engaged in trying to foist a high tariff on gloves into the bill in the interest of a friend named Littauer," the president told his wife, "and he has been threatening Aldrich and I believe will threaten me with defeating the bill unless this goes in. It is the greatest exhibition of tyranny that I have known of his attempting."[30]

The lumber schedule also proved a point of protectionist contention. The House bill had reduced the Dingley rate of $2 per thousand feet to $1 per thousand feet. The Senate restored the Dingley rate. Taft said that he would accept a rate of $1.25 per thousand feet on undressed lumber.

As the newspapers noted, "in all tariff revisions the issue finally gets down to one article on which everything depends. That is made the test. In this case it is hides." The president emphasized that he would not accept a bill without free hides. To that end, he mentioned a veto in private. Taft also warned that if the tariff were defeated, he would summon Congress back into special session to take up the subject again. In that session, the wool schedule would be addressed. The *Boston Transcript* said, "If the Payne Bill is defeated, wool and woolens will be among the first points of attack by the excited people."[31]

Taft decided that he had now to intervene in person to achieve passage of the tariff bill. On 29 July, he wrote a letter to Senator Aldrich specifying what it would take for him to accept the legislation. He said that he would not accept a duty higher than $1.25 on undressed lumber, he rejected the glove schedule that Cannon backed, and he reiterated his allegiance to free hides with the reductions in leather goods that the westerners were seeking. The letter was released to the newspapers, and political momentum swung toward the White House. "It turned out to be much more successful than some people thought," Taft wrote his wife, "and I hope it has not left any bad traces."[32]

The president's action broke the legislative stalemate, and on 31 July 1909, the House voted to accept the conference report. The result was tight, with only a five-vote margin for the administration on a motion to recommit the bill to the Ways and Means Committee. The Republicans had some votes in reserve, "but even at that it was a close vote." In the

Senate, there was last-minute confusion over the wording of the language producing reductions in the duties on boots and shoes. When that was resolved, the Senate voted to accept the conference report. Seven Republican insurgents, including Beveridge, Dolliver, and La Follette, voted no on final passage. Beveridge called his vote "good conscience and good politics."[33]

The small body of historical literature on what came to be known as the Payne–Aldrich Tariff Act conveys the impression that the congressional battle during the summer of 1909 fascinated the country. In fact, the reaction to the passage of the bill was mild, with editorial opinion leaning toward praise of Taft's leadership. "It should be generously conceded," wrote the editors of the *Wall Street Journal*, "that President Taft saved his party in some measure from indelible disgrace." On the opposing side, the Kansas City *Star*, a progressive Republican paper, deemed the bill "a flagrant betrayal of the people." The editors of the Washington *Post* said on 6 August that "it is easy to pick flaws in the bill, but it cannot be denied that, as a whole, it is as good as any tariff legislation that has preceded it."[34]

The key impact of the struggle lay in the tensions it revealed among Republicans. Protectionists in the party resented Taft's campaign for lower duties. Having voted to support the White House, they now wanted the president to provide them with political cover in his speeches and public statements. The insurgents, for their part, blamed Taft for not standing with them or even vetoing the bill. "I am convinced that a very large proportion of the people are with us," wrote Albert Cummins in mid-August. He believed that "we were doing what we could to secure even-handed justice."[35]

The problem for Taft was how to hold his fractured party together when the congressional session opened in December 1909. The president invited some insurgents to the White House as a peace gesture. At the same time, he disregarded the recommendations that the progressive senators and representatives made about census supervisors for the 1910 census tabulation. The progressives in the Wisconsin delegation, for example, found that their recommendations were ignored and these patronage positions allocated to Senator Isaac Stephenson, who had been a loyal Taft supporter during the tariff battle. These gestures of reprisal only solidified the feeling among the insurgents that they had done the right thing in opposing the Payne–Aldrich bill.[36]

The fissures in the Grand Old Party and the lingering bitterness over the tariff fight cast a shadow over the president's planned trip across the country beginning in mid-September. His route would take him through the upper Middle West, out to the Pacific Coast, and back across the Southwest and South. He had scheduled numerous speeches on what was to be almost a two-month journey. As was his habit, the president golfed and vacationed at his summer residence in Beverly, Massachusetts, during the second half of August. He did not spend much time preparing his speeches for his tour. Taft thanked a politician who volunteered to give him some speech ideas, "for I am starting out on this trip with no speeches at all, and a bareness of ideas that gives me a pallor every time I think of it."[37]

Although he had not developed specific ideas for speeches on his transcontinental sweep, Taft had received any number of political suggestions for what he ought to say when he visited the hometowns of prominent Republicans. "It is being recommended that as a subject for discourse he let the new tariff law alone." Pro-tariff conservatives very much wanted the president to endorse the Payne–Aldrich tariff and their support for the law. A former House member from Iowa told Taft that "it is highly important that you should not mince matters in the new Republican tariff bill when you speak in Iowa. The party must stand or fall upon what it has done, and I have no doubt that Congress and your administration have given us a good bill."[38]

Taft had scheduled a speech at Winona, Minnesota, the residence of James A. Tawney, a conservative from that state, and the only House member of the delegation to support the Payne–Aldrich law. Tawney wanted "a strong, forceful statement" that defended "the Payne tariff bill in my home city." He cautioned the president about commenting "concerning my vote on final passage of the bill." That would be seen, the congressman warned, "inferentially at least, as a criticism on the votes of my colleagues in the House and Senate." The president took Tawney's advice and decided to use his stop at Winona for a sustained defense of the Payne–Aldrich law.[39] The White House began assembling information about the various schedules in dispute. Taft obtained much of his data from Sereno Payne, the Ways and Means chair. He did not, however, develop a full draft of his proposed remarks that could be circulated for corrections and criticism. Instead, he intended to dictate the speech to a secretary while he was on the train heading west.

Taft opened his journey in Boston, where he praised Nelson Aldrich for his leadership in the tariff battle. As he headed into the Middle West, he told his wife that he was "able to dictate a speech last night and this morning which I shall deliver tonight on labor and the delays of the law." He moved on westward into Wisconsin, a state in which he found no opportunities to say a positive word about Senator La Follette. Meanwhile, he hoped "to be able to deliver a tariff speech at Winona but it will be a close shave." On 17 September, while his train rumbled toward the small Minnesota town where Tawney lived, "with a new statement just prepared by Chairman Payne of the house committee on ways and means, and with his own personal knowledge of all the intimate little details of the tariff fight in Washington still fresh in his mind, he sat down in the state room in his private car, Mayflower, and dictated to two stenographers, the speech he delivered tonight." He did not have time to consider the political implications of his words or to have someone caution him about the possible reaction to what he proposed to say.[40]

The audience in the Winona opera house was filled with supporters of Tawney, and they produced "cheers which could be heard down the street." The president reviewed the framing of the tariff law in the Ways and Means Committee and its subsequent history in the Senate. "The difference between the House bill and the Senate was much less than the newspapers represented," he said. He argued that of the 2,024 dutiable items in the Dingley law 654 went down in the new tariff law and 220 went up. He then went through various schedules to make his case. Of the wool schedule, he said that any attempt to change rates on that product would have resulted in the defeat of the bill. That result was "not a compliance with the terms of the platform as I interpret it and as it is generally understood."[41]

Following that sentence came the words that forever defined the Winona speech in the history of the administration of William Howard Taft. "On the whole, however, I am bound to say that I think the Payne tariff bill is the best tariff bill that the Republican party ever passed; that in it the party has conceded the necessity for following the changed conditions and reducing tariff rates accordingly."[42]

Once he had finished explaining his position on the tariff law, Taft proceeded to defend Tawney and other Republicans in Congress who had voted with the administration. He disclaimed any attempt to criticize the party members who had opposed the bill. "It is a question for each man to settle for himself." He went on to restate his fulsome praise of the Payne–Aldrich bill so that no doubt lingered about his position. "When I could say without hesitation that this is the best tariff bill that the Republican party has ever passed, and therefore the best tariff bill that has been passed at all, I do not feel that I could have reconciled any other course to my conscience than that of signing the bill, and I think Mr. Tawney feels the same way." He opposed any further effort to revise the tariff during his presidency and noted that opponents of the bill "insist that they are still Republicans and intend to carry on their battle in favor of lower duties and a lower revision within the lines of the party. That is their right and, in their view of things, is their duty." For his part, Taft thought that "we ought to give the present bill a chance."[43]

Reaction to Taft's remarks came at once. "It was a splendid endorsement of the bill and a strong aggressive speech," said one conservative Republican senator. Tawney himself said that the address "is making all good Republicans feel that the party once more has a leader." The pro-tariff wing of the party discussed how the speech might be disseminated either as a separate document or through a congressional frank.[44]

The response from the Republican progressives and the editorial pages of the country was more negative, as Taft should have expected. "While Taft's present attitude has given great cheer to the leading Standpatters," wrote Albert Cummins, "it has made our friends fighting mad." Albert Beveridge believed that "Taft's speech made the most unfortunate possible impression out here. I am so sorry for his own sake that he made it—and the impression grows worse as time goes on." The San Francisco *Call* concluded that "the lay mind will find it practically impossible to square the utterances of President Taft at Winona with the utterances of candidate and President-Elect Taft in 1908 and of President Taft no later than July 1909." The cynical Francis E. Warren observed that "the President in his Winona speech sort of hit everybody, much like the bull-in-the-china shop story."[45]

With the regular session of Congress a few months away, it made little sense for Taft to have alienated the progressives in the way that he did. If he was determined to do so, he might have laid the groundwork for his conclusions with a series of leaks and prepared stories from the White House building support for his position. Instead, he waited until the last moment, dashed off a hastily prepared text, and offhandedly dropped a political bomb. When it became clear that the speech had backfired on his presidency, Taft would concede that he might have phrased his praise of the tariff with more subtlety. "The comparative would have been a better description than the superlative," he said in 1911. He even excused himself on the grounds of haste, which was of course his own fault.[46]

The Winona experience indicated the problems Taft confronted in running the presidency as a one-man operation. For a two-month national tour, he needed an array of speeches for different occasions and audiences. Yet there was no thought of using a speechwriter at this time. Moreover, Taft had no close political advisers who could have cautioned him about the risks of what he proposed to say at Winona. Convinced of his own brilliance and indisposed to adapt his judicial working habits to the demands of the presidency, Taft relied on the methods that had brought him to the White House.

Another reason for the Winona outcome was the pressure of other issues on the president's agenda. As he moved across the country, he knew that an even more dangerous controversy loomed for his administration. The tariff fight might anger the progressive Republicans, but they hardly posed a direct challenge to his renomination and reelection. Picking a quarrel with Theodore Roosevelt over the issue of conservation offered just that dismaying prospect. By the time he embarked for the West, Taft knew that he might soon have to dismiss Roosevelt's chief ally in conservation matters, the chief forester, Gifford Pinchot, in a quarrel with the secretary of Interior, Richard A. Ballinger. One western conservationist wrote in late July, "It looks as though Ballinger were going to be Taft's escort to Hades." Soon the Ballinger–Pinchot controversy would overshadow even the clamor about the tariff.[47]

5

★ ★ ★ ★ ★

THE BALLINGER–PINCHOT
CONTROVERSY

As the conservation dispute between Richard A. Ballinger and Gifford Pinchot gathered momentum during the autumn of 1909, Elihu Root recognized that the issue "is pregnant with immense evil for the Administration and the Republican party."[1] With his usual shrewd judgment, Root went to the heart of the matter. For President William Howard Taft, a battle over conservation, the policy most identified with Theodore Roosevelt, posed dangers of a direct confrontation with his predecessor. Contrasting interpretations of executive power and the role of the federal government in conserving natural resources split Taft and Roosevelt in this field. More than any other topic during Taft's first year, the Ballinger–Pinchot contest drove a wedge into what remained of the friendship of the two presidents.

In the years that Taft and Roosevelt had known each other, they had not discussed in detail their differences over conservation policy. As secretary of war, Taft had argued that the federal government lacked the broad power over navigable rivers that Roosevelt and Pinchot had asserted regarding hydroelectric facilities. Taft did not share the view of many conservationists "who regard laws as obstacles," to be brushed aside at the whim of the president.[2] Taft did not put it to Roosevelt that way as a cabinet member, and the intellectual gulf between the two men on that point did not emerge. Once he was president, however, Taft soon made clear how much his convictions on conservation policy diverged from those of his predecessor.

With their shared views on conservation issues, Taft and Richard A.

Ballinger connected on a personal level during the early months of the new administration. Ballinger had put in "vigorous strokes" for Taft during the presidential campaign, and given his friendship with James R. Garfield and his previous experience in government, he seemed a natural choice to the incoming president. Their joint experience of having Roosevelt interfere with their respective department and agency in 1907 and 1908 gave them something in common to talk about. They were both lawyers and instinctive conservatives, and they had little patience with Pinchot's loose construction of the law and, in their minds, his willingness to go beyond powers that the Constitution granted to the federal government.[3]

Taft believed in giving his cabinet members wide discretion to run their departments. As a result, he did not pay much attention amid distractions of the tariff battle to what his new secretary of the interior did during the summer of 1909. Ballinger came into office suspicious of the role that Pinchot had played in shaping resource policy under Roosevelt. To avoid congressional oversight and bureaucratic delays, Pinchot and Roosevelt had devised a number of informal cooperative understandings between Agriculture and Interior over irrigation, Indian affairs, and forest reserves. These ententes had little basis in statute or regulations; they existed because like-minded officials tried to do what Theodore Roosevelt desired.[4]

Ballinger, whom Pinchot called "a stock, square-headed little man," saw these ad hoc arrangements as extralegal efforts to contain private development in the West.[5] He decided to replace key personnel in the Reclamation Service, which was charged with implementing the Newlands Irrigation Act of 1902. The shakeup included the service's director, Frederick H. Newell. In ways large and small, Ballinger sought to undo the procedures for expediting irrigation projects that had grown up in the Roosevelt years. His most overt step in the early weeks of his tenure came when he directed that withdrawals of land from private entry to be set aside for water power sites be overturned. The land in question was to be made available for private entry. Despite protests from Reclamation Service officials, Ballinger's change in policy took place at the end of March 1909. James R. Garfield wrote in his diary on 3 April that "the burden of the fight for the Roosevelt policies under this administration will fall on Gifford's shoulders. I hope he will be able to show Taft the follies his subordinates are ready to commit."[6]

Pinchot raised the subject with Taft in two personal interviews on 19 and 20 April. This intervention obtained a presidential reversal of what Ballinger had tried to do. The withdrawals of land were reinstated. Yet Pinchot's bureaucratic victory proved only a temporary respite. Soon the secretary of the interior took other steps to reverse what the Reclamation

Ballinger became embroiled in the great battle over conservation with forester Gifford Pinchot. Library of Congress.

Service had done earlier. James R. Garfield wrote in his diary on 11 June: "A serious attack is being made upon Newell & the Reclamation Service." Taft, on the other hand, thought that Garfield and Pinchot had made land reservations "without what Mr. Ballinger thought was legal grounds." By the middle of the summer of 1909, the tension between the Forest Service and Interior had spilled over into the newspapers. Ballinger was reported to have said that Pinchot "shall not run the Department of the Interior."[7]

These developments posed an acute dilemma for Taft. "I am sorry about the Pinchot–Ballinger business," he wrote in mid-August from Beverly, Massachusetts, where he was vacationing after the rigors of the Payne–Aldrich battle. "I think they misunderstand each other. But if they go on hitting each other I shall have to decide something between them."[8] The problem was what to decide. Giving Pinchot an endorsement would mean repudiating Ballinger and his policies. Because Taft held many of the same policy views that his secretary of the interior had advanced, that was never a realistic alternative. Both president and cabinet officer were convinced that Roosevelt had been heedless of the law, had brought some incompetent officials into the government, and was careless with public money. They were not about to endorse Pinchot's approach.

Taft also had scant personal respect for Pinchot and his bureaucratic style. He saw the Forester as overzealous in his commitment to conservation in the Roosevelt mode. Pinchot represented the freewheeling subordinate who had no regard for departmental lines of authority, used publicity to advance his ends, and verged on socialism in some of the goals of his conservation campaign. These traits damned him for Taft.

Then there was Roosevelt. Taft viewed his predecessor's indulgence of Pinchot as one of the key weaknesses in Roosevelt's record as president. As Taft wrote to his wife in October 1909: "I can't for a moment permit that complete demoralization of discipline that follows the reposing of such power in the hands of a subordinate. The heads of the Departments are the persons through whom I must act, and unless the bureau chiefs are subordinate to the heads it makes government of an efficient character impossible." That central element of presidential governance was, in Taft's mind, where Roosevelt had fallen short.[9]

Taft had a point about Roosevelt's approach to administration, but because he had not brought it up before, it was difficult to make a case without seeming to assail the former president directly. Yet Pinchot's disagreements with Ballinger sharpened the president's growing disillusion with his predecessor's performance. Although Taft understood that he needed to retain Roosevelt's friendship, at the same time, he did not wish to take the steps necessary to achieve that result. The two men did not communicate after Roosevelt left on his African hunting trip in March

1909. Each waited for the other to write first. The president was cordial to Roosevelt family members but would not write himself. In his mind, that would have meant compelling Roosevelt to comment on administration policy without full knowledge of the facts. A candid exchange of letters might not have worked, but Taft missed an opportunity to make his own case to Roosevelt by his standoffish method.[10]

Until August 1909, the Ballinger–Pinchot imbroglio was a conflict among bureaucrats that remained an inside Washington struggle. Newspapers interested in conservation issues covered the quarrel, but the points in dispute were hard for the average citizen to understand. Taft told reporters in July 1909 "that he did not intend allowing any stories going out from the White House which might in any way reflect on the policies of the former president." Then the Ballinger–Pinchot battle turned into a morality play that injured Taft and heightened expectations for a confrontation with Roosevelt.[11]

The catalyst for the shift from an internal quarrel to a potential scandal was a young government investigator named Louis R. Glavis. At twenty-seven in 1909, Glavis was an energetic chief of the field division of the General Land Office in Portland, Oregon. He seems to have had a nose for potential scandals, even some that did not exist. In the Ballinger–Pinchot case, Glavis took up the question of the claims of Clarence Cunningham, a promoter and investor, to coal lands in Alaska. The specific questions that arose from Cunningham's efforts to acquire these properties in Alaska are complex and intricate. Boiling them down to their essence as Glavis saw it in the summer of 1909, Ballinger was guilty of the appearance of a conflict of interest at the very least, or so Glavis charged. At worst, Glavis alleged that Ballinger had used his authority as commissioner of the land office and secretary of the interior to block investigations of the allegedly fraudulent Cunningham claims. Ballinger had as a private citizen represented the Cunningham claimants as their attorney and then supported them as secretary of the interior.[12]

Many words have been written about the substance of the Glavis charges. The dominant verdict is that Ballinger was indiscreet and inept in his handling of the Cunningham claims but neither dishonest nor criminal. The sensational nature of the Glavis allegations arose from their implied indictment of Taft for having appointed Ballinger in the first place and having supported him in the quarrels with Pinchot. In any event, Glavis spoke with Pinchot on 9 August. The forester suggested that Glavis take his charges to Taft, and he wrote two letters of introduction for the investigator to take to Beverly, Massachusetts. "This is clearly a matter for your personal attention," Pinchot wrote to Taft, "and my function ends with seeing that it reaches you." The president met with Glavis on 18 August and listened to what he had to say. Taft then wrote to the officials involved in the dispute, especially Ballinger, asking them to report to him about the merits of the charges that Glavis had made. While he waited for their comments, Taft told the editor of the *Washington Post* that "I do not regard the issue between Pinchot and Ballinger as serious, and have no doubt that when the whole matter is investigated it will be seen that they are both working for the same end, with some difference as to method and with some suspicion of each other which ought to be allayed." As a presidential prediction, this one proved inaccurate in the extreme.[13]

The process by which Taft decided to support Ballinger, reject the Glavis charges, and repudiate Pinchot became one of the key events of his presidency. By early September, the president was preparing for his extended tour of the nation that would commence within ten days. He was trying to write the speeches for his journey in his usual mode of procrastination. At the same time, he was worrying about his wife's health, playing golf daily, and recovering from the exertions of the Payne–Aldrich battle. Then the Ballinger controversy arrived, with all that it implied about relations with Theodore Roosevelt.

On 6 September, Taft met with Ballinger to review the questions at issue. They talked again the next day. At these conversations was Oscar Lawler, the assistant attorney general assigned to the Department of the Interior and an ally of Ballinger. With the time pressure that Taft faced, he asked "Mr. Lawler to prepare an opinion as if he were President." At the same time, the president stayed up late on the night of the 7th. He read "the contents of the entire record" until the early hours of the morning. During the three days that followed, he studied the materials in even more detail.[14]

Lawler's draft memorandum reached Taft on 12 September when Attorney General Wickersham came to Beverly to review the case. While Wickersham went over the documents, Taft read the Lawler manuscript. He deleted some language critical of Pinchot and Glavis and wrote the remainder of a statement of the case himself. The president and the attorney general then agreed on what the letter to Ballinger should say. They also decided that in addition to the letter, the attorney general should prepare a report that "should be dated prior to the date of my opinion so as to show that my decision was fortified by his summary of the evidence and his conclusions therefrom." The report actually was filed with other Ballinger-related materials in late October.[15]

Taft and Wickersham had not done anything that was unethical or that had not been practiced in the past with other government reports. However, there was some dissimulation inherent in the process. They were thus open to a charge of dishonesty in their procedure in the Ballinger case, should the attorney general's backdated report ever become public. The Lawler draft opinion would also serve, if it should be released, to show that Taft had made up his mind against Glavis in advance. It has been suggested that Taft was aware throughout the Ballinger–Pinchot episode that a congressional investigation might well ensue. If so, he was either careless or did not believe that such internal presidential documents would ever be part of a probe on Capitol Hill.

Taft's letter to Ballinger dated 13 September 1909 was released as the president departed on his national tour. In the document, Taft dismissed Glavis's charges that Ballinger had aided the Cunningham claimants to Alaska coal lands. The allegations were "only shreds of suspicions without any substantial evidence to sustain his attack." The president rejected any link between Ballinger's representation of the Cunninghams for a small fee of $250 while he was in private practice and his policies in office where he had recused himself from dealing with the claims.[16]

Then Taft authorized the dismissal of Glavis from the federal service and defended Ballinger's overall record on the conservation disputes that had arisen with Pinchot. At the same time, he wrote Pinchot a conciliatory letter asking him to remain in his post. His departure, the president added, would be "one of the greatest losses that my administration could sustain if you should leave it."[17]

The struggle over conservation within the administration was now public, and political observers grasped the problem that the battle posed for Taft's relations with Roosevelt. In the ensuing weeks, the president and Pinchot conferred about their differences in a meeting on 25 September in Salt Lake City while Taft was on his speaking campaign. Neither man changed his basic views. Taft told Pinchot that the Forester "wanted to have him set aside the will of Congress and make law," which Pinchot denied. For his part, Pinchot countered that "I would not make trouble if I could avoid it, but might be forced to, and he might be forced to fire me." The president meanwhile wrote privately that he proposed "to stand by" Ballinger "at whatever cost." Pinchot, Taft added, "is looking for martyrdom and it may be necessary to give it to him; but I prefer to let him use all the rope that he will."[18]

Coming as it did in the same month as the Winona tariff speech, the furor over Ballinger contributed to the impression of an administration in disarray. The president was off on his speaking junket without any kind of press apparatus or effective ability to respond to criticism from his enemies. Indeed, Taft was determined not to pay attention to what his adversaries were saying. During his trip, he instructed Fred Carpenter not to send him daily clippings from the *New York Times*. "I don't think their reading will do me any particular good, and would only be provocative of that sort of anger and contemptuous feeling that does not do anybody any good." It was understandable that Taft did not want to receive bad news. At the same time, there did not exist any mechanism within the White House operation for providing him with information about press opinion or for getting out his thoughts from his train as it moved through the West and South. Instead, he interpreted the trip as a continuing success. "I have had a great reception in the Northwest," he told his wife; "indeed from the time I left home it has been one continual acclaim."[19]

Others saw the overall result of the long journey as less effective. The muckraker Ida Tarbell wrote on 29 September: "Taft is done for, I fully believe. I have failed yet to meet a single person in whom he aroused the least interest. Not a man of discernment, but what shakes his head over him."[20] The Taft trip thus contributed to a growing popular sense that the president was not fully in touch with the government and its workings. His speeches were well attended, but he lacked the charisma that Roosevelt possessed. Accordingly, his appearances, although politely received, did not strengthen him in a political sense. One Indiana newspaper said, "The President is now sauntering around someplace in the South." The reporter for the *New York Times* who covered Taft on the trip told a friend after surveying the upper Middle West: "This country is suspicious and doubtful of Taft and mighty hopeful that Roosevelt will come back ready for another turn in the White House."[21]

Those progressive Republicans such as Pinchot and James R. Garfield who wanted Roosevelt to come back and challenge Taft in 1912 continued their efforts to make the public aware of the Glavis allegations and Ballinger's involvement. They turned to the popular magazines to get their case aired. The heyday of muckraking journalism was a few years in the past, but there were still venues where a juicy scandal in the executive branch could secure attention for a large-circulation magazine. Such a publication was *Collier's*. Rejecting any fee for his writing, Glavis, with much help from Pinchot and the Forest Service, prepared an article outlining the case against Ballinger. He restated the charges that he had earlier made to the president. In its published version, however, the piece came with a banner headline that asked: "Are the Guggenheims in charge of the Department of the Interior?" The Guggenheim mining interests were active in Alaska and had negotiated with the Cunningham group about coal lands once a railroad was constructed in the area. The railroad was not built, and the implication of overt or implicit Guggenheim involvement in the matter was false. Nor did Glavis level any specific criminal charge against Ballinger in the body of the article. The allegations boiled down to this: Ballinger had been in a position to help the Cunninghams, had accepted $250 to represent them before coming to Interior, and could have used his influence to help these claimants whose land holdings were riddled with fraud. There was abundant smoke from Glavis, and the public sensed that there must also be fire.[22]

As a result, the press clamored for Ballinger's scalp, or at the very least a congressional probe. Editors said that Taft had abandoned the Roosevelt policies on conservation, a charge the president rejected as an exaggeration. With Roosevelt in Africa, his potential return as a challenger to Taft seemed a guarantee of headlines and a fascinating story. The dilemma for Taft was that he now disagreed with Roosevelt's administrative methods. He could not say so in public without risking the damage that such a revelation would produce. Historians who have suggested that Taft should have dismissed Pinchot in September 1909 miss the plight of the president. Had he done so, he would have been asking for a confrontation with Roosevelt. Taft was caught in the bind that defined his presidency. He owed his office to a man in whose procedures and policies he now did not believe.

Pinchot, Garfield, and their allies also had an anomalous relationship with Taft. They had sincere faith in the Roosevelt policies on conservation and wished to see Taft adhere to them. They believed the president was betraying his professed allegiance to Roosevelt and conservation. At the same time, both Pinchot and Garfield had much to gain from a Roosevelt restoration. Garfield wanted to run for governor of Ohio, a race for which an endorsement from the former president would be valuable. He was unlikely to win the party's nomination as a pro-Taft candidate. For Pinchot, who missed the power he had wielded under Roosevelt, a return of the Rough Rider to the White House might mean a cabinet position for him with even more authority to serve the national interest as he defined it. A "return from Elba," as people now referred to a Roosevelt race in 1912, ideally suited Pinchot's political and personal needs.

By the time Taft returned from his swing around the country in November, the regular session of Congress was less than a month in the future. The prospect of an investigation loomed. With Democrats sensing the possibility of victory in the 1910 elections, the minority on Capitol Hill would press for such a probe. It would be difficult for the Republicans in an election year to rebuff such calls for an inquiry. Pinchot sensed his advantage in public relations terms and wanted to provoke Taft into firing him. He exchanged letters with the president in November. Pinchot said that Ballinger "had shown himself actively hostile to the conservation policies." Taft replied that what Pinchot had written had not "shaken in the slightest my confidence in Secretary Ballinger's good faith." The president said that he wanted Pinchot to stay on and hoped he would use his "influence to prevent further conflict between the departments by published criticisms in the newspapers."[23]

As Taft grappled with the effects of the Ballinger–Pinchot clash, his presidency was being defined in a manner that shaped the next three years. The impression took hold that Taft, for all of his talents and dedication, had a rare capacity for making egregious political mistakes. The Payne–Aldrich tariff and the Winona speech were two examples that progressive Republicans cited. Jonathan P. Dolliver quipped that Taft was "an amiable island; entirely surrounded by men who know exactly what they want."[24] The sense that Taft was unduly passive and lacking in Roosevelt's energy and determination grew in Washington. One Kansas Republican in Congress spoke of Taft's "gigantic quiescence" along with the hope that the president is "yet to bust loose."[25]

The president had no taste for image-making or spin, but both qualities were now expected in the aftermath of the Roosevelt presidency. His golf playing, for example, struck many commentators as elitist at a time when the game was the province of the wealthy members of country clubs. When the president was out on the course, the pictures that appeared emphasized his girth. Roosevelt had been careful to present an image of energy in a dignified way. He did not allow shots of himself playing tennis, for example. Taft's bulk simply did not photograph well in informal settings where his weight could not be disguised. Moreover, the president still believed that his deeds should speak for themselves and that it would be inappropriate to publicize his accomplishments. As he wrote in November to an Iowa friend, "You are quite right in saying that there is a cooperative knockers association against my administration, and that their chief stock in trade is misrepresenting what I have said." However, Taft continued "when the people are made to know what the facts are, our strength may grow stronger."[26]

When Congress met in December 1909, the calls for an inquiry into the charges against Secretary Ballinger grew more heated. The pressure resulted in congressional demands for the relevant documents in the case. Ballinger too asked for an investigation. With a congressional probe in the offing, Pinchot now faced a problem of his own. Two of his aides in the Forest Service had been leaking negative information to the press about Ballinger in defiance of Taft's public request that all such government infighting should cease. Pinchot began framing a letter to defend himself. Had he wanted to observe proper channels, Pinchot should have communicated with his boss, Secretary of Agriculture James Wilson, to obtain permission to comment on the case. His conservative advisers urged him to do just that. Instead, the forester laid out his plans to a Republican insurgent leader in the Senate, Jonathan P. Dolliver. Pinchot decided to send his views to Dolliver, knowing that to do so would likely mean his ouster from government service. The forester framed a provocative letter for public dissemination.

On 6 January 1910, Dolliver read Pinchot's letter to him on the Senate floor. Colleagues listened in surprise. In the missive, Pinchot conceded that his subordinates had released information to the press about Ballinger. He added that when Taft fired Glavis in September he had done so because of "a mistaken impression of facts."[27] For a member of the administration to defend insubordination and accuse the president of a mistake in judgment was a firing offense. As Taft wrote later, "I would not have removed Pinchot if I could have helped it, but the question had presented itself in such a way that if I were to maintain the dignity of my office I must do so."[28]

Taft consulted with his cabinet and Elihu Root about his decision. After reading the record of the president's dealings with Ballinger and Pinchot, Root concluded: "There is only one thing for you to do, and that you must do at once." The next day, Taft dismissed Pinchot and his two aides. "Your letter was in effect an improper appeal to Congress and the public to excuse in advance the guilt of your subordinates before I could act," Taft wrote, "and against my decision in the Glavis case before the whole evidence on which that was based could be considered." The president said he was charged "with the duty of maintaining that dignity and proper respect" for the president "on the part of my subordinates." Pinchot had "destroyed [his] usefulness as a helpful subordinate of the Government." Therefore he was removed immediately.[29]

The political impact of Pinchot's ouster was on everyone's mind in Washington. Henry Cabot Lodge wrote to Roosevelt in Africa that "no President could have tolerated such a letter as Pinchot sent to Dolliver." Roosevelt's eldest son told a friend, "I am very sorry about this Pinchot affair. I am afraid it complicates things for the President a great deal and I don't think he has handled it just right." Roosevelt himself learned of the firing ten days after it happened and told Lodge, "I most earnestly hope it is not true." When the former president heard a definitive account of the events, he invited Pinchot to visit him in Europe as Roosevelt made his way back to the United States. The cracks in the Roosevelt–Taft friendship had now begun to widen.[30]

Taft did not write Roosevelt himself to explain what had taken place. Whether that course would have done any good is an open question. Nonetheless, Taft erred in not making his own case to his predecessor and friend. Although in all probability it would not have changed anything, it might have delayed Roosevelt's disillusion with Taft's policies.

Instead, the president allowed Roosevelt to hear anti-Taft arguments without contradiction. As the spring of 1910 went on, Roosevelt became ever more open in what he said to friends regarding his disappointment with Taft. Meanwhile, as late as May 1910, Taft still was reluctant to explain to Roosevelt what his reasoning was. In a letter, the president said that the problem had caused him "a great deal of personal pain and suffering, but I am not going to say a word to you on that subject. You will have to look into that wholly for yourself without influence by the parties, if you would find the truth."[31] This passive approach from Taft left Roosevelt to obtain the truth of the episode on his own. Given the importance that Roosevelt attached to Gifford Pinchot's opinion, he was not likely to hear much that was favorable to the president.

The Ballinger–Pinchot investigation that Congress undertook during the spring of 1910 turned out to be a public relations disaster for the White House. That was not because the Pinchot forces proved their contentions of illegality against Ballinger. The controversy over lands in Alaska was so complex and hard to follow that the public never really understood all that had happened. Yet during the hearings, the actions of the president, Attorney General Wickersham, and Oscar Lawler became public. In an early example of the familiar Washington truism that the cover-up is usually worse than the crime itself, the strategy of Taft in shaping his September letters about Glavis and Ballinger came to light in the most damaging manner. The president's credibility suffered a severe blow as a result.

The management of *Collier's* hired Boston attorney Louis D. Brandeis to present the case for Glavis before the House–Senate committee investigating the issues between Ballinger and Pinchot. As Brandeis studied the documents that the White House had furnished to the panel, he became convinced that the report Wickersham had submitted, dated 13 September 1909, was too long and voluminous for the attorney general to have prepared in two days. He believed that the president and attorney general were not telling the truth about the process by which the report had been created and that they had backdated the document to enhance the credibility of what Wickersham had said. The problem was that he could not prove his contention.

As bad luck for Taft would have it, a government stenographer named Frederick M. Kerby came forward in February 1910 to reveal that he had assisted Oscar Lawler in drafting the preliminary report on the Glavis charges for President Taft. With that information in hand, Brandeis waited for the proper moment to make his disclosure. It came in April, when the committee asked Wickersham for materials relating to the investigation. The attorney general then discussed the process of postdating the document.

The Lawler report now became the focus of attention because it indicated that the Department of the Interior had in effect been asked to exonerate itself. On 15 May 1910, a statement from Kerby was published describing how he had worked with Lawler to create a letter on behalf of the president. When the news broke, the White House at first issued a response that said that the report was untrue. At the same time, Wickersham released a copy of the Lawler letter that Taft had used as a partial basis for his Glavis letter. A comparison of the two documents revealed that some of what the president said had been drawn from Lawler's draft. Taft now needed to make some explanation of the process by which the Glavis letter had been created. The president was behind the news cycle and his credibility was under attack.[32]

In a letter to the chair of the joint committee, Knute Nelson of Minnesota, dated 15 May 1910, the president explained what had happened. Once he did so, the aura of mystery and conspiracy about the events of September 1909 and the Glavis letter largely disappeared. As the main newspaper story put it, "this is a procedure common to all the Government officers, and if that had been admitted at the start it would have ended the whole hullabaloo at once. The opinion is general here that all of the magnitude which has been given to the incident is entirely due to the fact that the original charge that this was done was denied and that a mystery has been made of what did occur in the preparation of the letter of Sept. 13."[33]

That comment underlined the true significance of the Ballinger–Pinchot episode for the Taft presidency. A bureaucratic dispute had intensified during the late summer and early fall of 1909 into a controversy about the honesty of Secretary Ballinger. Taft's conclusions regarding the general lack of criminality and dishonesty on Ballinger's part track what historians of the case have also concluded. The secretary was maladroit and over his head as an official, but he had not done what Glavis charged him with doing. Yet Taft failed to mount an effective defense of his subordinate.

Pressed for time as he prepared for his national tour, Taft rushed through the preparation of his 13 September letter and took some shortcuts with Wickersham as they reached their joint decision about Glavis and Ballinger. If the president had said that he had instructed Lawler to draft a letter for his use and asked Wickersham to file a report based on the documents, all would have been out in the open. Instead, Taft and Wickersham, who had very little experience with electoral politics and public relations between them, acted as lawyers readying a case for court. They did not anticipate that their internal revelations would someday become public. Had someone with political insights been part of the process, they might have warned the president about the matter of appearances regarding their deliberations and the writing of the documents. But Taft did not have any such political adviser. Worse yet, he did not believe that he needed any such advice. He went ahead on his own to make his decision.

It thus appeared that Taft had acted in a deceitful manner and then attempted to cover up his actions. Pinchot said in a letter to Roosevelt, "it is a spectacle to make every decent American citizen squirm in his skin when the Attorney General of the United States falsifies an essential public document, and the President transmits the falsification to Congress."[34] Concealing the Lawler memorandum was also an error. In this case, Brandeis was correct when he said that the lying of the Taft administration was their worst mistake. Taft and Wickersham, for their part, did not believe that they had lied in September 1909, but the impression of ineptitude and blundering about was now becoming fixed in the public mind.

With the Payne–Aldrich tariff and the Winona speech as liabilities, as well as the Ballinger–Pinchot problems, William Howard Taft had not had a good year in 1909. In the sphere of foreign policy, his luck was not much better. The approach to international affairs that he and Philander Knox developed has become known through the derisory title of "dollar diplomacy." In his conduct in this area, Taft also encountered further difficulties that contributed to the sense that the administration had not yet established itself as a credible governing force with a clear idea of where it proposed to take the nation.

6

★ ★ ★ ★ ★

TAFT, KNOX, AND DOLLAR DIPLOMACY

Wedged between the foreign policy adventures of Theodore Roosevelt and the dramatic world statesmanship of Woodrow Wilson, William Howard Taft and his conduct of foreign policy seem lackluster and pedestrian. No wars, no major crises, no enduring doctrines, only the deriding label of "dollar diplomacy" remains of what Taft and his secretary of state, Philander Knox, tried to do. Because the president ceded so much authority to Knox, the White House sometimes seems only a supporting player in how foreign relations operated between 1909 and 1913.

Although Taft's efforts to reshape American foreign policy came to little, the unhappy result does not mean that the president lacked large ambitions. Taft saw himself as an important corrective to the Roosevelt policies that relied too much on balance of power politics and the implied threat of military force. With his knowledge of the world, acquired between 1900 and 1907 as a diplomatic troubleshooter for Roosevelt, Taft believed that he brought special experience to the foreign policy side of his new job.

In many respects, Taft had acquired as much expertise in world affairs as any president before him. He had governed the Philippines, visited Japan, China, and Russia, and traveled across Europe several times. Not since John Adams and John Quincy Adams had an incoming president been exposed to so many diverse cultures and met in person so many of the players in the countries he would deal with in office.

These experiences, fused with Taft's legal background, produced settled convictions about how the United States should behave as a world

President Taft allowed Philander Knox to be the main driving force in the administration's foreign policy. Library of Congress.

power. Economics and the law shaped Taft's thinking. The expansion of American trade was good for the country and the world. Capitalists should seek profit overseas to spread the blessing of capitalism. Treaties, international courts, procedures for arbitrating differences—all these methods would be conducive to a more peaceful and orderly globe. As attorneys, he and Knox believed that the world required more of the constructive spirit of the Anglo-Saxon bench and bar in addressing disputes among nations.

At the same time, the president viewed with skepticism the propensity of Roosevelt to wield a big stick. Although Taft defended the existence of the army and navy against peace advocates of disarmament, he did not think that the nation should build a more powerful fleet. Even though he had been secretary of war for four years, Taft had not emphasized the military aspects of the position. He left those chores to the regular army while he acted as the cabinet envoy for Roosevelt in such episodes as the intervention in Cuba in 1906 and the crisis with Japan over immigration in 1907. So Taft's instinctive tactic was to draft a note, much as he had once prepared a writ, rather than to mobilize a flotilla.[1]

This posture put him at odds with the approach of Theodore Roosevelt. Imbued with the strategic goals derived from the navalism of Admiral Alfred Thayer Mahan, Roosevelt saw the world as a network of alliances and powers in which the United States needed to function. In the case of Japan, for example, that meant recognizing the preeminent position of that nation in Asia. The Taft–Katsura agreement of 1905 that endorsed Japan's hegemony over Korea was one example of how Roosevelt conducted foreign policy. Given Taft's part in implementing Roosevelt's diplomatic initiatives in Asia and in Latin America, it may have seemed to the outgoing president that his successor shared these assumptions. Time would demonstrate that Taft did not think along those lines.

Because Taft delegated so much power to his secretary of state, historians have depicted Philander Knox as almost autonomous in foreign policy making between 1909 and 1913. His chief assistant, Francis Huntington Wilson, said "like a *cordon bleu chef* who allows no one to interfere in his kitchen, he had it tacitly understood that, outside of Congress, no official from the President down was to say or do anything that touched upon foreign relations without his approval in advance." That statement was true up to a point. Knox kept the president fully informed of his decisions and sought White House approval before making significant statements or initiatives. He and Taft worked as a team rather than as a hierarchy with Knox at the top.[2]

Knox emerged as the public image of the administration in world affairs. In an age before cameras and microphones, the diminutive Knox did not suffer because of his unprepossessing appearance, with a large head and ever-present cigar. He let his aide, Huntington Wilson, handle the press and cultivated the isolation that allowed him time to think about the issues before him. The secretary was not a devotee of long hours at his desk on the model of Elihu Root. Knox arranged to have the major newspapers delivered to his home before breakfast and then arrived at his office about 10:00 a.m. Department business went on until lunch, when Knox conferred with his chief aides. Then it was off to the golf course, often with the president, or to his stables for an afternoon ride on one of his expensive horses. When his schedule permitted, Knox left Washington for extended vacations.[3]

Despite Knox's relaxed working style, he was the driving force behind Taft's foreign policy. He and Huntington Wilson imposed their will on the State Department and made sure that all major decisions flowed through them. How good an architect of American diplomacy Knox was remains in dispute. The British, and especially the ambassador in Washington, James Bryce, believed the secretary of state was over his head in international affairs. Yet Knox reorganized the department into a series of geographical divisions that better reflected the priorities of diplomacy. He also gave State a clear direction. Whatever problems of execution arose in making foreign policy stemmed from the assumptions that Knox and Taft brought to the world arena.

During the Roosevelt presidency, Washington had pursued an approach in the Far East that recognized the preeminence of Japan in the region. That was the price Roosevelt was prepared to pay for Tokyo's willingness to accept American policies that excluded Japanese immigrants from the West Coast. Japan also recognized American rule in the Philippines. As a newspaper reporter told Secretary of State Elihu Root in September 1908 after a trip to the West Coast, residents that "have come to approve the diplomacy which has salved the sensibilities of the Japanese, while at the same time securing the stoppage of the entrance of objectionable Japanese labor." Believing that the United States should not risk war with Japan, Roosevelt thought it wiser, in the absence of significant American military power in Asia, to appease the political adversary while building up the American navy. If that also meant the ascendancy of Japan in Manchuria and on the Chinese mainland that was the result of China's weaknesses that the United States could not remedy.[4]

Taft and Knox thought Roosevelt's approach of deferring to Japan in Asia was wrong in principle and hurtful to China. The new president believed, as he said in Shanghai in 1907, that his country was committed to "seeking the permanent safety and peace of China, the preservation of Chinese territorial and administrative integrity," as well as the protection of all treaty rights and the maintenance of "equal and impartial trade with all parts of the Chinese Empire." These goals should be pursued through peaceful commerce, the rule of law, and diplomatic suasion. War with Japan was, in Taft's mind, improbable and unnecessary. Therefore, the projection of American power in the Pacific was unnecessary and, at a time when the government was running a deficit, expensive.[5]

Taft sought twin goals: promoting American trade in China and buttressing the Chinese empire itself. The decline in the nation's trade with China in the years before Taft took office bothered the new president. Only a small amount of the nation's total trade was with China in the first place. In 1909, exports to that country amounted to around $19 million, or just over 1 percent of the entire export business. Four years earlier, the amount of American exports had been $44 million. In the mind of Taft and Knox, however, the potential of the China market was one that capitalists should be able to tap, and the falling off in exports was a worrying trend to both men.

Assuming that American commerce was a benevolent economic force, the president saw no reason why other nations should not grant the United States access to markets in China. The president was also confident that the international community would recognize the wisdom of a strong, united China engaged in economic development with the rest of the world. China would accept the United States in this role "because she does not distrust our motives."[6]

For the president, the first priority in China was to improve American diplomatic representation in Peking. The incumbent minister was William Woodville Rockhill, the architect of the Open Door policy under John Hay and William McKinley. Schooled in the language of the country and an expert on Chinese life, Rockhill had been at his post since 1905. He shared the broad purposes of Roosevelt's policies toward Asia. Yet Taft had little use for Rockhill, whom he described as a "dilettante" without "the slightest interest in American trade or promoting it." All in all, Taft commented, he was "not a man of strength or force of action such as we need at Pekin."[7]

Unwilling to dump Rockhill from the diplomatic service and provoke a furor similar to the one surrounding the dismissal of Henry White, Taft shifted the diplomat to Russia. A search for a successor began at once. That process revealed some of the problems that plagued Taft for the next few years. Although willing to get rid of Rockhill, Taft did not have anyone else in mind before he took the step of transferring the veteran diplomat to St. Petersburg. The president turned first to Charles W. Fulton, a one-term senator from Oregon who had just been defeated for reelection. Fulton had no particular qualification, other than being from the West

Coast. Moreover, he was tainted with an involvement in the pervasive land frauds in his home state and was an opponent of Asian immigration as well. Happily, he declined the post. Taft then endeavored to persuade his old friend, John Hays Hammond, a wealthy mining engineer, to go to China. Hammond too refused.[8]

While Taft was searching for his minister to China, the new policy toward that country emerged during the spring and summer of 1909. The State Department learned in May that bankers from Great Britain, France, and Germany had agreed with China to lend money toward the construction of a railroad in the Yangtze Valley. Known as the Hukuang Loan, this financing arrangement did not include American participation. Knox protested against the exclusion of his country's moneymen and urged "full and frank cooperation among the powers with interests in China as best calculated to maintain the open door and integrity of China." Why the powers should do this for Washington was never made clear. Taft and Knox just assumed that the United States ought to be among the international participants. Because the loan had been signed on 6 June 1909, it was now up to the Chinese government to sanction an American role.[9]

When the Chinese decided not to let the Americans into the loan, Taft took dramatic personal action. On 15 July he wired the leader of China's government, Prince Chun, that he was "disturbed" at reports of Chinese opposition to the United States in the loan arrangements. Because of the "high importance" that the president assigned to the matter, he had turned to "this somewhat unusually direct communication." His move, Taft added, arose from "an intense personal interest in making the use of American capital in the development of China an instrument for the promotion of the welfare of China, and an increase in her material prosperity without entanglements or creating embarrassments affecting the growth of her independent political power and the preservation of her territorial integrity." China agreed in the face of Taft's message to allow Americans a part in the loan, but much negotiation remained to be done with the foreign bankers. Taft had a momentary public relations victory, but other problems with China soon appeared.[10]

It looked during the summer of 1909 as if the administration had found its minister to China. On 16 July, the White House announced that Charles R. Crane of Chicago, a wealthy manufacturer of plumbing and other industrial supplies, had decided to take the assignment to Peking. Taft had received strong recommendations on Crane's behalf from such progressives as William Kent, a former House member. His aim, Crane told reporters, "will be the aiding of American enterprise to secure and maintain an adequate foothold in a country which promises to be the richest market of the world." A happy Taft told his wife, "I think we really made a great find in him."[11]

Over the next two months, the Crane selection fell apart. The initial response in the press and with the public was positive. Crane had many friends among progressives, and they applauded the choice. In September, however, Crane's public comments on his assignment attracted unwelcome attention. Believing that Taft had told him to "let them have it out red hot," Crane made no secret of his pro-Russian and anti-Japanese views. In his first meeting with Taft, Crane had attributed some of the political discontent in Russia to the sinister influence of Jews. Although anti-Semitism was common throughout American society, Crane's words raised immediate warnings for the president. Jewish leaders in the United States opposed Russia's unwillingness to treat American Jews traveling in that country as they did other citizens of the United States. Crane's attitude could pose problems for the White House.[12]

Moreover, Crane seemed to believe that he was to conduct China policy on his own with only minimal supervision from the State Department. He spoke to a correspondent for a Chicago newspaper and leaked details of a possible official protest regarding a recent treaty between China and Japan. When this report was published, it caused a furor in Japan and an embarrassment to the administration. Knox decided that Crane would have to step down even as the new envoy was preparing to leave the United States for Peking.[13]

Crane's dismissal before he took up his new post was another public relations setback for the administration. Not wishing to emphasize Crane's anti-Japanese point of view or the dislike of Jews behind his pro-Russian opinions, the State Department left the reasons for his ouster obscure. "The whole 'truth about Crane' will probably never be known," Knox wrote a friendly editor. "Its disclosure would necessitate a divulgence of related matters affecting other countries." Coming as it did in the wake of the Winona speech and the Ballinger–Pinchot uproar, the Crane mess contributed to progressive disillusion with Taft and disappointment in the contrast between his diplomatic style and that of Theodore Roosevelt.[14]

In place of Crane, the White House selected William J. Calhoun, a veteran diplomat who had earlier served in Cuba and Latin America. "I think we are to be congratulated," Knox wrote the president.[15] With that task out of the way, Knox and the president resumed their efforts to find a more viable China policy than the one that Roosevelt had pursued. Knox soon launched an even more ambitious scheme to give the United States an equal chance in the Orient along with the other powers active on the Chinese mainland. Knox envisioned something like what John Hay had done with the original Open Door notes nine years earlier. He would lay down an attractive idea, obtain the support of the great powers in principle, and try to have the diplomatic momentum carry his plan to success. Consulting with the nations involved in advance was not Knox's approach.

Knox thought of his initiative as neutralizing the China problem. The continuing Russian–Japanese rivalry over competing railroads in Manchuria seemed the core of the issue. So in November 1909, Knox approached the British to see if they would endorse a "complete commercial neutralization" of these rail lines. The powers would furnish the money for the construction of the railroads and oversee their management; the Chinese would be the actual owner of the lines. In this way, the secretary of state contended, the Chinese would receive economic development and the international rivalries within China would be lessened.[16] The targets were, of course, Russia and Japan. Knox hoped to persuade the two countries that it was in their self-interest to step back into a less tense relationship over Manchurian railroads. If in the process American influence in China increased, so much the better. In the mind of Knox and the president, the United States did not have the selfish aims toward China that the other great powers displayed. As Taft told the Chinese minister in November 1909, "I want you to make it known to your government that it can trust us implicitly, for we do not want any of your territory. We only want your trade."[17]

Knox first worked with the British to gain endorsement of his proposal. London, which had an alliance with Japan, approved neutralization in principle (whatever that meant) but was sketchy about specifics. Germany and China also delivered similar broad agreement. Japan and Russia were the key players. The public learned of the Knox move in early January 1910 as word reached the press of American diplomats presenting the idea in world capitals. Even though Knox knew that Russia and Japan were likely to say no to his proposals, he told reporters that "the situation is regarded as very satisfactory."[18]

Within a few days, the Russians and the Japanese bluntly rejected the neutralization plan; the Knox diplomatic campaign had failed. The Knox proposal offered very little to either of the two countries that were neighbors of China and more involved with its diplomatic and political future. Why should they allow the United States an equal role in China's development and its railroads when Washington had no significant military presence in the region? As a British commentator put it later in 1910, the powers realized that they could resist "Mr. Knox's diplomatic activities in the Far East" because they faced no "serious risk of more than a verbal embroilment with the country he represents." With the neutralization idea, the Taft administration had brought Japan and Russia closer together, achieved no tangible economic gains, and stirred up nationalist feelings within China about the American presence in the country. After a year of Far Eastern diplomacy, the United States had little to show for what Taft and Knox had sought to accomplish.[19]

The other area where the Taft–Knox style of diplomacy proved controversial was in Latin America. Although Theodore Roosevelt and his secretary of state, Elihu Root, had followed policies that asserted American supremacy south of the border, they had done so in a manner that took into account Latin American sensibilities. Elihu Root in particular said that a condescending and bigoted attitude in public toward diplomats from the countries involved was unwise. Knox was less sympathetic to the feelings of Latin American envoys and thought that Root had achieved his results through a reliance "upon champagne and other alcoholic preservatives."[20]

Both Knox and Huntington Wilson believed that the United States should dominate Latin America and press forward with economic development in the area through extensive enlistment of United States business in helping countries behave in a rational and dependable manner. Selling naval vessels to South American nations, for example, helped the American arms industry and preempted European powers from seizing the markets for armaments. Battleships for Argentina thus became one of the leading instances for Taft and Knox of how diplomacy and economic development might work in unison. The two men took as their model what Roosevelt had imposed on the Dominican Republic as an outgrowth of the Roosevelt Corollary of 1904: management of customs revenues to ensure payment of international debts.[21]

The Taft administration sought to establish a network of treaties with countries such as Honduras and Nicaragua that fulfilled these obligations. Taft said in his 1909 annual message, for example, that in considering whether to support American enterprise "in a particular country," Washington would evaluate the extent to which its government "is in its administration and in its diplomacy faithful to the principles of moderation, equity and justice upon which alone depend international credit, in diplomacy as well as finance."[22]

The charge has been made that Taft and his State Department were doing the bidding of American business in shaping Latin American policy. Knox had been a lawyer for corporations, and these economic ties are often cited as evidence for his motivation in Nicaragua and other countries. Although both the president and Knox shared a commitment to capitalism in the manner of mainstream politicians of that time, they were more inclined to pressure the business community to support their cause in the region than to get their orders from Wall Street.

The main focus of the Latin American policy in 1909 was Nicaragua and its leader, José Santos Zelaya. In the eyes of the men in Washington, Zelaya was an unsavory, expansionist dictator who wished to make his nation the major power in Central America. The State Department saw him as intent on undermining Honduras, and he thereby threatened regional stability. Knox called him "a blot upon the history of Nicaragua," and the new administration made no secret of its desire to see that the Nicaraguan strongman should leave office forthwith.[23]

The secretary of state hoped that he could enlist Mexico in an effort to contain Zelaya. As he told a cabinet meeting on 16 March, "all action to be in conjunction with Mexico." What Knox and Taft did not perceive was that Mexico was quietly supporting Zelaya as a makeweight against the United States. At this early stage, Knox looked to the Dominican model as a way to maintain the financial credit of Nicaragua and Honduras. After Knox finished his remarks, Taft "endorsed the proposed action, and said he would even make a show of force in order to maintain peace and stop revolutions."[24]

Knox pursued the idea of a common approach with Mexico and the autocratic government of the aging Porfirio Diaz throughout 1909, but this initiative was based on a false hope that the Mexican government would make a de facto alliance with Washington to run Central America as Taft and Knox desired. The president met Diaz in lavish ceremonies in El Paso in October during Taft's cross-country trip as part of this courting process. Yet because Diaz and Zelaya had common interests and had cooperated in the past, such a shift in Mexican policy was never likely. Clinging to power, Diaz did not want to face the anti-American fervor such a move would evoke. As Knox wrote to Taft on 28 September, "Mexico has manifested no disposition to cooperate along the lines suggested."[25]

The chance for the Taft administration to act came during the fall of 1909, when a revolution against Zelaya occurred. In the ensuing struggle for power, Zelaya's forces captured and executed two Americans fighting with the rebels, led by Juan Estrada. After the killing of the two men, Knox broke off diplomatic relations with Nicaragua on 1 December 1909. In his annual message a few days later, the president wrote that the government was "intending to take such future steps as may be found most consistent with its dignity, its duty to American interests, and its moral obligations to Central America and to civilization." In a letter to Knox, Taft was even more candid. He reported how he had said to the Mexican ambassador that the United States sought "some formal right to compel peace between those Central American governments." He then added that he wanted "to have the right to knock their heads together until they should maintain peace between them."[26]

During 1910, as the various factions in Nicaragua jockeyed for power, the United States hoped for the success of Estrada and his forces. Military pressure through the presence of the navy and marines helped Estrada assume control and create a government by August. American diplomats moved in to negotiate arrangements for the United States to provide a customs receivership along the lines of the Dominican Republic. Estrada left office in May 1911, but not before his government agreed to the Knox–Castrillo convention of 6 June. The treaty set up a system in which the United States would supervise the country's customs and revenues. When Taft transmitted the convention to the Senate on 7 June 1911, he wrote that the agreement would help secure his goal toward Latin American countries of "a sound reorganization of their fiscal systems." That would in turn contribute "to the removal of conditions of turbulence and instability, enabling them by better established governments to take their rightful places among the law-abiding and progressive countries of the world."[27]

Earlier, the administration had developed a similar pact with Honduras with the same purpose in mind. By 1909, the Hondurans had run up a national debt of over $120,000,000, with annual customs revenues well below what would be needed to make substantial payments. A program for repaying the debt with loans from American bankers seemed the most feasible solution. However, domestic opposition within Honduras to American intrusion slowed the talks until late in 1910. Eventually the last resistance within the Honduran government to the treaty was removed when the State Department threatened to let the British seize the customhouses.[28]

The resulting treaty was signed on 10 January 1911 with language that would be repeated in the pact for Nicaragua later in the year. Taft sent the document to the Senate on 26 January 1911 with a message urging quick approval. Huntington Wilson wrote that "the principle we seek to act upon in Honduras is one we are bound to have to resort to in still other cases." Knox added his recommendation with a letter to the Foreign Relations Committee that included the terms of the loans to be made to Honduras.[29]

The fate of the Honduran Treaty was now uncertain. The Foreign Relations Committee approved it on 1 March 1911, but no action was taken in the Senate itself before the lawmakers adjourned on 4 March. The next Senate would see more Democrats in the chamber after the administration's reversals at the polls in November 1910. With the help of progressive Republicans suspicious of Taft and Knox, the Democrats could deny the administration the two-thirds vote needed to approve the pact.

Opposition within Honduras to the treaty provided ample ammunition to Senate critics of the State Department and the White House as well.

In its two major examples of dollar diplomacy in Central America, the Taft administration had little to show for its initiative as the president's term entered its third year.

Many years after the Taft administration, Elihu Root said of Knox and Latin America that the secretary's approach was "absolutely antithetical to all Spanish–American modes of thought and feeling and action, and pretty much everything he did with them was like mixing a Seidlitz powder." By 1910, that aspect of Knox's handling of foreign affairs was much discussed in Washington. Henry Cabot Lodge told Roosevelt that Knox "took that office without knowing anything about foreign affairs. He took it on the theory, as Root said, that he could be Secretary of State and do no work." An example of Knox's maladroitness toward Latin American opinion came in the Alsop claims case regarding Chile. The issue had been going on for years between the United States and Chile without much effect. With negotiations making progress and arbitrators having agreed on an amount that Chile was willing to pay, Knox sent a message that amounted to an ultimatum. The tone of the message offended the diplomatic representatives from Central and South America. As a press account later noted, even though the substance of the matter was settled, Knox's methods had "aroused and renewed old opposition, and created a situation very much less favorable to business generally than there was before."[30]

In December 1909, Andrew Carnegie, at a private off-the-record luncheon with Knox in attendance, compared the secretary of state's policies toward Latin America to those of Elihu Root in unfavorable terms. Carnegie "made it plain that, in his opinion, Mr. Knox had undone the work of Secretary Root in cultivating the confidence of the little republics in the good intentions of the United States." Knox, who was "not altogether pleased" to be under fire, responded with a defense of his approach to diplomacy. The news report said that "Mr. Carnegie's remarks, however, have simply given voice to the feeling the Latin Americans had but were afraid to express openly."[31]

Sensing a political opportunity, the Democrats took up Knox's record when the House debated the appropriations bill for diplomatic and consular offices in February 1910. Francis Burton Harrison of New York called the State Department decadent and the ambassadors "too often messenger boys in silk knee breeches with swords, who spend their time being photographed at the hosts of royalty or in playing the part of 'hands across the sea.'" Harrison added sarcastically that Knox had brought something new to his job: "dollar diplomacy," which judged an ambassador on the amount of American trade he promoted. The label had been bandied about Washington before Harrison's speech, but he gave public expression to the tagline for what Knox and Taft were trying to do. This phrase passed into the language, where it has remained ever since.[32]

President Taft came to Knox's defense in early May 1910 in a speech at a Grant Day dinner of the Americus Club in Pittsburgh, the secretary's hometown. Knox's insistence on a settlement of the Alsop claims with Chile "is not to be regarded in the slightest degree as an evidence of our lack of friendship for that Government or our earnest desire to maintain the friendliest relations with all South America." In addition, reaching back to when Knox was attorney general under Roosevelt, Taft said that the secretary of state had "shown the same capacity for guarding the interests of his client, the United States and her people, in dealing with foreign nations as he did in protecting their rights against the unlawful encroachments of domestic combinations of capital." The need that Taft felt to make such comments months after the Knox message to Chile underscored the persisting effects of what Knox had done.[33]

At bottom, the benevolent language of Taft and Knox toward Latin America masked a cold reality. The interests of the countries in the region were less compelling to American policy makers than the need to preserve the ascendancy of the United States toward its neighbors to the south. Only differences of degree distinguished the Taft approach from what Theodore Roosevelt had done and Woodrow Wilson would do later.

Taft's diplomacy in Central and South America as well as the maintenance of the Open Door in China had been a less than triumphant success for the administration. At the same time, the White House had also been engaged in high-stakes economic negotiations with Canada about the tariff policy for both countries. These talks had arisen because of provisions in the Payne–Aldrich tariff of 1909. In that law, a country that discriminated in its customs laws and tariff rates against the United States would face higher rates on goods imported into the American market. Canada had arranged a treaty with France in 1906 that provided lower tariffs on French imports into Canada than on comparable American products. American officials in the Treasury Department concluded that the Franco-Canadian pact did in fact trigger the provisions of the Payne–Aldrich law, unless the two countries could reach an accommodation before 31 March 1910. As a result, the Taft administration decided to open talks with the Canadians to see what might be worked out during March 1910. As the negotiations got under way, the governor general of Canada told the British ambassador in Washington, "both of us are searching for a decent excuse to help each other. The way out has not been found yet."[34]

The bilateral discussions led to an interim solution that allowed both countries to save face over the tariff issue without imposing trade restrictions on each other. At the same time, President Taft seized the opportunity to propose to the Canadians that they begin negotiations of "the consideration of readjustment of our trade relations upon the broader and more liberal lines which should obtain between countries so closely related geographically and racially, as indicated by the President in his recent public utterances." These commitments set the process in motion that would lead to the struggle for Canadian reciprocity, the second tariff battle of Taft's administration.[35]

The reasons for the president's receptivity to making tariff concessions to Canada have never been fully explained. At heart, Taft was never a high-tariff enthusiast. He was a nominal protectionist, but, like his brothers, he believed in free trade as a general concept. On practical grounds, the newspaper publishers who wanted lower duties on Canadian wood pulp and newsprint had been hammering away at him over the Payne–Aldrich tariff in their editorials and news columns. He also decided that achieving lower duties for American consumers would take some of the sting out of the Payne–Aldrich measure. In the process, he might embarrass the insurgent Republicans, who would now be confronted with lower duties on products that their constituents grew and marketed. It was a risky gamble for Taft, and one that in the end did not succeed. But it was a step that Theodore Roosevelt never contemplated, and it suggests that Taft was as adventurous in the use of presidential power in diplomacy and legislation as his predecessor.

Diplomacy in the Taft era proceeded by slow, incremental steps, without sudden breakthroughs or popular actions. As a result, what happened in foreign affairs during the first two years of his presidency did not offset the difficulties that the administration encountered on domestic matters. The Payne–Aldrich tariff and the Ballinger–Pinchot controversy were elements in the difficult situation that President Taft faced in late 1909 when the regular session of Congress assembled to tackle the main elements of the president's program for his party and the nation. Instead of clearing the agenda for lawmakers to engage in what Taft wanted them to do on trusts and railroad legislation, the battle over the tariff and the president's statement at Winona, Minnesota, had soured the atmosphere on Capitol Hill. Yet Taft approached the return of Congress with some optimism. He told critics of his cooperation with Speaker Cannon and Senator Aldrich: "the public asks a man to do something which he has no power to do except by associating with the Republican party and those who lead it in the House and Senate." Accordingly, "all I can do is to do the best I can to make the government as good as I can and secure as much legislation as I can in the right direction, and in doing so use those instruments which are indispensable to the passage of laws."[36]

7

★ ★ ★ ★ ★

TAFT AND CONGRESS, 1910

By the eve of the opening of the regular session of Congress in December 1909, the Taft administration and the Republican Party knew that they faced difficult prospects in the congressional elections of 1910. The elections in 1909 had not revealed any clear trend, but there were some discouraging portents. Despite Taft's efforts to crack the Solid South, the Democrats prevailed in Virginia in the face of a strong effort the Republicans made there. In Massachusetts, the protest against the Payne–Aldrich tariff led to Democratic gains and a reduction in the winning majority for the Republican gubernatorial candidate. As Henry Cabot Lodge observed about the result in his state, "we did very well to get through. The cry about high prices hurt us, and we did not discuss the tariff as we should have done, but we will fix that next year."[1]

The issue of the cost of living and higher prices would cut against Taft and the Republicans throughout the winter of 1910. James R. Garfield, no friend of Taft by this time, asserted that "the next few months will be the critical ones for this administration." With the rift among the Republicans, Democrats experienced a genuine optimism they had not felt for two decades. The Grand Old Party, wrote one Democrat, was "opening wide the door for the Democratic party, as we know it to enter into control of public affairs."[2]

The first year of Taft's presidency had brought a succession of setbacks and gaffes: the Winona speech, the Crane dismissal, and the Ballinger–Pinchot case. Each one could be explained or understood. Together, they conveyed a sense of an administration in disarray. Coupled with that perception was the charge from Roosevelt's allies that Taft had repudiated the policies of his predecessor. The public at large believed the president was too close to the unpopular figures of Nelson Aldrich and Joseph G. Cannon.

The nationwide speaking tour in the autumn of 1909 had not produced the results that Taft had expected. The remarks he delivered in the West and South were earnest and detailed; they did not provide much new information or fresh ideas. As time went on, the president's absences from Washington suggested an unwillingness to stay in the White House and do business. Henry Cabot Lodge told Roosevelt that "he fails now to interest the country. He goes away constantly; a great deal more than you ever did during the sessions of Congress, to make speeches, often on very unimportant occasions. He does not profit by it, he loses."[3]

Meanwhile, the divisions among Republicans grew more bitter. The president and the regulars wanted to use patronage as a way of compelling the progressives to behave themselves in the interest of party unity. "These gentlemen who profess to be Republicans and will yet do everything to bring the Democratic party into power can not expect me to assist them with patronage," Taft observed, "and I hope to make this as plain as I can before I get through." The problem with that strategy was that the progressives were well positioned within their home states to resist White House pressure. Reprisals against them through withholding appointments only added to the discontent among Republicans with the administration.[4]

Adding to the problems that Taft confronted was his continuing identification with Aldrich and Cannon as congressional leaders. The president hoped that Cannon would announce his retirement after the 1910 session, but that did not occur. In fact, the Speaker indicated his intention to run for another term. An exasperated president told a progressive critic: "I am trying to do the best I can with Congress as it is, and with the Senate as it is, and I am not to be driven by any set of circumstances into an attack upon those who are standing faithfully with me in attempting to redeem the pledges of the party." As Taft collaborated with the leaders to enact his agenda, however, he was, in the eyes of the public, pushed more and more into an alliance with the conservatives.[5]

While partisan passions intensified at the end of 1909, the president began writing his first annual message. He was not the kind of innovator who would have thought of delivering his remarks in person, as Woodrow Wilson was to do three and a half years later. Like a jurist in a judicial conference, Taft worked over a lengthy document in consultation with the cabinet. Despite their editorial efforts to pare it down, the message was so long that the president decided to deliver separate installments on the issues of trusts and conservation after the annual report had been sent to Congress. What Taft gained in thoroughness, he lost in popular interest and attention to what he proposed to accomplish during the regular session. In the years that followed, the president would continue the process of conveying the annual message in installments. This practice further diluted attention in the press about what Taft had to say.

The message went to Congress on 7 December 1909 and did not evoke great excitement as the clerks read the president's prose. "The galleries were not in demand by the public," and members moved in and out of the House chamber while the reading continued. Reaction broke down on partisan lines, though Republicans and Democrats noted the restrained tone of Taft's words in comparison with the rhetorical energy and strident approach of Theodore Roosevelt. One Democrat said the difference in the way the two presidents wrote was like the contrast between "fondling a hot stove lid and a refrigerated shad."[6]

In the message itself, Taft focused on the impact of the Payne–Aldrich tariff for future tariff policy. He did not favor further efforts to adjust tariff rates and disclaimed any attempt to engage in efforts to coerce trading partners through use of the minimum–maximum provisions of the new law. Using the authority given to him in the tariff law, he had named a board of experts to consider other revisions in the schedules.

The president also endorsed the enactment of legislation to create a system of postal savings banks. That innovation would enable individuals without access to banks, particularly immigrants, to put money aside in a government-backed institution. The proposal also sought to preempt Democratic calls for the government to guarantee bank deposits. On another budgetary matter, the president promised further cost cutting to bring revenues and expenditures of the government into balance. On foreign policy, he spent a good deal of time in the message on the situation in Nicaragua and American policy toward the government there.

Two statements in Taft's remarks attracted attention. When he talked about Latin America, he observed that in regard to unstable governments in that region, "the apprehension which gave rise to the Monroe Doctrine may be said to have nearly disappeared, and neither the doctrine as it exists nor any other doctrine of American policy should be permitted to operate for the perpetuation of irresponsible government, the escape of just obligations, or of the insidious allegation of dominating ambitions on the part of the United States."[7]

The Democrats jumped on this statement. "Foreign countries will not overlook this assertion," said John J. Fitzgerald, a House member from New York. "The country will hardly approve it." Henry Cabot Lodge believed that the "country at large neither noticed nor understood" what

Taft had said, "but I am still in a condition of dazed wonder as to why he said it or what he meant by it."[8]

In talking about the fiscal condition of the post office department, Taft noted that the low postage rate on second-class mail such as newspapers and magazines accounted for a large annual loss of $63 million. Therefore, he argued that Congress should raise rates on these publications' mailing rates. Having gone after the interests of the magazine publishers, he then added: "I very much doubt, however, the wisdom of a policy which constitutes so large a subsidy and requires additional taxation to meet it." The president had a point on the policy itself, but attacking the publishing business which did so much to shape public opinion was not an astute move. Coverage of the president and his record turned more negative in 1910 as a result.[9]

Editorial reaction to the message stressed the contrast with Roosevelt in the relative brevity of what the president had said and in its overall approach. The message, wrote the Pittsburgh *Gazette-Times*, "will make a strong appeal to the conservative and sober-minded people of this country because it is in such striking contrast to similar documents of recent years." That was the editorial consensus around the country. Only in a few instances did a dissenting note appear. Taft, said the Belleville (Illinois) *News-Democrat,* was "simply an amiable, obliging, good-natured nobody, accidentally landed in the President's chair. The Interests own him, and the Big Fellows control him."[10]

Little daunted because of the criticism of the Winona speech, Taft continued during the congressional session to praise the Payne–Aldrich tariff as "the best revenue getter we have ever had." He dismissed a growing popular unhappiness with inflation and rising consumer prices. "There has been some complaint about high prices," he said in Providence on 21 March, "but I do not think they have been so high as to cause suffering." To those who criticized him for going around the country to say such things, he responded, "I got into the Presidency by traveling, and I can't get over the habit."[11]

The president remained close to Nelson Aldrich as the Senate Republican leader, and his praise of the Rhode Island legislator irritated the progressives. Taft did little to conciliate the insurgents along the way. If anything, his anger about them intensified during the six months that lawmakers grappled with the president's agenda. "They are exceedingly malignant, and do not hesitate at times to say things right out against the administration," Taft told his brother Horace. "If I can beat them in the legislation that I am trying to get, I shall not be at all troubled that they have aligned themselves against me."[12]

Overall, the session did not bode well for the Republicans. For the first time in two decades, the political landscape favored the Democrats. Popular unease about the rising cost of living set off protests from angry consumers in several large cities. The index that measured the cost of living had stood at a level of 100 in 1898. By 1910, it had reached nearly 130. One magazine said that "Nearly the whole American people developed overnight last month into one stupendous debating society. The subject of debate is the cost of living."[13]

As prices went up, the Democrats attributed the change to the higher duties of the Payne–Aldrich measure. Congress discussed whether to hold formal hearings on the problem. The British ambassador noted that "the Republican party is anxious to at least appear to be doing something to relieve the strain before the November elections arrive."[14] An indication of the shift in electoral attitudes came in March, when a special election occurred in a Massachusetts district that was regarded as safely Republican. A low-tariff Democrat won the seat and convinced at least one conservative senator "that we are to get a tremendous trouncing next fall so far as the National House of Representatives is concerned."[15]

The feuding among Republicans contributed to the sour political atmosphere. Taft issued his two supplements to the annual message about corporations and interstate commerce on 7 January and conservation on 14 January. The first presidential offering came on the day that Taft fired Pinchot for his letter to Senator Dolliver. The second, sent to Congress a week later, seemed anticlimactic in light of Pinchot's ouster from government service. In neither case did the president receive the attention he was seeking for his agenda.

In the interstate commerce message, Taft asked for changes in the Hepburn Act of 1906, which had strengthened the authority of the Interstate Commerce Commission over railroad rates. From his perspective as a former federal judge, the key recommendation was for a new court of commerce to hear railroad rate cases more quickly. The president argued that such a panel would enable rulings that were "as speedy as the nature of the circumstances will admit" and would also promote uniformity in court decisions about railroads in general. As the attorney general put it, "it is far more important to have speedy decisions and certainty introduced into law and regulation, than it is to seek absolute accuracy through long, tedious and conflicting legal proceedings."[16]

The advocacy of the commerce court put the president into conflict with Roosevelt's approach to railroad regulation. In the Hepburn Act, Roosevelt had endeavored to restrict the power of the judiciary to review rulings of the Interstate Commerce Commission. Now Taft wanted to put judges back into the process. In 1912, Roosevelt would call the new panel "the mischievous Commerce Court, the creation of which represented a long step backwards, of benefit only to the trusts themselves."[17]

The rest of the administration's railroad program, drafted by the attorney general, gave enhanced power to the Interstate Commerce Commission to suspend a proposed rate on its own authority for sixty days. The commission would also be able to review rate agreements of competing companies, and provision was made to oversee the issuance of railroad securities and bonds. The measure did not contain a favorite progressive idea: establishing the physical value of railroad property as the basis for rate making.

The Republican progressives were cool to Taft's ideas. "This commerce court," wrote Joseph L. Bristow, "is for the purpose of placing Federal judges, appointed for life, over the Interstate Commerce Commission and vesting in them far more power and authority than the Federal judges now have over its rulings." Albert B. Cummins of Iowa was very suspicious of the president's motives because Taft had asked him not to submit any amendments to the administration's proposal. Dolliver told Aldrich that the bill was "bunc."[18] The White House faced rebellious Republicans eager to reshape the railroad reform bill to their liking.

Taft also requested that Congress enact a national incorporation law to assist in the regulation of large corporations. On the enforcement of the Sherman Antitrust Act, he had no patience with the distinctions that Roosevelt had tried to make between corporations that behaved in a socially responsible way and those that did not. Taft recognized that some people believed that "a line may be drawn between 'good trusts' and 'bad trusts,'" but he believed that the public and corporations should "rid themselves of the idea that such a distinction is practicable or can be introduced into the statute."[19] Such comments illustrated the extent to which Taft further distanced himself from his predecessor.

From the outset, it was evident that the administration's approach to corporations and their regulation would have a difficult time. Progressive opposition was to be expected. However, the business community also reacted negatively to the proposal. Stock prices fell on Wall Street, and there was grumbling about White House policies. "I am quite aware that since the first of January a great chill has come over the business community," wrote Wickersham, "and I am not surprised by it." Businessmen, he added, had misread Taft's intentions about antitrust law and its enforcement. Still, the backlash from conservatives in and out of Congress added to the problems that confronted the president's legislative program.[20]

Within weeks, it became apparent that Taft would have to limit his priorities for the session to those bills lawmakers would pass. On 20

February, the White House said that the president wanted a railroad law, legislation to regulate the issuance of injunctions in labor disputes, a measure to admit New Mexico and Arizona into the union, and a law to allocate authority to the executive to withdraw public land from settlement for the purposes of conservation. Meanwhile, the president's plan for postal savings banks seemed on the way to safe passage. The announcement, said the *Washington Post*, "is received by Republican leaders with unmixed feelings of relief."[21]

These gestures did not ease the apprehensions of the progressive Republicans about the proposed railroad measure. Cummins led the assault in the Senate when debate opened on the administration's bill on 18 March. The president was on the road to a speech in Rochester, New York, and he told his wife that the Iowa senator was "very vicious and very anxious to defeat legislation." From that point on, the insurgents had the initiative in the upper house and the administration forces played from behind.[22]

Taft's absence occurred at the same time that the opposition to Speaker Cannon in the House brought a dramatic reduction in his power. Seeing an opportunity to restrict Cannon's authority, his adversaries, led by George W. Norris of Nebraska, offered a resolution to limit the power of the presiding officer over the rules committee and various other elements that had maintained Cannon's dominance. A point of order was raised against the Norris resolution. Once the Speaker ruled on the point of order, the members would vote on whether to sustain that position. A vote on the question would actually be a vote on whether to keep Cannon's power as it had been. Because the debate came on St. Patrick's day with members absent, both the pro- and anti-Cannon forces played for time. When the balloting occurred on 19 March, the Speaker's ruling was overturned and the Norris resolution adopted. An effort to oust Cannon from the Speakership failed. The larger point, of course, was that Cannon's dictatorial management of the House had been broken.[23]

Taft did not like the Speaker and was pleased with the result of the House rebellion against him. During the first year of his tenure, however, the president had become so identified with Cannon that he gained very little in popular approval from the reduction in the Speaker's power. The White House thought that with Cannon removed as a target for insurgent anger, the chances of getting the Republican legislative program through the House might improve. Instead, the battle over Cannon underlined the extent of Republican disunity and further bolstered the chances of the Democrats in the fall elections.

The absence of the president during the Cannon struggle was symptomatic of Taft's propensity to get out of Washington as much as he could during the winter and spring of 1910. Archie Butt wrote in early April that "the President takes these trips just as a dipsomaniac goes on periodical sprees." Although the experience tired out his aides, "he returns from them refreshed and invigorated. It is almost freakish, the ghoulish delight he gets from traveling."[24]

Although it helped Taft relax, his compulsion to travel outside Washington worsened his relations with Congress. Republicans complained that he was away from Washington when they most needed him to be present. Even his brother Charles warned him that he was moving around too much. "This excessive amount of railroad travel must wear on you a great deal. It prevents you from taking your regular exercises in the morning; then comes the added danger of accident. I just wish you would cut it out."[25]

His journeys also provided a tempting target for the Democrats, who continued their efforts to cut back on his travel appropriations. The pictures of Taft at baseball games, in automobiles, and speaking around the country contributed to the perception of a chief executive often bored with the intricacies of the legislative process. "The truth is," wrote a Republican senator, "while President Taft is a lovable and delightful man, he is not impressing himself upon the country in a strong way. He is obsessed with the idea that he must keep on the move and make speeches, and all that is hurting him instead of helping him."[26]

Throughout the congressional session, Taft hammered his argument that party loyalty required Republican lawmakers to support the presidential program. When Senator Julius Caesar Burrows of Michigan wavered in his endorsement of the postal savings bill, Taft told him, "I thought you were an Administration senator." When Burrows responded, "I am an Administration Senator, but—," the president replied: "There is no 'but' in it. The way to be an Administration Senator is to vote with the Administration."[27]

The same ideological message came from the president and the cabinet. In February, speaking at a Lincoln Day dinner of the Republican Club of the City of New York, Taft told his partisan audience that there were divisions among Republicans. As the Grand Old Party approached the congressional elections, he hoped that "the settlement of these internal questions can be effected without such a breach of the party as to prevent our presenting an unbroken front to the enemy." In the process of reform that Theodore Roosevelt had pursued, party organizations came under assault and "the leaders of the party organization are subjected to the severest attacks and to the questioning of their motives without any adequate evidence to justify it."[28]

Two months later, in a major speech presented as an official statement of administration policy, Attorney General Wickersham made the president's argument in a more direct manner. At Chicago, appearing before the Hamilton Club, Wickersham said: "I speak to an assembly of loyal Republicans. I am sure I voice your thought when I say the time of running with the hare and hunting with the hounds is over and every one must choose whether or not he is for the president and the Republican party. He that 'hath no stomach for the fight, let him depart.' Treason has ever consisted in giving aid and comfort to the enemy."[29]

Far from being persuaded to become more loyal, the Republican insurgents reacted with outrage to Wickersham's remarks. "The speech," said Albert Beveridge, "voices the real sentiments of the Administration" and has "made things much worse than ever." La Follette said that he would not have his Republicanism impugned by someone "known to the public chiefly as an attorney for the big business and financial interests of New York." Because the speech had been presented to the press as an authoritative statement of administration policy, it undercut any attempt Taft made at the time to conciliate the progressives through White House conferences.[30]

As the congressional session proceeded during the spring of 1910, the proximity to the elections brought the Republicans back together. Greater unity enabled Taft to achieve some elements of his policy goals. The postal savings bank bill was enacted. The president saw his conservation bill enacted, and he signed, with some reluctance, the rivers and harbors bill. The Republican record also included a modest campaign finance measure and gave the executive $100,000 for an investigation of how the cost of government could be pared down.

In the case of railroad legislation that became the Mann–Elkins act, Taft realized his goal of a commerce court, though its powers were less extensive than he had proposed. The rest of the railroad bill bore more of the imprint of Cummins and the insurgents than it did of the administration. When the railroads sought to raise rates in late May, Taft and Wickersham got political credit for jawboning the lines into rescinding their increases. As for the railroad measure itself, the insurgents obtained the advantage over the conservative leadership in the Senate. By granting greater power over rates to the Interstate Commerce Commission, the Mann–Elkins law was more restrictive on the railroads than Taft and Wickersham had envisioned.

The president was generally pleased with how the regular session of Congress had fared. "I think things are coming our way a little more than heretofore," he wrote on 11 June 1910, "and I am as pleased as Punch about the postal savings bill." He believed that "the leaders of the House and the Senate" did not intend to pass either postal savings or the railroad bill, "and would not have done so if I had not made a fuss about it and insisted." Taft was glad to praise the Republican Congress in a letter for the fall election campaign.[31]

As a legislative leader in 1910, the president had used all the political tools at his disposal. He had wielded patronage against dissidents, had summoned lawmakers to the White House for conferences and social events, and had dabbled in state politics to launch candidates against the insurgents. In so doing, he had put together a creditable record of bills passed and issues engaged. "I am elated at the legislation which has been enacted by this Congress," the president proclaimed. "It has fulfilled the pledges of the party. It is a great satisfaction to me that we have accomplished so much." The editors of the *Washington Post* said that "the President could take his vacation with the consciousness of a duty well done."[32]

What Taft had not been able to do was to heal the fissures within the Republican Party. For the Grand Old Party, that result meant a difficult situation as the incumbents faced the voters. The railroad bill had little immediate relief for consumers pressed hard with high prices, nor did the postal savings measure address the discontent over the tariff. "Unless something unforeseen occurs or Roosevelt shall come and prove the peacemaker, we are sure to lose the House this year and almost as sure to lose the Presidency in 1912—unless, as General Grant always said, the Democrats act the fool in our favor at the right time," wrote a longtime party insider in April 1910.[33]

The president thus did not gain all that much in a political sense from the session of Congress in 1910 despite his genuine accomplishments as a legislative leader. The revelations about Gifford Pinchot and the Glavis document backdating had been a public relations setback. Reviewing the president's performance after a year in office, the Newark *Evening News* concluded: "the people do not want a lawyer in the White House. They want a leader." The outcome of the congressional session did little to counteract that harsh conclusion in the public mind.[34]

Throughout his first year, the shadow of Theodore Roosevelt had been ever present on the White House for William Howard Taft. Now, after a year of hunting in Africa and a triumphal procession through Europe in the spring of 1910, Roosevelt was preparing to return to the United States. In the time he was away, much had changed in his relationship with President Taft. The problem for Taft was simple. Theodore Roosevelt's support could not ensure that Taft's presidency would be a success. Roosevelt's opposition, however, would be the most damaging blow the administration could receive.

When Roosevelt left for Africa in March 1909, Taft sent him a letter before his departure. In it, the new president wished his predecessor well on his journey, then concluded, "I do nothing in the Executive Office without considering what you would do under the same circumstances and without having in a sense a mental talk with you over the pros and cons of the situation." Although some in the public might in time think that Taft had "fallen away from your ideals," the president assured Roosevelt that "you know me better and will understand that I am still working away on the same old plan and hope to realize in some measure the results that we both hold valuable and worth striving for."[35]

To this letter, Roosevelt responded with a brief wire that read, "am deeply touched by your gift and even more by your letter. Greatly appreciate it, Everything will turn out all right, old man." There would not be another direct communication between the two men for a year, until Taft wrote Roosevelt in May 1910 to get him current on what happened while the former president was away.[36]

On Roosevelt's side, he was on a hunting trip and far from civilization. Writing to Taft would have been difficult, but he managed to correspond with others during his year outside of the country. If Roosevelt could comment on current events as Henry Cabot Lodge presented them to him, he could well have done the same with the president. As an ex-president, Roosevelt had gone to Africa for the express purpose of not seeming to interfere in Taft's administration. So his silence could be defended on that ground. Still, Roosevelt carried his self-denial to an extreme. He did not think it necessary to give his old friend at least some moral support in a job that only they knew from the inside.

Taft's approach to corresponding with Roosevelt seems equally odd. The president was a facile author of letters that he dictated to his secretaries. It would not have taken much time to have dashed off notes to Roosevelt on a regular basis, say twice a month. There would have been the difficulty of maintaining the confidentiality of these communications, but the president had the diplomatic service or alternatively the Roosevelt family as practical conduits. Taft had time to write letters arranging golf games. Keeping Theodore Roosevelt in the loop should have commanded a higher priority in the president's mind.

As for Roosevelt himself, what hard news he received during 1909 came from the office of the *Outlook* and the letters of friends such as Henry Cabot Lodge and especially Gifford Pinchot. In late December, Pinchot wrote a lengthy letter laying out the case against Taft. "The general tendency shown in these examples cannot be mistaken," Pinchot said. "It is away from the Roosevelt policies and the people, and in favor of the special interests and the few."[37] Lodge also wrote extensively with his take on Taft's performance in office. "This Administration," wrote Lodge in late December 1909, "without doing anything wrong, is not strong in the country and is losing its hold." The Massachusetts senator added that if the Republicans lost the House in 1910, "a situation will arise which neither you or any one in your place can control" relative to 1912.[38]

By late March 1910, Roosevelt was in Egypt and on his way to Italy, where Gifford Pinchot would meet him to discuss politics. Pinchot took with him letters about Taft from a number of prominent Republicans and journalists. The overall tone about the president was negative. "President Taft, up-to-date, has been a failure," wrote William L. Ward of New York. "You can find very few people in any walk of life who will say a good word for him. He wobbles and has allowed the Republican party to become disintegrated." The Kansas City newspaper publisher William Rockhill Nelson told Roosevelt that "the American people want an executive in the President's office, not a judge who hears arguments on all sides and finally gives his opinion on a technicality." The mail did not contain any sustained defense of what Taft had done or the problems he had encountered. Even Henry Cabot Lodge, while stating that Taft "is sound and right in his policies," added that "he has got himself in difficulties more than once by speaking decisively" about "one policy or some appointment before he has stopped to think about it."[39]

Gifford Pinchot saw Roosevelt in mid-April at Porto Maurizo, Italy, and noted in his diary, "One of the best and most satisfactory talks with T.R. I ever had. Lasted nearly all day, and till about 10:30 at night." A meeting with Elihu Root did not sway Roosevelt from his emerging negative appraisal of Taft. By early May, Roosevelt was telling Lodge, "For a year after Taft took office, for a year and a quarter after he had been elected, I would not let myself think ill of anything he did. I finally had to admit that he had gone wrong on certain points; and then I also had to admit to myself that deep down underneath I had known all along he was wrong, on points as to which I had tried to deceive myself, by loudly proclaiming to myself, that he was right." For the moment, Roosevelt pledged to keep silent about his feelings, but the statements he made to Pinchot and the letters he wrote combined to make it very difficult for him to give Taft even rhetorical support in public. For Roosevelt, the ouster of Henry White rankled. The president had not asked Congress to keep the Country Life Commission alive. Instead, this initiative, so close to Roosevelt's thinking, had been allowed to die out. There was little that Taft had done that, in Roosevelt's mind, represented a continuation of his policies.[40]

The imminent return of Roosevelt led Taft to consider what his attitude would be toward this impending event. He found an interim answer when King Edward VII of Great Britain died in May. Taft appointed Roosevelt to represent the American government at the funeral ceremonies. Selection to this diplomatic mission, while welcome, did not remove Roosevelt's doubts about Taft as the former president prepared to return home in mid-June.

During these weeks, the president eased out Fred W. Carpenter as his personal secretary. The replacement, Charles Dyer Norton, was a Chicago insurance executive serving as assistant secretary of the treasury. Norton did not prove to be a wise choice. He had a propensity for intrigue without the skills to carry out his schemes in a deft political way. Norton encouraged that side of Taft as well, and their machinations would provide some embarrassment for the administration during the summer of 1910.[41]

Roosevelt was going to have an elaborate public reception when his ship reached New York City on 18 June 1910. After discussing whether he should attend in person, Taft decided to send Archie Butt instead with personal greetings. The suave Butt helped Taft draft a letter to Roosevelt, dated 26 May 1910, that endeavored to get the personal relations of the two men back on a friendly basis. The letter itself stressed the impact of Mrs. Taft's illness on her husband before it turned to policy matters. Taft defended his course on the tariff and criticized the insurgents for their obstructive tactics. "The fight for a year to move on and comply with our party promises has been a hard one." Taft also finessed the issue of the Ballinger–Pinchot controversy when he urged that Roosevelt look into the matter himself to make up his mind. The president missed a chance to lay out the case for his policies, perhaps because he knew his predecessor would disagree with his actions.[42]

The letter reached Roosevelt in England just before he sailed for home. In his reply, Roosevelt wrote that "what I have felt it best to do was to say absolutely nothing—and indeed to keep my mind open as I kept my mouth shut!" The letter was friendly enough, if a little restrained in its tone. Roosevelt declined the invitation to come stay at the White House on the grounds that former presidents should not come to the executive mansion, or indeed even Washington itself. That rationale struck Taft as implausible, and he concluded that Roosevelt did not wish to see him.[43]

Roosevelt was pleased when Butt and two members of the cabinet showed up in New York to greet him. The day itself was an occasion that emphasized Roosevelt's continuing popularity. Henry Cabot Lodge caught the spirit of the moment. "No band, no procession, just a man in a carriage and the most tremendous crowd that my eye ever rested on for the whole five miles. It was one steady roar of applause, entirely spontaneous and no organization about it,—one of the most remarkable things I ever saw."[44] Roosevelt told reporters that he had nothing to say for the public and would henceforth not make political statements.

The two men did talk at the president's summer home at Beverly,

Massachusetts, on 30 June 1910 with Henry Cabot Lodge and Butt there, as well as Mrs. Taft. The advance billing for the event in the press was intense. As the editors of the *Washington Post* put it, "no conference of recent years which had for its object the good of the Republican party has aroused such exceptional interest as attaches to that arranged for today."[45]

The president wrote his nephew that "I am going to see Mr. Roosevelt this afternoon. I have no reason to suppose that his attitude will be hostile." The only record of the event is from Archie Butt and the occasion was pleasant and, beyond a discussion of the New York Republican situation, nonpolitical. Roosevelt spoke of his dealings with the crowned heads of Europe at the funeral of Edward VII in an amusing manner. The two principals never got down to the issues on which they disagreed. Roosevelt told the waiting reporters that nothing of consequence had happened. As for the president, he called it "another corner turned."[46]

In a sense, Taft was right. A significant episode in his presidency had come to an end. From 1 July 1910 onward, the deterioration of the Taft–Roosevelt relationship would accelerate; two years later, the one-time friends were bitter enemies. The summer of 1910 would see the opening stages of that process, one in which Taft found himself off balance and on the defensive against the man with whom he had once been so close. Even the modest successes that Taft had in the regular session of Congress faded in importance as the charismatic Roosevelt imposed his presence on the Republican Party. As a result, Taft's presidential administration never recovered from the return of Roosevelt to the center stage of American politics.

8

★ ★ ★ ★ ★

TAFT, ROOSEVELT, AND THE
1910 ELECTION

At the time of his late June meeting with Theodore Roosevelt, President William Howard Taft had reached the high point of his administration. His success with Congress during the regular session enabled him to restore some of the prestige that had slipped away in 1909. There was a sense that the president had found his footing after a difficult first year. As one reporter noted in July 1910, "The president has got all over his discouraged spell of the winter and thinks he has the world by the short hair." Although political signs still pointed toward trouble for the Republicans, Taft felt some optimism about his party's chances with the voters.[1]

In an interview for *McClure's Magazine,* the president laid out what he saw as the accomplishments of his first year in office. Coming after Theodore Roosevelt, "it was the business of the administration following his to make" the changes "in the operations and powers of Federal Government" permanent ones. He reiterated his praise of the Payne–Aldrich tariff, and he explained how the corporate tax in the tariff bill, the Mann–Elkins law, and the federal incorporation bill would, in his mind "place the corporations of this country upon an entirely new basis." He said there was no evidence of wrongdoing on the part of Secretary of the Interior Richard Ballinger, and he defended his conservation policies. In the finances of the government, a $60 million deficit had become a $35 million surplus. Summing up his goals, he had but "one aim in the Presidency—to make a broad and permanent advance in the powers of the Federal Government and their enforcement."[2]

Contributing to Taft's upbeat mood was his new secretary, Charles

Dyer Norton. Once in the White House, Norton fed Taft's penchant for partisan intrigue. Reluctant to be seen behaving like a politician, Taft adopted a lofty stance above the conflict while at the same time launching several covert moves to discomfort his Republican adversaries. When these schemes faltered, Taft backed away from them, but he could not always erase the traces of what he had done. The White House initiatives contributed to the increasing tension between Roosevelt and Taft that festered during the summer of 1910.

The conclusion of the regular session of Congress saw the president and the insurgents as divided as they had been when lawmakers had gathered in December 1909. A progressive boycott of a White House signing ceremony left Taft irritated at the Republican dissidents. "If they can get along without me," the president said, "I presume I can do the same without them." Rather than conciliating his adversaries within the Grand Old Party, he sought to defeat them in the primaries and state conventions of that election year summer.[3]

By pursuing that course, however, Taft encouraged these party apostates to turn to Roosevelt for support. The more that the insurgents made pilgrimages to Oyster Bay, New York, where the former president lived, the more that the incumbent president, the cabinet, and party regulars bristled. Internal warfare became the rule for Republicans in 1910, with the unstated prospect of a Roosevelt run for the nomination in 1912 just beneath the surface. Watching their rivals behaving with such unexpected discord, the happy Democrats believed that the chances of retaking the House of Representatives improved daily.

To maintain his dominance within the party, the president made common cause with Aldrich and Cannon. The Republican Senate leader had announced that he would not seek another term but was still interested in reforming the banking system. Aldrich thus urged Taft to defeat insurgents who had to face the voters in the fall. Among the key targets were Albert J. Beveridge and the two Iowa senators, Albert B. Cummins and Jonathan P. Dolliver. The president called Beveridge "a liar and an egotist and so self-absorbed that he can not be depended on for anything, and I really am not particularly concerned whether he is elected in Indiana or not."[4]

The party was split in Indiana over Beveridge's stand against the Payne–Aldrich law. Even unified Republicans would have been in trouble against the resurgent Indiana Democrats who had united behind John Worth Kern, the running mate of William Jennings Bryan in 1908. Divisions over prohibition in the wet state further crippled the GOP there. By the spring, it was evident that Beveridge was in trouble. His friend

Dolliver told him that "you stand on the firing line, at the bloody angle, in a nation-wide fight for good government and honest legislation." Beveridge secured renomination to the Senate from the state convention, while his opponents, Congressman James E. Watson and Senator James Hemenway succeeded in electing several pro-tariff conservatives to run for the House. At the end of the summer, as the national tide ran toward the Democrats, the chances of Beveridge retaining his seat seemed slight.[5]

Taft had dabbled in Iowa politics even before he became president. His distaste for the maverick Republicanism of Cummins and Dolliver had grown in the aftermath of the legislative battles over the tariff in 1909 and railroads in 1910. Taft hoped to see Dolliver and Cummins rebuked within the party and to have conservative House members from Iowa nominated. In February 1910, the president met with allies among conservative Iowa Republicans to work out joint action against the senators and to block an endorsement for them at the Republican state convention the following summer. The group agreed to set up Taft Republican clubs aimed at "uniting the Republican Party of Iowa under President Taft's leadership." It was this program that Taft asked Senator Aldrich to fund.[6]

The problem for the administration, however, was that both senators remained popular with their constituents. "You need not have the slightest fear of lack of support on the part of the people," Henry Wallace of *Wallace's Farmer* (and the grandfather of the future vice president) told Dolliver, "how ever much standpat politicians may desire your scalp." Dolliver attacked the White House and high-tariff Republicans in a major speech during June, to popular acclaim. "The President is in error," Dolliver said. "It is not necessary for men to swallow down every tariff law that is set before them or 'in conscience abandon the party.'"[7]

Taft took some temporary gratification when the incumbent conservative governor, B. F. Carroll, was renominated in the June primaries. The president was informed, "Our friends have carried Iowa." The conservatives claimed victory in the eastern press, and Taft exulted over the apparent success of his cause. An angry Senator Cummins, aware of the gains of his faction on the local level, resolved "to give the President less endorsement than he has hitherto had, even in the strongest progressive conventions."[8]

When the state convention met in early August, Cummins and his allies prevailed in what the press called "a rout" against the president. The progressives approved in the platform only "such efforts as President Taft and his advisers have made to fulfill the promises of the National platform, and which have been in harmony with the declarations of this convention." Dolliver's death from heart disease a few weeks later removed one critic of the president, but as a political venture, Taft's efforts in Iowa had failed as the fall of 1910 opened.[9]

As administration attacks on insurgent Republicans intensified during the summer, those politicians naturally looked to Theodore Roosevelt as a potential ally. Resting at his home in Oyster Bay, New York, before a speaking tour of the West in late August, the former president welcomed a series of Republican reformers for personal consultations. In Taft's mind, his one-time friend had rebuffed the several invitations to the White House and now had the temerity to receive, amid a wave of publicity, those who attacked the administration. The president found the resulting spectacle hard to accept. He spoke in private about "the sage at Oyster Bay." Taft warned his cabinet members not to comment on statements emanating from Roosevelt's camp about encounters with the insurgents. As Charles Norton told a newspaper publisher, "Our position is that we don't know what Oyster Bay is going to do and we don't give a damn."[10]

In fact, Norton, like his boss, worried about what Roosevelt might do in the fall election campaign. To change the dynamic in favor of the White House, Taft's secretary decided to dabble in Republican politics himself. That he acted with at least the knowledge of the president seems likely. When the scheme fell apart, Taft distanced himself from the wreckage. Norton identified Secretary Ballinger, Senator Aldrich, and Speaker Cannon as political drags on the president's popularity. Working with Senator Winthrop Murray Crane of Massachusetts, Norton proposed to have Ballinger resign and seek a U.S. Senate seat from his home state of Washington. Aldrich would be repudiated, and Cannon would announce his retirement from politics. These moves, one reporter speculated, would conciliate Roosevelt and perhaps make possible an endorsement of the president for 1912.[11]

On 13 August, national newspapers carried dispatches out of Taft's summer residence in Beverly, Massachusetts, announcing a major change in the priorities of the administration. Aldrich would continue with his plan to leave the Senate, Ballinger would resign in mid-September, and Cannon would step down too. "I have not heard that Mr. Cannon would be a candidate," was the quote attributed to Taft. A press report continued: "That Beverly is being made the headquarters of the movement to set the Republican house in order is now generally admitted. The various moves are being made quietly but effectively."[12]

In practice, the Norton scheme proved to be neither quiet nor effective. The reaction among the progressives was suspicion, while the conservatives felt betrayed. One newspaper reporter concluded that "Taft is a stranded whale" who had chosen to cut his ties with Ballinger and

Charles D. Norton's tenure as Taft's secretary was filled with controversy, and he departed after a year in the post. Library of Congress.

Cannon a year too late. Within a day, reports disclosed that progressives were as dubious about the leadership of Crane as they had earlier been of Aldrich. The key to Norton's maneuvers was the departure of Ballinger. The secretary declined to step aside, and the president refused to ask him to go. Once that central element faltered, the rest of the proposed scenario fell apart. Taft wrote to Aldrich to dismiss everything as a "flubdub," which he blamed on reporters who were advancing "a thought to save the administration against itself."[13]

Neither the defeat in Iowa and other states nor the breakup of the Norton venture, embarrassing as they were for Taft, brought the president into direct conflict with Roosevelt. The actions of conservative Republicans in New York, however, led to an imbroglio that further eroded relations between Taft and his predecessor. The roots of this episode lay in the complex politics of the Empire State. Governor Charles Evans Hughes, first elected in 1906, had by 1910 become the target of the wrath of the regulars in his state. They regarded the governor as self-righteous and hypocritical. As one observer wrote to Roosevelt, Hughes "has never been anything but a preacher of the crusade, never a leader except in the intellectual sense, not a constructive statesman because of his lack of knowledge of human conditions."[14]

By the spring of 1910, Hughes was on his way out of New York and on to a seat on the United States Supreme Court. Taft would have six appointments to the high court. The first came in October 1909, when Justice Rufus Peckham died, and Taft named his old friend, Horace Lurton, a federal appeals court judge from Tennessee, to replace him. Then in April 1910, David J. Brewer died, and Taft offered the post to Hughes. They agreed that Hughes would remain in office until mid-October, when he could resign and take his seat on the Supreme Court. The news of the appointment made Hughes a lame-duck governor, but he still had priorities that he wanted the New York legislature to adopt.[15]

The major reform that Hughes sought called for a direct primary to put nominations for political office in the hands of the voters. The Republican conservatives wanted no part of such a proposal. Hughes had called a special session in June to deal with the issue. To gain support for his program, the governor turned to Roosevelt. Although the former president had told reporters covering him that he would have nothing to say about politics upon his return from Europe, his self-denying stance did not last long. Governor Hughes saw Roosevelt at the commencement ceremonies at Harvard University on 29 June. After an intense conversation, he persuaded Roosevelt to endorse the nomination bill then before the lawmakers in Albany. Roosevelt wired Lloyd Griscom, a former diplomat who now chaired the New York County Republican Committee. The measure

Hughes was proposing, Roosevelt said, "meets the need of the situation. I believe the people demand it. I most earnestly hope that it will be enacted into law."[16]

Taft too favored the direct primary legislation. He sent letters to prominent New York Republicans asking them to "help put through the Hughes compromise primary bill, which the interests of the party clearly require."[17] Roosevelt thus saw the New York controversy as one where he and the president could stand together behind reform and in the process heal some of the wounds of the party. He did not take into account the anger that the regulars felt about Hughes, and even more their suspicions about Roosevelt's own intentions. Might the former president, the regulars asked themselves, be trying to get control of New York as a prelude to a presidential run in 1912? "We must stand up and hold matters together or the party is busted," wrote Vice President James S. Sherman. "It may mean temporary defeat but what of it? It would mean more than temporary defeat if we did not stand up."[18]

The anger of the regulars against Hughes contributed to the defeat of the direct nominations bill on 30 June. They supplied the Republican votes to kill the measure. William A. Barnes Jr., the leader of the opposition to Roosevelt, proclaimed, "Teddy is licked to a frazzle. We no longer worship the gods, we laugh at them." With the nominations issue decided, Republican attention then shifted to the upcoming state convention and the gubernatorial nominee for the fall campaign. "I want," Roosevelt told reporters, "to find the best man for the office; the man who is most acceptable to the rank and file of the republican party and the independent voters."[19]

A movement began, led by Griscom, to have Roosevelt serve as the temporary chair of the state convention. From that post, the former president could sway delegates toward his hand-picked candidate and set the tone for the fall campaign. The regulars decided that they had to block Roosevelt's selection "to carry on a successful State Convention that will be looked on as a Taft convention." Another conservative told the *New York Times* "that he would face defeat for his party at the polls rather than to bow to dictation from Beverly or Sagamore Hill."[20]

To make sure that he had presidential support for Roosevelt's candidacy, Griscom went to see Taft at Beverly and floated the idea of the temporary chair position going to the former president. After their discussion, Taft wired Sherman, asking him to promote party unity "by a full conference with Mr. Roosevelt and reasonable concessions with reference to platforms and candidates." The president did not come out for Roosevelt as the temporary chair. The resulting ambiguity gave the conservatives enough wiggle room to go ahead with their own plans. Taft talked on the phone with Sherman, and although he avoided any direct commitment to regulars, Taft felt, as Archie Butt put it, "a hope that they would not let Mr. Roosevelt dominate the convention." Taft's mind told him not to alienate his predecessor; his feelings tempted him to encourage Sherman and his allies to block Roosevelt's candidacy.[21]

The result was that Sherman, Barnes, and the others went ahead with their intention to rebuff Roosevelt's hopes. On 15 August, the key members of the Republican state committee, led by Timothy L. Woodruff and Barnes, met at Sherry's Restaurant at 525 Fifth Avenue and laid their plans for the formal meeting of the committee the next day. Their ploy was to select Vice President Sherman as temporary chair. His national office and link to the president would trump Roosevelt's popularity. To what extent Taft was in on the scheme is not clear. The president may have been engaging in another one of his political maneuvers. If Sherman won and Roosevelt backed down, the result would be good for the White House. If Roosevelt protested, Taft would have grounds to deny any involvement. That Roosevelt might have suspicions about the president's good faith was not in Taft's mind.

At the state committee meeting on 16 August, the Sherman nomination was made. Griscom countered with Roosevelt's name. The panel voted 20 to 15 not to recommend the former president to the convention at Saratoga on 27 September. When Taft received the news that Sherman had been designated, Archie Butt was there to record the reaction. "Have you seen the newspapers this afternoon?" Taft said. "They have defeated Theodore." Norton and the president laughed over the news, much to Butt's dismay.[22]

Back in New York, Roosevelt reiterated to the press his desire for the selection as the GOP candidate for governor of "the right kind of man on a clear-cut progressive platform." Griscom issued a statement that relieved Taft of any responsibility for the selection of Sherman. Nonetheless, the episode stirred Roosevelt's ire. He wrote to friends what Griscom had told him about a meeting with Taft. The president had supported Woodruff, Barnes, and Sherman because they controlled the delegates for 1912 and Taft "must of course go with the side that was most apt to give him the delegates."[23]

Taft was now in a dilemma. On the one hand, Woodruff was telling Sherman that "the President must stand by us and be actively on our side" to prevent Roosevelt from shattering the New York party. But Taft also knew that if he threw in with the regulars and confronted the former president in a public fight, his whole administration would be in peril. Taft had to step back from an identification with the regulars and their intrigues. On 22 August, Taft released to the press a letter he had written to Griscom outlining his part in what had happened. Any suggestion that the president had wished to see Roosevelt beaten for the temporary chairmanship was "wholly untrue." Taft once again urged that all interested Republicans work out a compromise on the direct nominations issue.[24]

When the letter was published, the press hurried to get Roosevelt's reaction. "I am very glad to see President Taft's letter," he said, "and am pleased with it." However, the White House also learned more of Roosevelt's true feelings. During his trip west in late August, Roosevelt spoke with a Republican in Toledo, Ohio. That gentleman reported to Taft that he said to Roosevelt "how every body was pleased with your letter *in re* selection of Mr. Sherman as Chairman." To which Roosevelt responded: "Yes, that was all right, but it came a little slow."[25]

The incident intensified Roosevelt's desire to defeat his political enemies in his home state. "I am sorry that the 'Old Guard' have put themselves in such shape that I shall have to go in and try to smash them," he wrote to a Kansas newspaper publisher. In the White House, the strategy was to wait in the confidence that Taft had prevailed in the public relations battle with the former president. "Everyone on the inside," wrote Norton, "every intelligent newspaper man who was there—knows of the ravings, the innuendoes, the near open denunciation. The calm truth was too much for him."[26]

Roosevelt departed for the West on 23 August with the desire to set the agenda for the Republicans through what became known as his political creed of the New Nationalism. Taft looked for some word from Roosevelt indicating that he accepted personally the president's assurance expressed in the letter to Griscom about his actions in the battle over the temporary chairmanship. By this time, Taft had also heard a garbled version of the issue surrounding his November 1908 letter to Roosevelt in which Charles P. Taft had been mentioned as an equal force in getting Taft into the White House. The president believed that the offending phrase had been in the letter he had sent to Roosevelt at the time the former president departed for Africa. A fellow passenger of Roosevelt's had informed Taft that Roosevelt was complaining about the coupling of his brother and the former president even then. Taft expressed his hurt feelings to those who came to see him, and these comments found their way back to Roosevelt. The inability of the two men to keep straight the facts of their own interaction added to the political confusion. By late August 1910, their rapport, once so strong, had almost disappeared.[27]

While Roosevelt was delivering his speeches on his cross-country tour, Taft did his part for the Republican congressional campaign. He prepared a lengthy defense of the party's record in Congress through a public letter to William B. McKinley of Illinois, the chair of the National

Congressional Republican Committee. Taft noted that Republican faction-alism was much in the news but that in its legislative work, "the present Congress has not only fulfilled many party pledges, but it has by its course set higher the standard of party responsibility for such pledges than ever before in the history of American parties." He praised the reductions in government expenditures and looked forward to more constructive legis-lation in 1911. Republicans, he concluded, were "the party of construction and progress," while the Democrats were "the party of obstruction and negation."[28]

Taft's campaign document did not attract much attention in late Au-gust 1910. Theodore Roosevelt had achieved extensive press coverage with his western tour and enunciation of the New Nationalism. In a se-ries of speeches, he attacked the judiciary for insulating business from effective supervision, spoke out for more regulatory legislation, and made clear by implication his philosophical differences with the White House. Though he said nothing critical of Taft as such, there were phrases in his addresses that observers took as implied slights of the incumbent. At Osa-watomie, Kansas, on 31 August, for example, he told his audience: "No man is worth his salt in public life who makes on the stump a pledge which he does not keep after election; and, if he makes such a pledge and does not keep it, hunt him out of public life."[29]

From the perspective of President Taft, the program that Roosevelt promulgated during his western tour was deeply disturbing. On a personal level, Taft noted that Roosevelt, "in most of these speeches . . . has utterly ignored me." As he told Elihu Root, "the difficulty about the speeches is their tone, and the conditions under which they are delivered," espe-cially in the attacks on the courts. Philosophically, the president found the New Nationalism to be replete with "wild ideas" and "a threat that would startle most conservative institutions." What Roosevelt proposed, Taft concluded, would require drastic changes in the Constitution or a revolution in society. The prospect of a Roosevelt candidacy in 1912 now seemed more and more probable in the minds of Taft and his advisers.[30]

As the Republicans contemplated defeat in the fall campaign, there were efforts to reconcile Taft and Roosevelt in some public way to per-suade voters that all was well within the Grand Old Party. The National Conservation Congress met in St. Paul, Minnesota, on 5 September 1910. Organizers hoped that Taft and Roosevelt might meet there and talk out their differences. Taft ensured that such an encounter did not happen. In-stead, the president appeared on 5 September, and Roosevelt spoke the next day. They made flattering references to each other without speaking about the subjects that divided them.[31]

Two weeks later, a conference did occur, but that too widened the breach rather than resolving any hard feelings. Taft was attending the meeting of the Yale University Corporation on 19 September in New Haven, Connecticut. It was arranged that Roosevelt should cross Long Island Sound from Oyster Bay by motorboat and have lunch and a conference with the president. The weather conspired against the plans. Choppy waves and winds forced *The Tarpon,* on which Roosevelt traveled, to put in at Stamford, Connecticut, and the former president made his journey the rest of the way by car.[32]

The two men met in private and agreed that the Republican state convention to be held eight days later would endorse the president's record and the concept of direct nominations. The meeting did not address the question of Taft's candidacy in 1912. The Ohio state convention had recently taken that step, but the president, as far as New York was concerned, "did not think he should be made an issue." When Roosevelt left, he told the press, "I had a very pleasant interview with the President and an entirely satisfactory talk on the New York situation." Roosevelt reiterated his position relative to the New York regulars. "There will be no compromise in any way. This is a fight for decency in politics as against bossism."[33]

Had the conference been reported in a matter-of-fact manner, there might have been better feeling between the two camps. However, a dispute began about whether Roosevelt or Taft had in effect sought the meeting in the first place. Roosevelt believed that Charles D. Norton had asked Lloyd Griscom to make the arrangements. Taft was certain that Griscom and another friend of Taft's had been the ones asking for the meeting on Roosevelt's behalf. After the session, Norton informed the press that Roosevelt's request "was a source of much gratification to Mr. Taft and his friends. That his aid should be sought at this time, and in the manner that it was, following a somewhat recent attitude of an almost complete ignoring of his administration or existence, probably gave the president much satisfaction."[34]

Reading these news stories, Roosevelt became angry at the spin that the White House put on his participation in the New Haven conference. He issued a statement of his own, denying, through Griscom, that he had asked for a conference. Taft was not amused. "It was perfectly characteristic," he told his wife, "that after having sought the interview, as he undoubtedly did, our friend should at once advertise that it was not at his instance, but at Griscom's, or wearing around to the point of showing that it was at my instance. But this playing for position and small politics and the manipulation of daily telegrams, all have no attraction for me. They only furnish me amusement in revealing his present character, which is a development of that which I knew, but a development in a direction that I did not expect."[35]

Taft's reaction, although understandable from his perspective, overlooked that Norton had tried to win political points at Roosevelt's expense in the way he portrayed what had happened at New Haven. Like many other politicians, Taft tended to see his moves as justified and the responses of his adversaries as evidence of deeper plans or unworthy motives. He never considered having a joint appearance with Roosevelt to emphasize their mutual regard, if only for public consumption. The unwillingness of the two men to be seen together attested to how much the one-time friends had drawn apart by the autumn of 1910.

The remainder of the fall campaign went badly for Taft, Roosevelt, and the Republicans. In New York, the former president did secure control of the state convention at Saratoga and obtain the nomination of his choice for governor, Henry L. Stimson. Stimson, a former U.S. attorney in the Roosevelt administration, was also a good choice from Taft's perspective. Unfortunately, Stimson was a lackluster candidate who did not have the touch with New York voters. At the Saratoga meeting, the platform endorsed Taft's record and the Payne–Aldrich tariff, much to the dismay of Roosevelt's progressive supporters in the West.[36]

Across the country, it was a bad year for Republicans almost everywhere. Representative James A. Tawney, whom Taft had tried to help in the Winona speech, was defeated in the Republican primary. Beveridge's prospects in Indiana dimmed as the balloting neared. La Follette prevailed in Wisconsin. "This is the most confused campaign I have ever known," wrote James R. Garfield. "Everyone at sea & our people discontented & resentful over Taft's failure to keep his promise to carry along the Roosevelt policies."[37]

The president did what he could to help the Grand Old Party in his home state of Ohio and elsewhere in the Middle West. He sought without success to get Roosevelt to campaign in Ohio. "If he doesn't do it," Taft wrote, "I shall think he is lacking in spirit of reciprocity." Roosevelt found time for a brief trip South in early October and then worked in an appearance for Beveridge. During the latter part of the month, he focused on Stimson and New York and did not spend any time on Ohio.[38]

In ways both conscious and inept, Taft sought to promote Republican unity. For the moment, he got over his disdain for Senator Cummins and offered to write a letter endorsing his reelection in Iowa. The administration also said that with the primary elections at an end, Taft would no longer withhold patronage from rebellious Republicans. "The President has concluded that it is his duty now to treat all Republican Senators and

Congressmen alike, without distinction." This letter from Norton to an Iowa conservative was given out to the press by mistake. It confirmed that Taft had been using patronage as a weapon, and it embarrassed the White House. "The incident has caused me much personal distress," Norton wrote. The secretary had told Taft when he started the job that he only wanted to stay for a year. By September 1910, he and the president were grasping just how political and subtle the post of White House secretary really was.[39]

Even with greater exertions from Roosevelt and more activity from Taft himself, the Republicans faced a licking in the 1910 elections. Unhappiness with the high cost of living, associated as it was with resentment over the Payne–Aldrich tariff, gave the Democrats an issue on which they were united against the party in power. The Democrats had good candidates in John Worth Kern running against Beveridge for the Senate in Indiana, Woodrow Wilson seeking the governorship in New Jersey, and John A. Dix opposing Stimson in New York. There was also evidence that Roosevelt lacked the popular appeal in the Northeast that he had possessed at the time he returned from Europe.

On election day, 8 November 1910, the Democrats achieved a stunning triumph that brought them back into power in the House of Representatives for the first time since 1894. The country, said Elihu Root, was like a "man in bed. He wants to roll over. He doesn't know why he wants to roll over, but he just does; and he'll do it."[40] When the election returns were all tabulated, the Republicans had lost fifty-eight seats and the Democrats had a working majority of sixty-seven members. The GOP dropped ten seats in the Senate. The Republicans remained in control by a count of fifty-one to forty-one, but enough progressive Republican senators would defect on a particular issue to endanger the GOP majority. The progressive Republicans survived the onslaught; the conservatives had more difficulty. As Gifford Pinchot put it, "where the administration was a factor in the campaign, as in Ohio and New York, the Democrats won. Where the Republicans did not support the administration, as in California, Kansas, and Wisconsin, the Republicans won." The mainstream of the party, however, blamed inflation and the adroit use the Democrats made of that issue for the general outcome. "There is no doubt," wrote Henry Cabot Lodge, "that the cry of the cost of living was what gave the Democrats their general victory throughout the country."[41]

The extent of the Republican debacle introduced sober reality into the dispute between Taft and Roosevelt. The president told a friend that "the coolness will wear away and our old relations will be restored, I hope, in the course of a year." Chastened by the defeat of Henry Stimson in New York and the personal attacks on him from conservatives, Roosevelt concluded that the result of the election was "the doing away with the talk of nominating me in 1912." His only option, he wrote to an English friend, was "to do what we can with Taft, face probable defeat in 1912, and then endeavor to reorganize under really capable and sanely progressive leadership."[42]

In that spirit, the two men began to correspond again. Roosevelt addressed him as "Mr. President" and advised him about issues relating to the progress on the Panama Canal and diplomatic questions regarding Japan. His letters were friendly and helpful, and a delicate rapprochement between the two men emerged in the final weeks of 1910. Whether their new friendliness could endure as the presidential campaign of 1912 neared was a question that neither man wished to confront.

Taft now faced a situation that a Republican president had not encountered for two decades, since Benjamin Harrison dealt with a Democratic House of Representatives after the elections of 1890. The president looked to reunite the Republicans through "a working agreement with all elements of the party." Inevitably, the loss of the House and the rebuke to the GOP cast a shadow over the prospects for Taft's reelection in 1912. Once the Democrats under the new Speaker, Champ Clark of Missouri, took over, the difficulties of the White House in managing events would increase. As Taft would soon learn, the easy part of his administration was behind him, and constant troubles lay ahead.[43]

Amid the political turmoil of 1909–1910, the administration had pursued a number of discrete initiatives that were less at the forefront of public discussion than the tariff and Theodore Roosevelt. Several of these activities added credibility to Taft's claims of administrative success. As the editor of the *American Review of Reviews*, Albert Shaw, wrote before the elections, the mistakes of the Taft presidency "were of the kind to absorb attention and to obscure the solid merits of an administration which has very much indeed to its credit." A review of Taft as an administrator reflects the accuracy of Shaw's judgment.[44]

9

★ ★ ★ ★ ★

TAFT AS ADMINISTRATOR

Because he has been perceived as a failed president, William Howard Taft's record as an administrator has not come in for much scrutiny. Yet in the day-to-day conduct of the presidency, Taft was more of an innovator than Theodore Roosevelt and Woodrow Wilson in his vision of how the federal government and the role of president should be changed. Roosevelt was a superb improviser who relied on his personality, a cadre of gifted subordinates, and a mastery of public opinion. He was not, however, systematic in his approach to the duties of his position. Wilson conducted the presidency more in the manner of a small law office, leaving his cabinet officials to run their departments without much beyond general guidance from the top.

Taft endeavored to make the government efficient. The commission on efficiency laid the foundation for subsequent efforts to impose more budgetary discipline on Congress and the executive branch. Cabinet members such as Secretary of the Navy George von Lengerke Meyer and Secretary of War Henry L. Stimson endeavored to transform their departments to reflect the possible challenges of a modern war. Meyer had more success than Stimson, but both men reflected Taft's purpose to make the government more effective. Within the presidency itself, Taft changed the record-keeping practices of the office and added other modernizing details to the institution.

Taft also greatly influenced the future of the judiciary. Fate enabled him to make six Supreme Court appointments in a single four-year term. The president used that opportunity to turn the Court in a conservative

President Taft (at right, holding program) at a Shakespeare performance.
Coburn Collection, Hargrett Library, University of Georgia.

direction that endured until the second term of Franklin D. Roosevelt. In lower-court appointments, Taft acted as a kind of one-man search committee who sought out judges sympathetic to his conservative views. In this area where he felt so much at home, Taft used his appointing power to produce nominees who shared his suspicion about progressive principles and an activist judiciary.

Contrary to the notion that Taft slept through significant parts of his presidency because of sleep apnea and was otherwise sickly at key moments, the president worked hard at his job. He had the capacity to dictate letters and memoranda at a high rate of efficiency, as his presidential letter books attest. His tendency to defer tasks to the last moment and then to work at an intense pace was still present. Often he complained that he could not remain ahead of his workload. In his haste, he sometimes made statements that worked against his own interests, as at Winona in 1909 and later on Canadian reciprocity in 1911.

Taft sought in a determined manner to trim federal spending throughout his term. During Roosevelt's last full year in office, the deficit reached $57 million. In 1909, the red ink totaled more than $89 million. With customs revenues down because of the Panic of 1907, Taft looked to the Payne–Aldrich tariff to increase receipts. Once in office, the president pushed his budget-cutting agenda. In his first annual message, he wrote that "perhaps the most important question presented to the Administration is that of economy in expenditures and sufficiency of revenue." He warned of a deficit in 1910 in excess of $73 million and recounted that he had "directed the heads of Departments in their preparation of their estimates to make them as low as possible consistent with imperative government necessity." In the case of the military services, Taft sought "a reduction of ten millions in the Navy and as much more in the Army." The cabinet, under the lead of the treasury secretary, went over appropriations requests in July 1909 and cut costs by $50 million. By the time the president sent his message to Capitol Hill, the amount of savings stood at nearly $43 million, with a budget surplus projected for 1911.[1]

Taft realized that the federal government had no budget mechanism to keep revenues and spending in balance. The executive branch did not have the means to decide what the government ought to spend each year and no weapons to compel Congress to go along. Clearly, the government needed a way to manage its finances, but there was strong resistance among lawmakers to any attempt to interfere with their historical control of the federal purse.[2]

The recurrent efforts of the Democrats in Congress to cut back on the president's travel funds reflected this tension. During the Payne–Aldrich special session, the opposition objected to the $25,000 allocated for Taft's travels. Democrats said that a recent $25,000 increase in the president's salary had been adopted to deal with travel costs. While the money went through, the Democrats returned to the subject in 1910. When Republicans charged southern Democrats with accepting Taft's hospitality on his trips and then voting against his travel expenses, a partisan battle erupted in the House. Taft had to write a public letter to calm the situation. Persuading lawmakers to cede power to the presidency to manage finances would not be an easy proposition.[3]

The legislative branch did agree to allocate funds to the president for a survey on how government spending might be trimmed in the interest of "greater efficiency and economy." Taft asked his secretary, Charles D. Norton, to explore that objective during the summer of 1910. The eager Norton envisioned his task in wide-ranging terms. He made sure that control of the project remained in the hands of the president and kept the work of the probe out of public view. The manager of the endeavor was Dr. Frederick Cleveland from the Bureau of Municipal Research in New York City. He directed a five-member committee that was dubbed the Commission on Economy and Efficiency. The goal of the panel soon evolved into an effort to give the president the authority to direct and oversee all aspects of the executive branch. The president himself indicated that "I will look in on important conferences whenever it may be advantageous."[4]

The commission conducted an extensive inquiry into every phase of the workings of the executive departments. They recommended combining agencies for greater efficiency. Among the most controversial of their suggestions were consolidating agencies within the Treasury Department and the combining of the Navy and War Departments into a single Defense Department. Once the president had control over the budget and a workable bureaucratic structure for the executive, the White House could set policy and then carry it out in practice. The work of the commission led Taft to create a budget system of his own in 1911. He instructed agencies and departments to obey his instructions in framing their appropriation requests for the following year.[5]

Taft formally presented the case for a federal budget to Congress in June 1912 in a lengthy message transmitting the findings of the commission on that point.[6] Lawmakers answered by amending the 1912 appropriations bill to forbid the president from taking the actions Taft had instituted and to instruct the executive agencies to oppose what the president had ordered. For their part, the cabinet secretaries exploited to the fullest the discretion that Taft gave them about running their departments. They responded slowly to presidential directives, and as the administration wound down in 1912, they tried to run out the clock with their agency's power undiminished. Although Taft claimed that it was "entirely competent for the President to submit a budget," he failed to persuade Congress of the wisdom of what he and the efficiency commission had sought to accomplish. The most he could do was to set precedents on which subsequent budget reformers would capitalize.[7]

In his general dealings with his departments, Taft produced mixed results over his four years in office. Franklin MacVeagh and the Treasury Department became almost an independent entity over which the president had little control. Frank Hitchcock and the Post Office Department, usually a patronage arm of the White House, also went their own way. In the process, they sparked recurrent complaints to the president about what Hitchcock's methods were doing to the Republican chances at the polls. The president was consistent in his application of the theory of cabinet government, often at the expense of his own partisan interests.

When Taft took office, the army and navy had serious problems of structure and mission that Theodore Roosevelt had not been able to resolve, or in some instances even to address. George von Lengerke Meyer at the Navy Department proved an effective administrator who made some needed changes in the operation of the fleet during his four years. The War Department under Jacob M. Dickinson and then Henry L. Stimson became a more difficult proposition when it came to genuine reform. When Taft left office, the United States did not have even the semblance of a modern army in place a year and a half before World War I erupted in Europe. Because the United States did not face a threat from a foreign power during this period, the weakness of the army and the problems of the navy did not have the urgency they would acquire a few years later. As a result, Taft's administration escaped the problems that plagued Woodrow Wilson during World War I.

In the case of the navy, George Meyer took over a fighting force in which Theodore Roosevelt had made important improvements during his nearly eight years in office. There were more modern vessels, the state of naval gunnery had improved, and the fleet had sailed round the world in 1908–1909. Yet beneath that impressive facade, serious organizational problems persisted. As an institution, the navy faced a bitter divide between the line officers who sailed the ships and the bureau chiefs who ran the daily routine of the shipyards, supply facilities, and personnel. Roosevelt had attempted to resolve these conflicts toward the end of his presidency without success. They remained in place for Meyer to deal with when he assumed his duties in March 1909.[8]

Meyer had been ambassador to Italy and to Russia before returning to the United States to serve as postmaster general from 1907 to 1909. Meyer was fifty-one when he took over the navy post. He had risen through Massachusetts politics in the 1880s and 1890s while running his father's merchant business. He served several terms as speaker of the Massachusetts House of Representatives and then caught President McKinley's eye in 1900. Dispatched to Italy as ambassador, he did well enough to earn a promotion to Russia in 1905. His friendship with Theodore Roosevelt and Henry Cabot Lodge won him these opportunities. His abilities made Meyer a valued member of two cabinets. Urbane and sophisticated, Meyer struck Taft as he did Lodge as "a very valuable man."[9]

Meyer needed all his skills when dealing with the entrenched naval bureaucracy ashore in Washington and around the country. The bureau system, which had been in place since 1842, had allowed the officers who ran these bureaucracies to build up ties with members of Congress who benefitted from naval appropriations in a series of interlocking and cozy relationships. From the outset, Meyer sided with line officers such as gunnery expert William S. Sims. The new secretary saw the major task of the fleet as fighting and winning wars, and he believed that "the navy yards existed for the needs of the active fleet, and that the fleet is not for the purpose of making work for the navy yards." That posture put him at once into conflict with key members of the hierarchy of the service.[10]

With the free rein that Taft gave his cabinet heads, Meyer set about in 1909 remedying the defects he saw in the structure of the navy's organization. He created a series of boards that recommended changes in the way the navy operated. The cumulative effect of these panels was to bring forward changes in line with earlier reforms that the service had not adopted. During the fall of 1909, a number of recommendations came to Meyer. He adopted them and announced their implementation. The navy was reorganized into four divisions that were designed to supersede the bureaus. The secretary stressed the importance of preparing for military action as the key purpose of the various components of the navy. Meyer was taking on the dug-in bureaucracy and its congressional supporters. A writer on naval affairs praised what the secretary of the navy had done: "No Secretary has ever shown so much courage and discernment in grappling with these ancient troubles, nor has dealt with them so quickly, as has Mr. Secretary Meyer."[11]

When Congress came back in December 1909, the committees that oversaw the navy held hearings on what Meyer had done. The secretary proved to be an effective advocate for his reforms. Meyer needed all the political clout he could amass. The president was determined to pursue economy in government, and he asked the navy for cuts in its budget. One area where many in Congress saw a logical source of reduced spending was in the appropriations for new battleships. Meyer had to fight hard to obtain congressional approval of the administration's request for two new battleships during the spring of 1910. He also achieved White House support for the ouster of the navy's paymaster, who had assembled a fund that he dispensed at his own discretion. Taft backed up his subordinate in this power struggle within the navy.

During his first two years in office, George Meyer had accomplished major changes in the navy, improved its efficiency, and streamlined its budget. His new methods kept the fleet at sea in an effective manner while providing for needed repairs to vessels on a sustained basis. Time would show that the power of the bureaus had not been curbed in any meaningful way. Yet Meyer had made progress in other areas. What he had achieved was enough to persuade the *London Times* that "the United States, in a word, has begun to possess a thinking Department capable of grappling with the control of a modern navy."[12]

Taft was not so fortunate in his secretary of war. His old friend and southern Democrat, Jacob M. Dickinson, faced a task that was in some respects even more taxing than the one that Secretary Meyer had confronted with the navy. The navy, after all, had to show itself on the oceans and thus had an incentive to bear comparisons with the fleets of other nations. The army, in contrast, did not confront any serious armed threat to its existence in 1909. The prospect of an invasion seemed improbable, not to say remote. The army thus had little reason to ponder its deficiencies in comparison with the huge armies of Europe. Those forces would never, or so the thinking in the army went, present themselves on the North American continent. If someone had suggested that American forces might have to fight in Europe, that person would have been regarded as delusional.[13]

Despite the efforts of Elihu Root as secretary of war between 1899 and 1903 to improve the army's war-fighting capability, the military remained burdened with red-tape-laden, out-of-date practices, and a lack of direction under Taft between 1904 and 1908 and his successor, Luke E. Wright. The adjutant general, Fred C. Ainsworth, was the dominant officer in the army because of his mastery of the bureaucracy and his ties with Congress. Mobilizing even a regiment for active duty would have taxed the army to the limit. Dickinson did not do anything to remedy the situation during his two years in office. He traveled to army posts around the country, inspected the Panama Canal Zone, and made a world tour of foreign armies in 1910. When he resigned in 1911, newspapers noted criticism that he had "applied himself too closely to the details of routine business in his department."[14]

From the first, Dickinson seemed out of place for the post he held. Family cares, including an ailing son, weighed on his mind. Business issues involving his home in Tennessee also troubled him. In the spring of 1910, the president observed, "I fear Dickinson is not as elastic as I thought he was. He also seems much older than I thought, somehow."[15] Archie Butt, on the other hand, thought that Dickinson was a better administrator at the War Department than Taft had been. A year later, when the army had trouble mobilizing on the border in the wake of upheavals in Mexico, it was time for Dickinson to go. The press of Dickinson's family financial matters made it an opportune moment to effect a change. To some extent, Dickinson was being disingenuous about his motives. He did not wish to get caught in the emerging tension between Taft and Roosevelt, and his business worries provided a convenient rationale for his withdrawal. The selection of Henry L. Stimson occurred in May 1911. The questions of reforming the army and modernizing its practices became key issues for Taft during the last two years of his presidency.

Running through all of Taft's chores as an administrator was the ever-present issue of political patronage and the appointments a president had to make on a daily basis. The president devoted detailed attention to these matters in two key areas: the selection of candidates for government positions in the South, and the naming of federal judges, especially to the United States Supreme Court. Taft failed in his efforts to penetrate the Democratic South and build a Republican presence there by favoring whites over blacks in patronage. In the area of the judiciary, Taft named five new Supreme Court justices, elevated another to chief justice, and reshaped the high court for a generation.

The president did not adopt a hands-off approach to his relationship with the Department of Justice and Attorney General George Wickersham in the area of judicial nominations. Taft acted as his own attorney general when it came to making these selections. He had definite ideas of the kind of men he wanted on the federal bench at all levels. As he wrote early in his administration, "I am very anxious to raise the standard of Federal District Judges in the South, and I do not propose to appoint anyone whom I do not know to be a lawyer of the first class, if I can find such a one."[16] He brought the same knowledge of the legal profession in all the states to the task of naming jurists at every level in the federal system.

Taft believed that he was an objective appraiser of legal talent who sought only people of the highest quality. His ideological commitments, however, governed his judgment when assessing who was a good lawyer and who was not. He looked for men like himself and often allowed friendship or emotion to affect how he decided that a candidate was a "first class" nominee. His celebrated accomplishment in having "rehabilitated" the Supreme Court with his six nominees offers the best example of Taft at work as a judge of future judges. The president's view at the outset of his administration was of a Supreme Court in crisis because of its aging members. He wrote in caustic terms about the situation when he took office. "The condition of the Supreme Court is pitiable, and yet those old fools hold on with a tenacity that is most discouraging." The chief justice, Melville W. Fuller, was "almost senile," while other justices were either lazy or deaf. "It is most discouraging to the active men on the bench."[17]

To revive the Court, Taft intended to name younger men in their mid-fifties who could be on the bench for more than a decade. He also wanted judicial conservatives who did not take an expansive view of national power. The process turned out to be a convoluted one that got the president the conservatives he sought. Yet the quality of the judges that Taft selected was, with the exception of Charles Evans Hughes, not as high as it could have been. Taft's remaking of the Supreme Court influenced the direction that law took in the United States for more than a generation, but his choices fell well short of overall excellence.

The shortcomings of Taft's approach emerged when he made his first nomination to the Supreme Court. Rufus Peckham died on 24 October 1909, and Taft immediately thought of his old friend, Horace H. Lurton of Tennessee, whom he had known when they were on the federal bench in the 1890s. The problem was Lurton's age; he was sixty-five and would soon be sixty-six. Yet as Taft told the secretary of war, "there was nothing that I had so much at heart in my whole administration as Lurton's appointment." The president rationalized that Lurton's experience as a judge justified the choice, even though it meant abandoning the criteria that Taft himself had established. In the end, friendship mattered most, and Taft "strained a point" to get the nomination made.[18]

Having selected a Tennessee Democrat for his first Supreme Court pick, the president went a more safely Republican route when his second opportunity arose with the death of David J. Brewer in March 1910. Charles Evans Hughes was in the last year of his second term as governor of New York. He did not plan to run for another term, much to his relief and that of regular Republicans in New York State. The president had seen Hughes in action in 1909 and had tabbed him as a potential Supreme Court nominee. Such a move would also eliminate Hughes as a possible rival for the nomination in 1912. Taft offered the governor the place with the implied opportunity to become chief justice if that seat should become vacant. Hughes accepted, and the Senate confirmed his nomination within a week.

The run of openings on the Supreme Court continued with the death of Chief Justice Melville W. Fuller on 4 July 1910 and the resignation of Justice William H. Moody on 20 November 1910. Taft now had the chance to fill two more vacancies and to select a new chief justice. For the chief justice slot, Taft elevated Justice Edward Douglass White. In doing so, the president selected another Democrat, a man who had fought for the Confederacy, and a Roman Catholic. White was also sixty-five years old. On the other side, Taft admired White's attitude toward antitrust issues, and his appointment furthered Taft's desire to woo southern Democrats. At the same time, appointing Hughes, who was only forty-eight, would likely have meant foreclosing any possibility for Taft to be chief justice during his lifetime.[19]

To take the two places that now were vacant, Taft chose Willis Van Devanter, a federal judge and former Wyoming lawyer who was the protégé of Senator Francis E. Warren of Wyoming. Van Devanter had already shown some of the difficulties in writing opinions that would characterize his work on the Supreme Court, but his conservative views and western background impressed the president.

The other seat in 1910 went to Joseph R. Lamar of Augusta, Georgia, a city where Taft had played golf and where he had many friends. Lamar was a qualified candidate, but his proximity to Taft's social circles did not do him any harm. The president had visited with the Lamars in Augusta during his national tour during the fall of 1909 and had told his wife that the couple were "very nice people." Another Southern Democrat, Lamar fit in with Taft's strategy of courting votes from that region. He enjoyed strong endorsement from his home state and possessed the judicial experience that Taft valued so highly.[20]

With the death of Justice John Marshall Harlan in October 1911, Taft obtained his final Supreme Court appointment. He selected Mahlon Pitney of New Jersey, a former member of Congress and a judge on the New Jersey Supreme Court between 1901 and 1908 before becoming chancellor of the state. Pitney had made some rulings against labor organizations and thus fulfilled Taft's desire to select a conservative for the place.

Taft was proud of his six choices for the Supreme Court. On his way out of office, the president recalled that he had told these jurists, "Damn you, if any of you die, I'll disown you."[21] In some degree, Taft did have a significant influence on how the Supreme Court developed during the decades that followed. White remained chief justice until his death in 1921, though he was not a notably successful leader of the Court. Van Devanter stayed for twenty-six years, into the Court fight of the New Deal era. He was an important intellectual figure in the conservative wing of the Court, though not a writer of notable opinions. Lurton and Lamar died during the Wilson administration. Only Charles Evans Hughes was an outstanding nominee and he, of course, departed in 1916 to run for president against Woodrow Wilson. He then succeeded Taft as chief justice in 1930. For all the time that Taft devoted to the judiciary, he was not a president who infused the Supreme Court with excellent selections. Favoritism to men he knew such as Lurton and Lamar and a desire to preserve his own chance to be chief justice one day, as in the case of White, governed his decisions.

Picking Supreme Court justices was the exercise of the presidential appointing power at its most intense level. Other patronage choices represented more of the everyday workings of national politics. In the case of Taft, however, his designation of federal officials in the South became entwined with his campaign to make the Republican Party a viable alternative to the Democrats in that region. To accomplish that goal meant, for the president, a reduction in the number of African American appointees in the South. The president believed that there was a potential reservoir of white Democrats who could be persuaded to vote Republican once the race issue was removed. So he hoped to construct a "reputable Republican party with which independent Democrats may be glad to ally themselves."[22]

Such a proposed course brought Taft to the sensitive and perennial question of the role of black Americans within the Republican Party. He shared with most GOP politicians conflicted views about African

Americans. He paid some deference to the commitments to racial fairness embodied in the Fourteenth and Fifteenth Amendments. As president-elect, he criticized efforts to deprive blacks of suffrage in Maryland in December 1908. At the same time, Taft held the prevalent white view that blacks required supervision in politics to succeed. In 1906, he alluded to them as "political children" and spoke of the "ignorant black" in contrast to those members of the race who were "thrifty" and "educated." By being sympathetic to the racist views of white Democrats who spoke in these terms about African Americans in the South, Taft signaled that he intended to reorient the Republicans toward a lily-white policy in making patronage appointments.[23]

Predictably, white southerners praised Taft for his intentions regarding a reduced role for blacks in Republican affairs. If he followed such an approach, argued Walter Hines Page of the *World's Work,* the president would "prevent the repetition of the ignorant rule of either race."[24] In his inaugural address, the new president made it evident that blacks would not be named to federal positions in the South against the wishes of the white majority. That commitment meant an end to black office holding in the South to the degree that Taft could accomplish it as president. The policy, however, put Taft at odds with black Republicans, especially Booker T. Washington and his allies. Taft reasoned that Washington and other blacks had no place to go politically because the Democrats remained as racist as ever in the South.

The patronage policies that Taft adopted in the South from March 1909 through the end of 1910 wooed white Democrats. The selection of Jacob M. Dickinson of Tennessee was an earnest of that intention. At the same time, even before taking office, Taft eased out William D. Crum, the black collector of customs at Charleston, South Carolina, whom Roosevelt had named in 1902 and who had been retained in his post despite intense southern white protests. Once he was in the White House, Taft acted to remove black incumbents from patronage slots. In Louisiana, Mississippi, South Carolina, and other southern states during 1909, blacks were ousted from the jobs they had held under the Roosevelt administration. The 1910 census in the South, for example, was to go forward without naming blacks to any of the boards that did the work.

The response to Taft's policy among black Republicans was negative, as Booker T. Washington recognized. One of his correspondents said that blacks "feel that they have less friends about the White House, than in 50 years." By March 1910, the president was telling black politicians that "I have not done all I ought to do or all I hope to do in the matter of recognition of colored men, but positions are very hard to find. Nobody resigns and nobody dies." Despite these assurances, the president's restrictive approach toward African American appointments continued, and black anger persisted.[25]

In 1910, as protests from blacks mounted, Taft made some appointments in Washington to assuage his critics. One notable selection was the appointment of William H. Lewis as an assistant attorney general. Lewis was the first African American to hold such a high-level position. Several other blacks were named to offices such as the register of the treasury, the recorder of deeds for the District of Columbia, and the collector of customs at Georgetown. On the larger point of preventing nominations of blacks to offices in the South, Taft remained committed to his exclusionary approach.

Although there was editorial approval across the white South for what the president was doing, his appeasement of segregationists did not result in any shift in voting allegiances. The 1910 elections were a disaster for the Republicans, and the Democrats retained their usual dominance in southern races. Outside the South, black voters joined whites in the North in rejecting Taft and the Republicans. Taft had sacrificed the civil rights standing of his party, such as it was, by 1909–1910, for the illusion that southern Democrats might abandon their distaste for Republicans over the race issue. The political conversion that Taft had looked for from his southern friends never happened. As he noted wryly, they would do anything for him but vote Republican. Like Roosevelt before him and Woodrow Wilson after him, Taft reflected the attitudes of white Americans toward black people and contributed to the racism and oppression of the early twentieth century.

In contrast with his condescending and dismissive attitude toward black Americans, Taft used his office and executive authority in ways that served the interest of Jews. The president said in several public addresses that Jews in the United States made a valuable contribution to the national life. In March 1910, he told opponents of immigration restriction that in the Jewish community of New York City "there was no part of the country in which the real, true spirit of patriotism prevailed more deeply than there."[26] Taft attributed his tolerance to his upbringing in Cincinnati: the Unitarian church he attended was across the street from a synagogue. The two institutions sometimes "exchanged ministers" and "I came to feel that the Jews were a very important part, as they were, of the citizenship of Cincinnati."[27]

In 1911, speaking to the B'Nai B'Rith in Washington, the president criticized the blackballing of Jews from the Metropolitan Club in Washington. There were, he said, "the small-headed men who occasionally get into a directory" who then "manifest their greatness by using a blackball and shutting out men of importance in the community." In response to the president's veiled attack on the Metropolitan Club, several officials in the administration resigned their membership in protest of the organization's exclusionary policies.[28]

The president took visible action in another case involving a Jewish enlisted man in the army who was up for promotion to lieutenant. Frank Bloom had gone into the army when he could not get into West Point, and his record caused him to be recommended to take an examination for a commission as a lieutenant. His commanding officer, Colonel Joseph Garrard, came out against allowing Bloom to take the test. The colonel did not "desire him in my command as an officer and a social and personal associate." The colonel added that "From an experience of many years I have found, except in a few cases, few communities where Jews are received as desirable associates." When the matter was brought to Taft's attention, the president said that he resented "as commander-in-chief of the army and navy, that any officer of either should permit himself in an official document to give evidence of such unfounded and narrow race prejudice as that contained in this statement."[29]

Bloom was allowed to take another examination, which he passed in the fall of 1911. Meanwhile, the War Department, acting on Taft's instructions, informed Colonel Garrard "that he has not the moral right to exert influence in his official position to bar the advancement of a courageous and efficient young man, simply because that man was of Jewish race." The Jewish leader, Simon Wolf, who had brought the case to Taft's attention, believed that the president had not "during my acquaintance" displayed "a finer sense of American citizenship and patriotism" than in the Bloom matter. The benefits that the president gained from his intervention on behalf of the young soldier assisted him when he and the Jewish community engaged issues of immigration and the status of Jews in Russia later in his administration.[30]

When it came to issues involving women and politics, President Taft displayed attitudes that clashed with the views of the women who sought suffrage. In the years of his presidency, several states, most notably California, adopted women's suffrage. Taft's wife favored the reform but doubted the wisdom of women running for office. His daughter held more advanced views on women voting. The president devised a convoluted rationale for his coolness to women having the ballot. These ideas led to an awkward situation when he addressed the National American Woman Suffrage Association in Washington 14 April 1910.

The audience greeted him with cheers and listened to his speech with attention. He told the women of his own early experience in favor of suffrage, but he noted that his position had changed. Wondering whether "women as a class would exercise the franchise," he said that "the theory that Hottentots or any uneducated and altogether unintelligent class is fitted for self-government is a theory I wholly dissent from." Moreover, should women get the vote "it may be exercised by that part of the class least desirable as political constituents and may be neglected by many of those who are intelligent and patriotic and would be most desirable as members of the electorate."[31]

The implied comparison of suffrage advocates to a nomadic African tribe rankled the audience, and there were hisses heard in the hall. His words about the "least desirable" also irritated some listeners, who complained about his "wobbly stand" on suffrage. Fearful of a backlash against the hissing, the delegates passed a resolution thanking the president for coming to speak to them but did not offer any kind of apology for the vocal displeasure of some. "I did not expect to hear a cultivated gentleman say what President Taft did last night about the Hottentots," observed Anna Howard Shaw, the president of the association.[32]

These events made the president an unlikely politician to make a significant appointment of a woman during his administration. However, the exigencies of the 1912 election and his desire for another term moved Taft in an unexpected direction. During the Roosevelt administration, advocates of the regulation of child labor proposed that a federal children's bureau with investigative authority be created as a first step. Just before he left office in 1909, Roosevelt endorsed the idea in a message to Congress. Bills to establish the bureau moved through Congress in 1911 and 1912. Early in January 1912, the Senate acted. The House then granted its approval in early April. Taft signed the measure on 9 April 1912.[33]

In selecting the head of the new agency, Taft consulted with leaders of the National Child Labor Committee. They in turn suggested Julia Lathrop, a fifty-three-year-old Illinois resident with extensive experience in the settlement house field and with children's issues. The president made sure that she possessed "the special qualities, the special training, and the administrative ability which make her preeminently fitted for the building up of the Bureau on the right lines." He announced her appointment on 17 April 1912. Her supporters praised the choice, and Taft claimed credit for the bureau in his reelection campaign. Almost by chance, the president had picked "the first woman to head a federal bureau."[34]

The good judgment that Taft showed in the establishment of the Children's Bureau deserted him in the most celebrated pardon case of his administration. The pardon case surrounding the jailed financier Charles W. Morse exemplified the president's problems in dealing with awkward issues. Morse had been convicted in 1908 on charges of misappropriating funds from the Bank of North America, which he controlled. He received a fifteen-year jail sentence for his crimes. A wealthy business operator

After Congress created the Children's Bureau in 1912, the president named a prominent reformer, Julia Lathrop, to head the agency. She became the first woman to head such a part of the federal government. Library of Congress.

who had earlier run an ice trust (a monopoly of the marketing of ice) in New York City, Morse had found that the weed of crime bore bitter fruit. He hired two lawyers, one of whom was Harry Daugherty, the future attorney general under Warren G. Harding, to obtain a pardon for him. Daugherty was an Ohioan and reportedly close to President Taft.[35]

The Morse family and his attorneys mounted an effective public relations campaign on behalf of a pardon for the jailed financier. He could not be paroled until he had served one third of his sentence, and a pardon was his best opportunity. His wife argued for clemency on the basis of the length of his sentence; in addition, "he had only been guilty of a technical violation of the national bank laws." Taft turned down Morse's pardon request in May 1911 and noted that his fraudulent transactions had caused "severe losses to the bank, which forced it into liquidation."[36]

Having lost on the merits of Morse's crime, his lawyers and family turned to the argument of failing health. Stories appeared in the

135

newspapers that the convict was mortally ill and would die within days or weeks if not released. There are some indications that Morse was faking his symptoms and ingesting substances that produced signs of illness. With cash to spread around, Morse could easily have swayed physicians to report that he was on the brink of dying. Reports reached the White House from Harry Daugherty and others that Morse could only survive a few weeks if he did not receive a prompt pardon.[37]

By early January 1912, the president had ample reports from army doctors that Morse would soon die even if he was pardoned. Moved by these statements, and aware of the public support for clemency for the financier, Taft granted a pardon on 18 January. The White House statement predicted that Morse would only live a month if he remained in prison and could not live more than six months once he was released. Morse left the country, ostensibly to take the waters and restore his health. Within a year, he was back in the business world and he lived on until 1933. Almost a year after the pardon, Taft remarked ruefully in a lecture: "This shakes one's faith in expert examinations."[38]

Further revelations about Morse while Taft was still alive suggested that the president had been gulled into his pardon action. The involvement of Daugherty in the case and his presumed influence in Ohio politics may have shaped Taft's ultimate decision to grant the pardon at a time when the president's political fortunes were in jeopardy in his home state. Several years later, Taft and Wickersham wrote letters defending Daugherty's behavior in the Morse case when the Ohioan was seeking a United States Senate seat. Had Morse been an indigent defendant without the means to mount a publicity campaign in his behalf, the president would never have acted as he did. In this instance, Taft lacked the strength of will to do the right thing and compounded his error with his subsequent endorsement of Daugherty as a senatorial candidate.[39]

Another high-profile controversy that Taft confronted as president involved the role of Harvey Washington Wiley, the chief of the Bureau of Chemistry in the Department of Agriculture. Wiley had been a major figure in the enactment of the Pure Food and Drugs Law of 1906 and was much identified with its enforcement in the years that followed. Wiley and Theodore Roosevelt had been at odds over the manner in which the bureau chief pursued manufacturers of catsup and other products. Roosevelt concluded that the abrasive Wiley had committed "errors of judgment," but the bureaucrat was so well entrenched in his position that the outgoing president took no further action against him.[40]

Unlike his course with Gifford Pinchot, Taft endeavored not to alienate the imperious Wiley. The president ruled against him in a case involving the definition of whiskey but did so in a way that left Wiley little grounds for protest. There were further quarrels over the question of benzoate of soda as a food preservative in catsup, as well as infighting within the board charged with the inspection of food. Wiley believed he was under siege from his bureaucratic adversaries.[41]

At that point in the early months of 1911, an issue arose about Wiley's appointment of an expert witness as a government employee at a rate of $1,600 per year. The move was a way of getting around the limit on what such a consultant could be paid on a daily basis. An internal investigation by people unfriendly to Wiley produced a recommendation that the witness be fired and Wiley resign. Attorney General George Wickersham agreed and recommended to the president that Wiley be ousted. Taft responded with a letter exonerating Wiley and leaving him in office. A few months later, after another flare-up between Wiley and Secretary of Agriculture James Wilson, Wiley resigned. He supported Woodrow Wilson in the 1912 election. On the whole, Taft managed the volatile Wiley with greater skill than he had shown during the Pinchot controversy.[42]

As an administrator, Taft did not create the intense loyalty that Roosevelt evoked from his subordinates as president. He functioned in an efficient and capable manner. Some of his ideas, such as the efficiency commission and the budget system, represented constructive initiatives that foreshadowed important innovations by later presidents. His selection of Meyer and later Stimson for cabinet posts attest to his wisdom in choosing who held these key portfolios. But in the end, Taft was a no more than adequate custodian of the administrative phase of the presidency. Of course, Taft did not seek to do more than to execute the duties of his office in a quasi-judicial manner. In that sense, he provided the kind of lawyerlike implementation of policy that suffused his tenure in the White House. Once he departed, few traces of his influence on the presidency remained.

10

★ ★ ★ ★ ★

RECIPROCITY, REVOLUTION,
AND ARBITRATION

The day after the Republican defeat in the congressional elections of 1910, President Taft departed on a long-planned inspection tour of the Canal Zone in Panama. Theodore Roosevelt had made a similar trip while he was president, and so the precedent against chief executives leaving the continental United States during their term of office was breaking down. The trip was scheduled to last two weeks, after which Taft would commence work on his annual message to Congress. Friends of the president told reporters that the repudiation Theodore Roosevelt had suffered in New York had led to "a revival of confidence" about Taft's chances for renomination in 1912. Yet the Republicans and the White House now confronted revitalized Democrats who for the first time in two decades sensed that they now had a realistic chance to recapture the presidency.[1]

There remained the lame-duck session of Congress that would start in early December and expire on 4 March 1911. In the Taft years, the political calendar did not call for much legislative activity during the third year of a presidency. After Congress adjourned in March, lawmakers would not reconvene until December for a long session that extended into the presidential election year of 1912. House Democrats would at that time see the fruits of their 1910 election success. During the 1910–1911 short session, the new majority elected its leaders and established its rules in contemplation of its accession to power in the House in December.

An emerging political scandal further crippled the Republicans going into the lame-duck session. William Lorimer had been elected to the Senate in 1909 after a long struggle in the Illinois legislature. In 1910, the press in Chicago charged that bribery had been involved in Lorimer's selection. Republican insurgents took up the Lorimer case and sought his ouster. Taft too believed that Lorimer's election was tainted. However, the support of conservative senators enabled Lorimer to stave off penalties in the winter of 1911. The case would plague Taft throughout the remainder of the year.[2]

Thus, for both parties, the session that commenced on 4 December 1910 seemed to offer more problems than opportunities. In his annual message, read on 6 December, the president took a cautious tone and did not seek much new legislation. He discussed the need for banking reform and a national incorporation law. He also wrote about the findings of the temporary board to review schedules of the tariff that the Payne–Aldrich tariff law had established. In passing, Taft mentioned the ongoing negotiations with Canada about reciprocal tariffs and hoped that when talks resumed in January, "the aspiration of both Governments for a mutually advantageous measure of reciprocity will be realized."[3]

Out of public view, the negotiators for the two countries met on 7 January in Washington. During the next two weeks, the discussions went forward until an agreement was secured on 16 January. The reciprocity understanding put a large number of agricultural products on the free list of each country. On balance, Canada's farm products gained entrance to the American market. American manufacturers secured some lower rates of duty from Canada. On a key point, newspaper publishers in the United States received the benefit of getting Canadian print paper and wood pulp free of duties. To implement the deal, the participants agreed not to go the route of a treaty. Obtaining two thirds of the Senate would be for the Taft White House a difficult task. Instead, the two nations decided to seek enabling legislation from Congress and the Canadian parliament. Official announcement of the reciprocity arrangement came on 21 January 1911. The president promised to send in a formal message in support on 26 January 1911, and the British ambassador told London: "Legislation in Congress to give effect to agreement very doubtful, and may not be possible for many months."[4]

In his message, Taft laid out the specifics of the deal with Canada and included supporting data for the legislators to consider. His letter made a clear and thoughtful case for the accord. Unfortunately, the president also committed another one of his untimely gaffes. He said of Canada that "the Dominion has greatly prospered. It has an active, aggressive and intelligent people. They are coming to the parting of the ways."[5] By that last sentence, Taft seems to have meant that Canada should choose between friendly trade relations with the United States or remain behind high tariff walls. In Canada, however, "the parting of the ways" came to imply

THE TRYST AT THE WALL.

Pyramus (President Taft). "I SEE A VOICE: NOW WILL I TO THE CHINK,
TO SPY AN I CAN HEAR MY THISBE'S FACE.
THISBE!"
Thisbe (Sir Wilfrid Laurier).   "MY LOVE! THOU ART MY LOVE, I THINK."
Pyramus. "THINK WHAT THOU WILT, I AM THY LOVER'S GRACE."
Midsummer Night's Dream, Act V., Scene 1.

The British humor journal *Punch* depicted Taft and the Canadian prime minister, Wilfred Laurier, as classical lovers as they negotiated over trade policy during the spring of 1910. Author's collection.

absorption by the United States—not a popular thought. The opposition to the Liberal government that had made the reciprocity agreement seized on Taft's statement as a key element in its campaign against the entire program.

While the president discussed the economic gains that the American people would receive from freer access to Canadian products, he also argued for a larger vision that included "good feeling between kindred peoples." Taft saw what he had done as the fulfillment of the goals of his administration to help American consumers and foster greater amity with Canada. He knew that he confronted political risks in his course, but he believed that he was acting in the public interest.[6]

To shore up his base, Taft turned to Theodore Roosevelt. The two men had regained a measure of their former intimacy after the election. Newspapers reported with some exaggeration that they talked on the phone on a regular basis. When the reciprocity agreement was pending, Taft wrote Roosevelt to fill him in on developments. In a letter of 10 January 1911, Taft reminded his predecessor that he had always "been a low tariff and downward revision man." He had defended the Payne–Aldrich tariff, he added, because above all it was to some degree a downward revision. Because these changes were based on the idea of imposing tariffs when the cost of production in the United States was lower than in its trading partner, it made no sense to have tariffs with Canada, where production costs were essentially the same on both sides of the border. Taft warned that the agreement "will cause a great commotion" and that "it may break the Republican Party for a while." He did not ask outright for Roosevelt's support, but the thought was implicit in the letter.[7]

In his answer, Roosevelt said that "it seems to me what you propose to do with Canada is admirable from every standpoint." Roosevelt shared the president's belief in free trade with Canada for much the same reasons. "Whether Canada will accept such reciprocity I do not know, but it is greatly to your credit to make the effort. It may damage the Republican Party for a while, but it will surely benefit the party in the end, especially if you tackle wool, cotton etc., as you propose." Roosevelt would come to regret having written this endorsement of Canadian reciprocity once opposition to it appeared among his friends in the progressive wing of the Republicans.[8]

As with any presidential decision, Taft also operated from political considerations. The British ambassador noted that reciprocity "makes attractive concessions to the consumer and to that 'cost of living' cry which has so seriously damaged the Republican party, and ought, therefore, to secure the support of the representatives of the large towns."[9] If insurgent Republicans opposed the agreement on the grounds that it hurt their farming constituents, then their anti–high tariff stance on the Payne–Aldrich tariff would seem hypocritical. "Whatever happens," Taft wrote to his brother, "it will be admitted, I think, that I have added considerably to the interest of the present session."[10]

What Taft had not reckoned with enough was the resistance that Canadian reciprocity produced among protectionist Republicans. "The republican party has stood for Protection to all interests agricultural as well as industry," wrote one industrialist; "if we do not hang together we hang separate." The president's adoption of the position of low-tariff Republicans and free-trade Democrats outraged the defenders of the protective system. "The course of President Taft is enough to make any of us ill," concluded the director of the Home Market Club to a protectionist leader, "and I can now see that he is impossible, and that you have been right from the beginning in so regarding him."[11]

The insurgent Republicans reacted as Taft had expected they would. La Follette expressed his dislike for the agreement, as did Senator Knute Nelson of Minnesota. The understanding with Canada, he wrote, "puts everything the farmer raises on the free list, while everything he buys has a duty on it. There is no reciprocity in it for him."[12] These progressives united with the standpatters in the Senate to try to block the measure from being acted on before the adjournment date of 4 March. As Moses Clapp, also a Minnesota Republican in the Senate, put it, "a tariff measure like this never ought to be rushed through Congress without any discussion."[13]

It was a long shot to push the reciprocity measure through Congress before adjournment when everything favored those who wanted to defeat the bill. The president's campaign for the legislation in the House encountered difficulty among Republicans and strong support from the Democrats. Leading Republicans on the House Ways and Means Committee declined to support it, and the committee Republicans split six for and six against when the bill went through on 11 February, with six Democrats making up the 12 to 7 majority. The solid Democratic backing enabled the bill to pass the House three days later on a vote of 321 to 92. Of the Republicans, 78 voted for the bill, with 87 opposed. During the debate, the incoming Speaker, Champ Clark of Missouri, said, "I look forward to the time when the American flag will fly over every square foot of British North America up to the North Pole." Taft rushed a letter to Capitol Hill to repair the damage Clark had done. "This agreement, if it becomes law," he said, "has no political significance. No thought of future political annexation was in the minds of the negotiators on either side. Canada is now and will remain a political unit."[14]

The next obstacle was the Senate, where advocates of delay had the clock and the calendar on their side. The unlikely coalition of progressives and standpatters "are determined that no vote shall be taken on the reciprocity agreement," wrote Winthrop Murray Crane of Massachusetts on 17 February 1911, "and as there is no one heartily in favor of it, I presume their views will prevail."[15] By now Taft had decided that it would be necessary to call Congress into special session to deal with Canadian reciprocity. Although Democratic House leaders were initially opposed, they recognized that the special session would do more damage to the deeply divided Republicans. The Democrats could bring up bills to lower tariff rates on individual products that, if Taft vetoed them, would help their cause. In the Senate, meanwhile, the session sputtered to a close with no action on the reciprocity measure. Taft announced that he would summon Congress back into session on 4 April 1911 to resume deliberations on Canadian reciprocity.

The reciprocity agreement with Canada was a sound piece of public policy that drew on the precedents of William McKinley and Theodore Roosevelt. However, Taft had not prepared the ground for support of his initiative. He had done little to alert congressional leaders to what he and the Canadians were doing. Vice President Sherman, no friend of reciprocity, predicted that in a special session, "things will be ripped wide open." Although public opinion favored what the president had proposed, his situation on Capitol Hill was in more doubt. He could force the measure through at a special session, but the price would be a renewed Democratic emphasis "upon a general revision of the tariff along revenue or free trade lines." That discussion would help the opposition and further divide Taft's party.[16]

As the lawmakers ended their work in early March, a foreign policy crisis emerged as Mexico stood on the brink of revolution. Taft had supported the autocratic regime of Porfirio Diaz as the best means of maintaining political stability in that country. In 1909, on the eve of his meeting with Diaz at El Paso, the president had warned his wife that "we have two billions American capital in Mexico that will be greatly endangered if Diaz were to die and his government go to pieces." The president added: "I can only hope and pray that his demise does not come until after I am out of office."[17]

Unfortunately for Taft, the Diaz regime was under severe challenge by the winter of 1911 as discontent with his oppressive government mounted across Mexico. Revolutionary sentiment, associated with Francisco Madero, a leading opponent of Diaz with moderate views on social change, gathered momentum throughout 1910, and the country experienced violent outbreaks of popular resistance to the Diaz government. The American ambassador in Mexico City, Henry Lane Wilson, detested the

Mexican revolutionaries and filed frequent, heated reports critical of the rebels. He had been equally dismissive of the Diaz regime in late 1910 and thought that American intervention to preserve stability in Mexico might become necessary. Throughout 1911 and 1912, the White House received a distorted perspective on the course of the fighting in Mexico and the chances for the revolutionaries to create a viable government. President Taft would make policy toward Mexico despite the information he was being sent from his chief representative within the country.[18]

In mid-February 1911, Wilson told the Department of State that "the revolutionary situation in a general way is becoming worse." Then several weeks later, the ambassador came to Washington to confer with the president and report on the spread of revolutionary passions in Mexico. An alarmed Taft heard that "all of Mexico was boiling" with the likelihood that Americans in Mexico and their economic interests would be at risk. Secretary of State Knox was away from the department in Florida, so Taft had to respond on his own. He met with Secretary of the Navy Meyer and Secretary of War Dickinson, along with the commanding officers of the army and navy, to work out a suitable strategy. Although Taft had little desire to intervene in Mexico, he thought—and his advisers agreed—that some show of American force was appropriate under the volatile circumstances then existing south of the border.[19]

To that end, Taft decided to dispatch 20,000 troops to Texas, where they could conduct maneuvers as events in Mexico unfolded. The president did not want to go into Mexico and would not do so "without express Congressional approval." There was little sentiment on Capitol Hill for such an adventure. The news of the partial mobilization of the army caused a sensation in newspapers in both Mexico and the United States. Theodore Roosevelt, ever bellicose, volunteered to raise a regiment, should war break out with Mexico and even Japan. War talk surged through newspaper columns for several days.[20]

In fact, Taft sought to dampen such expectations. The White House stressed the routine nature of what the army was doing and leaked information to friendly newspaper publishers about the president's true intentions. Taft was convinced that diplomatic obscurity was the right approach and that the impact of troops in Texas "would be quite as great whether we were to express our purpose or left it to be inferred."[21] When the navy sent some of its smaller ships into Mexican waters without informing the president, Taft told Secretary Meyer to "see that these small fry do not appear any more in Mexican ports and that you will keep all your maneuvers to the north of the borderline."[22] The navy said that ship movements were part of the replacement of vessels in Panama and did not contradict Taft's policy toward Mexico. The episode demonstrated, however, that Taft intended to wield his power as commander in chief as he saw fit without interference from the navy.

By the time Congress convened for the special session on 4 April, the Mexican issue had subsided. The underlying problems had not gone away, and the departure of Diaz to exile in May 1911 and the accession of Madero to the presidency would keep tensions high between the two countries. Still, Taft assured his worried correspondents that "I am not going to be pushed into intervention in Mexico until conditions are such as to leave no doubt in the minds of people that intervention ought to be undertaken. The burdensome consequences of such action no one appreciates more than I do." The abrupt nature of Taft's decision and the inability of the White House to explain in a clear way what the president's intentions were added to the public confusion. "The U.S. Gov't have made a mess of their Mexican business," wrote the British ambassador. "Never was there a slacker & worse organized State Dept."[23]

The new Congress that came back to Washington in April faced Republican expectations that the Democratic majority would blow their opportunity, as they had done in the past. The press anticipated a similar result. Instead, the majority chose Champ Clark as Speaker and proceeded to enact business with efficiency. Democratic assertiveness in the Senate dimmed prospects for the two treaties with Honduras and Nicaragua as the session proceeded. Republicans remained skeptical that the Democrats could stick together. As Vice President Sherman put it, if the Democrats could "get through the two sessions of Congress intervening before the next general election without tipping over the milk pail and dropping the bread and butter, butter side down, they will have established a new record."[24]

With the lawmakers once again in session, the president too made some moves to buttress his political position. His secretary, Charles D. Norton, had proved to be a liability to the White House. The ill-fated initiative against Roosevelt during the summer of 1910 and the release of the "Norton letter" about patronage at that time had undermined Norton's usefulness. In addition, the officious Norton was unpopular with the White House staff, who chafed at his memos banning loud talking and other indiscretions. By the winter of 1911, Norton had made it clear that he wanted to return to private banking in the near future. When he campaigned on Capitol Hill to raise the salary of his position from $6,000 to $10,000 per year, he informed lawmakers that he would not gain personally from the change. Taft had also let him know that there was no chance Norton could succeed Franklin MacVeagh at the Treasury Department. Senator Winthrop Murray Crane told Archie Butt that Norton had made

Charles D. Hilles became a trusted adviser to the president
and the main architect of Taft's renomination campaign in
1911–1912. Author's collection.

the president "almost hateful in the eyes of the House and Senate and
with every public man who was his friend."[25]

To succeed Norton, Taft turned to Charles Dewey Hilles, also an assistant secretary of the treasury but with political skills honed in New
York Republican affairs. Forty-four years old in 1911, Hilles had been a
passionate supporter of the president's nomination in 1908. He brought

conservative views, political insight, and personal efficiency to the post. For the first time, Taft had an aide who could handle the demands of the president's schedule and keep track of the partisan dimensions of key issues. With the presidential nomination in the balance, Taft needed someone like Hilles, a de facto White House chief of staff, to manage a campaign against a likely challenge from Robert La Follette and the possible threat of Theodore Roosevelt.

As he settled into the job, Hilles talked with the president about what should be done to sew up the Republican delegate votes for 1912. Taft turned to a tested answer: presidential travel. He planned for a cross-country tour during the autumn of 1911 that, although nonpartisan on the surface, would give the chief executive the chance to communicate to Republican leaders in key states. Hilles would go along to do the work of lining up support for 1912. Other initiatives for the presidential race were also discussed and arranged for the summer of 1911.

At the time Hilles was named, Taft also made a move on his cabinet that many in the Republican ranks regarded as long overdue. Richard A. Ballinger had been a liability since the hearings on his dispute with Gifford Pinchot had been held during the winter and spring of 1910. The efforts of Norton and others to secure Ballinger's resignation during the summer of 1910 had also weakened the secretary's position. By early March 1911, Ballinger gave up and told Taft of his willingness to step down. In an exchange of letters, Taft vented some of his anger about how Ballinger had been treated in the press and the political arena. His critics had "showered" Ballinger "with suspicion" and used "pettifogging methods" against his record. "The result has been a cruel tragedy."[26]

Ballinger's replacement was Walter L. Fisher, a prominent Chicago attorney who had been an associate of Gifford Pinchot on resource questions. According to James R. Garfield, the president promised Fisher "an absolutely free hand" in running the department. Appointing one of Ballinger's critics while denouncing the alleged conspiracy against his secretary of the interior left Taft in a somewhat awkward position with the public. Garfield called it "just another one of Taft's incomprehensible actions displaying again his absolute lack of political sagacity as well as dense ignorance regarding conservation questions." The Fisher appointment did, however, make it more difficult for Pinchot and his allies to blast the administration on conservation matters.[27]

A month later, Taft confounded his critics once again with another cabinet change. His first secretary of war, Jacob M. Dickinson, had not proved a strong figure in the post. The army bureaucracy had captured him, as it had done so many of his predecessors. Facing family problems and personal financial questions, Dickinson wanted to depart. The question arose of who would follow him. The president considered a number of candidates, including his longtime friend in New York City, Otto Bannard. Then Franklin MacVeagh offered the name of Henry L. Stimson, the defeated gubernatorial candidate from New York in 1910. Hilles went to see Stimson on 11 May to make the formal offer. Stimson asked why the president had thought of him, and Hilles replied that Taft "believed he had the training, and talent, and taste, and tact for public affairs, and that his achievements in New York entitled him to be called higher."[28]

Several political factors helped to persuade Taft that Stimson was the proper choice. Given the New Yorker's closeness to Roosevelt, the nomination was bound to please the former president. Stimson had been the district attorney for the Southern District of New York during Roosevelt's administration and had prosecuted several high-profile cases against such corporate malefactors as the Sugar Trust. He was also identified with clean politics in the Empire State and thus would separate the White House from some of the less savory conservatives, such as William A. Barnes Jr. and even Vice President Sherman. Both Taft's brother, Henry Waters Taft, and George Wickersham had opposed Stimson's election in 1910. The president looked forward with ironic delight to the first cabinet meeting when Stimson and Sherman became colleagues.

These moves strengthened Taft politically during the spring of 1911 as the debate over Canadian reciprocity heated up in Congress. The president mobilized the powers of his office behind that controversial initiative. He went out on the road to sell his program to the nation. His most notable speech came on 27 April in New York at a dinner for the Associated Press and the American Newspaper Publishers Association. "The talk of annexation is bosh," Taft said. "Everyone who knows anything about it realizes that it is bosh." He warned that the moment was critical for action. "Unless it is now decided favorably to reciprocity, it is exceedingly probable that no such opportunity will ever again come to the United States." As a result, "we must take it now or give it up forever."[29]

In the course of his remarks, Taft alluded to Canada's ties with Great Britain as "light and almost imperceptible." In reality, he went on, "the control exercised from England by Executive or Parliament is imponderable." Taft's attempt to quash talk of annexation now only provided more ammunition to the opponents of the agreement in Canada. His earlier remark about "the parting of the ways," along with Champ Clark's indiscretions, supplied the context in which Taft's New York speech occurred. "Taft, who is a dear good fellow," wrote James Bryce, "is no politician and made a speech last Thursday in New York singularly indiscreet so far as Canada and Gt. Britain are concerned."[30]

Taft's immediate problem was not the reaction of London and Ottawa but getting Congress to approve his reciprocity legislation. "Confidentially, I believe that the President will be sorry that he ever called an extra session before another month goes by," wrote a Wisconsin Republican in early April. Two months later, the progressive editor, William Allen White, observed, "what a genius for fumbling Taft is! Here is an issue on which he might have rallied the American nation to himself, on which he might have united his party and might have demonstrated himself a leader on a great issue. Instead of that he finds himself advocating a bill which has absolutely no friends anywhere, so drawn that it alienates every source of strength that he might hope for and so manifestly unjust that no public man cares to stand for it."[31]

Despite the critics among both conservative and progressive Republicans, Taft pressed ahead with reciprocity. The House still favored the measure with the coalition of Democrats and sympathetic Republicans holding together to pass the enabling legislation on 21 April. There were 201 Democrats and 67 Republicans in favor. Ten Democrats joined 78 Republicans and one independent in voting against reciprocity. The president had called wavering Republicans to bring them over for the bill, but his efforts had swayed few GOP members. When reciprocity went to the Senate, Taft faced a very confused parliamentary situation. The Republican members of the upper house had little enthusiasm for Taft's initiative. In the two years since 1909 and the Payne–Aldrich tariff, they had suffered losses during the elections of 1910. The departure of Nelson Aldrich to private life had left the Senate majority with much less effective leadership in Eugene Hale of Maine and Jacob H. Gallinger of New Hampshire. Although few GOP lawmakers expected to lose the Senate in 1912, they knew that their prospects were far from bright. Beneath the surface of party harmony, there were simmering resentments at the way the president had muscled through railroad, postal savings, and other progressive laws in 1910. Now he wanted them to reduce the tariff in ways that the Democrats applauded and protectionists resisted. His posture legitimized Democratic efforts to lower the tariff on other products during the special session. One defeated senator, Chauncey M. Depew of New York, compared Taft to a judge who looked at Congress as a jury. "In regard to the Reciprocity Treaty with Canada, he would have been satisfied with a vote. Whichever way the vote had gone there would have been no extra session. But it is the practice of judges when the jury say they cannot agree to send them out again and again and again. So, in this case, Congress, not having taken a vote and presented a verdict, they are called together and will be kept together until they do."[32]

The Senate, in its usual deliberate way, spent the next month holding hearings on Canadian reciprocity in the Finance Committee, which was stacked with opponents of the agreement. It was evident that the process of deciding on Taft's tariff proposal would drag on through the summer, much as had happened two years earlier. The expectation was that the president would in the end prevail, thanks to Democrats and loyal Republicans. As the weeks slipped away, prospects for the agreement turned sour in Canada. The Conservative Party in that country saw a chance to win a general election and would not support legislative action. "It is I fear," wrote Governor General Lord Grey, "as useless for Taft to hope that the Reciprocity agreement may pass the Canadian Parliament soon as it wd be to hope for the moon to place itself within his reach."[33]

To complicate matters still further for the president, he was planning to ask the Senate to take up a foreign policy initiative to which he was deeply committed. At the same time, what Taft had in mind was certain to outrage Theodore Roosevelt. The submission of international disputes to arbitration was an idea that advocates of peace advanced with great fervor during the first decade of the twentieth century. Andrew Carnegie, the former steel magnate, was a particular exponent of this approach, and he wrote the president often to press the case for arbitration. The concept, which involved submission of disputes among nations to an international court, also appealed to the president and Philander Knox. As attorneys, they gravitated toward a judicial procedure that would have parties presenting their positions before a panel of expert jurists. In the words of a British diplomat, for Knox, "a treaty is a contract, diplomacy is litigation, and the countries interested parties to a suit."[34]

In late June 1910, Knox gave a speech on "The Spirit and Purposes of American Diplomacy" at the University of Pennsylvania. His goal was to "bring out its altruism and unselfishness" as a nation. During his remarks, the secretary said that "we have reached a point when it is evident that the future holds in store a time when wars shall cease; when the nations of the world shall realize a federation as real and vital as that now existing between the component parts of a single State." He related that the United States had "loyally submitted ourselves to the control of the ideas of peace and to principles of international comity and good will."[35]

President Taft made it clear during 1910 that he favored arbitration treaties of a wide scope. While cautioning peace advocates of the need for a strong national defense in the absence of international understanding, he also, unlike Theodore Roosevelt, was prepared to refer "matters of national honor" to a court of arbitration. He looked toward "the development of a code of international equity which nations will recognize as affording a better method of settling international controversies than war." With the British, the Taft administration began negotiations for an international prize court to resolve disputes about fishing rights and other territorial questions in North America. The president hoped to build on that precedent in seeking arbitration treaties.[36]

He began with inquiries to European powers in late 1910, but not much came of those initial steps. Early in 1911, the government initiated talks with Great Britain about such a treaty. Inevitably, word leaked out regarding the discussions of the pact and its provisions. Theodore Roosevelt wrote for the *Outlook* an attack on the principle of arbitration treaties. "The United States," he wrote, "ought never specifically to bind itself to arbitrate questions respecting its honor, independence, and integrity." A treaty with Great Britain was possible, moreover, because the two nations knew that they would never have a dispute that could lead to war. Roosevelt did not mention Taft's name anywhere in the article, but the clear thrust of it was to accuse the president of being naive and foolish. The fragile entente that had existed between Roosevelt and Taft was once again under intense pressure.[37]

Another sign of the underlying tension between the two men came three weeks later, when they both attended the jubilee celebration for James Cardinal Gibbons of Baltimore in that city. As the two men sat together laughing and joking about the other speakers, the crowd erupted in spontaneous applause. That was the last time the two men would be in each other's company for four years. After the event, the Associated Press carried a story that Roosevelt would endorse the president for renomination in 1912. Roosevelt felt compelled to issue a denial. "There is no truth in the report that I have agreed to support any man for President in 1912. I have neither made any such statement nor even discussed the matter. The story is made out of whole cloth."[38]

The source for the alleged commitment was the secretary of the navy, George von Lengerke Meyer. The Associated Press expanded Meyer's comments about Roosevelt, whatever they were, into a pledge to support Taft. Roosevelt blamed the White House and the Associated Press for the confusion, and he decided not to accept the invitation of the president to attend the celebration of the Tafts' twenty-fifth wedding anniversary two weeks later on 19 June. The episode, about which Taft seems to have had no knowledge, marked an acceleration of bad feeling on Roosevelt's side that continued throughout the summer of 1911.

By that time, Roosevelt was already backing away from his earlier support of the Canadian reciprocity agreement. In March, he indicated that it was unfortunate how the negotiations with Canada had worked out, but he remained in favor of the Taft program. In June, although still in support, he was calling the reciprocity bill "very badly drawn," even while telling English friends, "I hope and believe it will go through." Once the measure passed Congress, he said that "I did not like all the details" because it was "a far better measure for Canada than for the United States; because it helps the Canadian agriculturalist and the American manufacturer, and I most emphatically believe that it is for the advantage of a country to help the man who works on the soil." Roosevelt's progressive supporters in the Middle West hoped he would go even further, and in time he did.[39]

As Roosevelt's letter suggests, Taft did succeed in obtaining passage of the legislation to implement the reciprocity deal. The Senate took up the measure on 13 June, and more than a month of debate followed in the stifling heat of a Washington summer. The president now had a primitive air-conditioning apparatus in the White House and was more comfortable than the lawmakers in the eighty degrees of his office. There remained no doubt that the Canadian bill would pass, which it did on 22 July, by a vote of 53 in favor to 27 against. The Republicans were split. Twenty-one members either voted for the bill or were paired in favor. Twenty-eight stood against either by vote or by pair. All but four of the 41 Democrats expressed approval of the legislation. The insurgent Republicans, in their opposition to the bill, had lost some standing with the public.

The president praised the Democrats for their vote, but his final domestic victory with Congress left his party in disarray. Meanwhile, there were disturbing reports of developments in Canadian politics. The Laurier government was in trouble with its electorate for its economic involvement with the United States. For William Howard Taft as president, even when he succeeded, events conspired to turn his triumphs into defeats. In one area, however—his renomination for president in 1912—the summer of 1911 saw the beginnings of his determined campaign to control the Republican Party and thwart the ambitions of Theodore Roosevelt.

11

★ ★ ★ ★ ★

TOWARD A BREAK
WITH ROOSEVELT

Amid the travails of the spring and summer of 1911, President Taft enjoyed one rewarding personal moment. On 19 June, he and Mrs. Taft observed their twenty-fifth wedding anniversary in a gala celebration on the White House grounds. It signaled something of a return to the lime-light for the first lady after her May 1909 stroke. In broad terms, the first lady's health had improved during these two years. She had been able to carry forward her initiatives to improve Washington as a cultural center. Her musicales with important classical artists and other activities as a so-cial leader in Washington had received positive press notice. However, when she suffered another small stroke during a visit to New York City in May 1911, her doctors warned her not to take part in the anniversary festivities.

As the day approached, however, Mrs. Taft was able to take her place in the receiving line for the more than 8,000 guests. The first lady and the president stayed until one in the morning and listened to the bands and the revelry. The wife of a Democratic member of the House said that "the wedding [anniversary] was a prodigious affair, the company promiscuous to a degree."[1]

The president and his wife invited descendants of all the former chief executives to join them in the gala event. Presents showered in on the presidential couple from across the United States and from European roy-alty. Newspapers reported that "people are already wondering what Pres-ident and Mrs. Taft will do with the wondrous array of gorgeous presents" that they received. One of the gifts was from Theodore Roosevelt, but the

Taken at the time of the Taft's twenty-fifth wedding anniversary in June 1911, the photo shows Charles Taft (second row, left), Helen Taft, and Robert A. Taft standing behind their parents. Library of Congress.

former president, still miffed about the episode in Baltimore two weeks before, refused to attend the event itself. A year later, Taft and Roosevelt would be locked in political combat at the Republican National Convention as the party split itself into two battling factions.[2]

While Roosevelt seethed, the president began the work of securing the GOP nomination. He and Charles Hilles decided that he should begin the process of lining up support from within the party. On the surface, matters looked promising for Taft. The progressive Republicans had turned to Senator Robert M. La Follette of Wisconsin as their choice to run against the president on the assumption that Roosevelt would not be entering the race. Early in 1911, the National Progressive Republican League had been formed as a vehicle for change and a way to test the sentiment for the Wisconsin senator. Although there had been much activity and some fund raising, La Follette's candidacy had not caught on. During the summer he announced that he would make the race, but the news stirred little excitement in political circles. The Wisconsin senator had almost no backing in the Northeast, South, and Middle Atlantic states.

The real menace, in Taft's mind, was Roosevelt. For the moment, that aspect of Republican politics seemed to be under control. Although Roosevelt declined to endorse the president as the White House expected him to do, he also made clear to friends that he did not anticipate becoming a candidate and did not want such efforts to go on in his behalf. He told a sympathetic reporter that "as far as I can now see, no situation could arise which would make it possible for me to accept a nomination next year."[3] Nonetheless, there was always the possibility that Roosevelt could change his mind. He was disgruntled about arbitration, still unhappy regarding Taft's conservation policies, and privately critical of the president.

If Taft wished to be sure of renomination, it was necessary for him to get his campaign under way at an early date. Accordingly, Hilles began sounding out sympathetic Republicans regarding ways to disseminate news about the president and to line up potential adherents. In early June, Hilles initiated correspondence with potential backers asking them "for an expression of their views as to the success of President Taft's administration, and as to his availability for 1912."[4] These moves soon made their way into the press, and reports were optimistic about the president's chances.

To provide publicity for Taft and to test sentiment among Republicans in the country at large, the president planned for an extensive speech-making tour of the country during the autumn of 1911. As during the autumn of 1909, the speeches would be on nonpartisan topics including his campaign for the arbitration treaties. The opportunity would arise to meet with Republican leaders in states where Roosevelt might be strong. Hilles would be measuring sentiment and conferring with party officials while the president met the public. "I hope we shall put a crimp in the inflated boom of the opposition in a few States," the president's secretary wrote as his boss readied for his departure.[5]

These moves, which did not receive much public attention, put Taft in a stronger position going into the nominating season. With Roosevelt on the sidelines and Senator La Follette's campaign struggling to gain any traction, the president was establishing an ascendancy within the Republican organization that would be indispensable during the months ahead. Taft used patronage and his authority with party regulars to create a coalition that could withstand challenges from the progressives. He and Hilles grasped the point that an incumbent president had the capacity to achieve renomination even when his prospects for the general election seemed uncertain.

Throughout the special session on reciprocity in the summer of 1911, Taft jousted with the Democrats over the tariff. The opposition, mindful of the persistent discontent about the higher cost of living, saw a winning issue in pushing bills to reduce the tariff that Taft would have to veto. They knew that there was not a two-thirds majority to override Taft's veto, but that did not matter. The point was to demonstrate to the public that the Democrats were behind legislation to put products that farmers purchased on the free list and to reduce rates on wool and cotton. Such gestures created themes that could carry over into 1912, when both Speaker Champ Clark and Oscar W. Underwood, chair of Ways and Means, expected to seek the Democratic presidential nomination.

The summer of congressional tariff warfare gave the Democrats the opportunity to make their case. Speakers declaimed on the iniquities of the protective tariff, especially Schedule K, on wool and wool products, which was the most notorious example of a protected product and industry. The union between western sheep raisers and eastern woolen manufacturers was at the center of Republican protectionism. A Republican newspaper satirist caught the passions that the now-forgotten Schedule K once aroused:

> What's the cause of human woe?
> Schedule K;
> Why do festive microbes grow?
> Schedule K;
> What's the reason flies abound
> And that snakes are sometimes found,
> And some folks go harem-gowned?
> Schedule K.[6]

There was never any chance that President Taft was going to sign these Democratic bills to lower tariff duties. Although he was a believer in reduced rates within the framework of Republican dominance, he was a protectionist. It would have been political suicide for him to have endorsed the Democrats' handiwork. The efforts of his political enemies brought out Taft's underlying sympathy for the principles of tariff protection. Of the farmers free list bill, he wrote his wife that the measure was "such a fraud that I would not hesitate to veto it on general principles. It is a pretense of helping the farmer it is wrong in principle."[7]

When the bills reached his desk in August 1911, he sent back to the Congress three biting veto messages. The president did not issue ringing defenses of the protectionist policy. Instead, he faulted legislators for not postponing their decisions until his tariff commission provided detailed information about what rate reductions might cost the government and the consumer. Taft was consistent in his position, but he did not offer his fellow Republicans much to rally around when they defended the White House.

The continuing controversy over the election of Senator William Lorimer of Illinois also acted as a drag on the White House, even though the president was not a defender of the embattled lawmaker. The opposition to the Illinois senator, particularly among the Democrats, suggested that Taft had wanted to see him elected to help in passing the Payne–Aldrich tariff in 1909. Taft fired back that such was not the case. "I never sought Lorimer's election and only said when asked in respect to it that I would not interfere and did not object to him or any other Republican."[8]

The Democrats in the House also probed Taft over an army major, Beecher B. Ray, who had while on leave campaigned for the president in 1908 among members of railroad unions. Democrats wanted to know about the links between the military and the Republicans. This little-known episode kept the president awake in the Washington heat. He felt himself being subjected to a "mild sort of political blackmail" by the controversial officer. The Democratic attempt to connect Taft with these various scandals contributed to the acerbic atmosphere in Washington during the summer of 1911.[9]

Democratic attacks on the tariff and his links with Senator Lorimer were a nuisance to the president, but they did not affect his renomination prospects. The reappearance of the issues surrounding the Ballinger–Pinchot controversy strained the relations between the White House and Theodore Roosevelt during the summer of 1911. Coupled with Roosevelt's assaults on the president's arbitration treaties, the dustup over the fate of Controller Bay in Alaska started the process that culminated in Roosevelt's presidential candidacy.

In late October 1910, Taft had issued an executive order returning 12,800 acres in the Chugach National Forest around Controller Bay in Alaska to the public domain. Six months later, Robert La Follette and other conservation critics of the president alleged that Taft's action had benefitted the interests of the Guggenheims, who were seeking a monopoly of coal lands in the area. There were also charges that Taft had acted in secret to give Richard S. Ryan, who was affiliated with the Controller Railway and Navigation Company, an unfair advantage in filing claims on the newly opened lands.[10]

Roosevelt wrote an article for the *Outlook* that appeared in the magazine's issue of 22 July 1911. In it he assailed the president's decision to restore the land to the public domain and give private interests control of the bay, which offered access to the coal lands. "It was the imperative duty of the Government service to keep this outlet free and not to dispose of it to any individual or individuals." Alaska, Roosevelt added, "must be developed. It must not be developed through the Government's conniving at lawbreaking on a gigantic scale by great corporations." Taft began preparing a response to Roosevelt designed to persuade the public that "nothing but venom prompts the attack on me in respect to it."[11]

In his message, released to the press on 26 July 1911, Taft defended his actions and rebutted the claims of his opponents. He sought to show that Roosevelt and James R. Garfield had in 1907 taken steps similar to what Taft had recently done. The president explained the propriety of his decisions and then added in his conclusions a cautionary note. The public should be warned "of the demoralization that has been produced by the hysterical suspicions of good people and the unscrupulous and corrupt misrepresentations of the wicked." Taft did not state into which of these two categories Theodore Roosevelt might fall. Roosevelt and Pinchot fired back at the president for the remainder of the summer. The chances of another rapprochement between Taft and Roosevelt were fading.[12]

The issue of international arbitration treaties further soured the political atmosphere between the two men. The White House announced the signing of pacts with Great Britain and France on 3 August 1911 in ceremonies staged for the greatest political effect. As written, these pacts specified that any "justiciable dispute" could be part of the arbitration process. Taft and Knox wanted to make their initiative as far-reaching as they could. Earlier arbitration treaties under William McKinley and Roosevelt had put questions of vital issues and national honor outside of what could be arbitrated. Initially, the treaties were quite popular, and Taft gained political points for his support of the concept of international peace. He and Knox believed that what they had done represented a significant step forward toward "the end that war might be eliminated as a means for adjustment of international disagreements."[13]

As he had earlier indicated in May 1911 when the treaty negotiations were disclosed, Theodore Roosevelt believed that the administration had blundered. "I must say I do not think much of the peace and arbitration treaty," he wrote to one English friend. To another, he said that "as a model for world treaties, for treaties between us or you and every other nation, I think it is absurd." Early in September, Roosevelt launched a public attack on the treaties, again in the *Outlook*. He denounced the idea of allowing non-Americans to decide questions of national honor or vital interest. He was especially scathing of the concept in the treaty that a Joint High Commission could decide against the United States in arbitration. "It is difficult to characterize this provision truthfully without seeming to be offensive. Merely to speak of it as silly comes far short of saying what should be said."[14]

Taft adopted an attitude of wry amusement about Roosevelt's strictures in private. "I don't think the Colonel has greatly injured our cause and certainly not as much as he has hurt himself." The president said that on his nationwide tour, he would talk about the treaties "and shall not notice the personal tone of his remarks. With the intimation that he could be offensive in describing the treaties he refers to them as silly and hypocritical. It is curious how unfitted he is for courteous debate—I don't wonder he prefers the battle axe." By the autumn of 1911, almost nothing of the old personal esteem remained between the two men.[15]

As for Taft himself, the president felt more confident about his chances for renomination on the eve of his national tour. His one announced rival, Senator La Follette, had still not achieved traction in his half-hearted presidential race. Outside of Wisconsin and its neighboring states, little enthusiasm was evident for "Battle Bob." The senator's wavering course on reciprocity undercut his claims to be a genuine reformer. A survey in the *New York Times* in mid-August speculated that Taft would have almost 800 delegates of the 1,100 to be present at the Republican National Convention. The most La Follette could expect to gain would be 250 or so. A first-ballot nomination for the president seemed assured.[16]

Of course, if Theodore Roosevelt made the race, Taft's problems would increase at once. Though he was now disillusioned with his former protégé, Roosevelt informed friends in public and private that he did not expect to be a candidate. He wrote his oldest son that "I do not care for Taft, indeed I think less of him as time goes on, in spite of the fact that I believe he is improving his position before the people. He is a flubdub with a streak of the second-rate and the common in him, and he has not the slightest idea of what is necessary if this country is to make social and industrial progress." To the dismay of associates such as Pinchot and James R. Garfield, Roosevelt remained firm in his insistence that he not be a candidate.[17]

Though Taft saw a reasonably clear path to the Republican nomination, his chances against a Democratic nominee seemed less promising. The congressional session had left the Democrats feeling optimistic about 1912, and Woodrow Wilson continued to impress people as the presumed front runner. Speaker Champ Clark also had wide support among Democrats. Taft had encountered Wilson while making a speech in New Jersey in August 1911. "The managers were much afraid he would be called on for a speech," the president told his wife. "He is a good deal of a 'butter in.' They called Wilson 'Dr. Syntax,' 'the open mouth,' and 'I would Run.'" Taft recognized Wilson's ability as a speaker and knew he would have a difficult race with the likely candidates among the Democrats.[18]

To bolster his own case, Taft spoke at Hamilton, Massachusetts, on 26 August 1911 in a fighting speech that took on the Democratic congressional leadership and La Follette. The tariff bills that he had vetoed represented "tariff for politics only" from the opposition party. He then went on to ask his audience, "do not this session and its results demonstrate that our present National system of business, which is based on the principle of protection, needs for its reasonable continuance, the guarding support of the Republican Party?" The Democrats offered "reckless legislation" in an effort to force a veto to create "popular hostility toward the Executive and the party of which he was the head."[19] As he wrote to George Meyer two days later, "I am starting on a long trip, and it is going to be hard work, but I feel there is some necessity for it. We have a gambler's chance of winning next year, and I ought not to lose any opportunity to improve it."[20]

The president left on his western trip on 15 September with a planned arrival back in Washington around 1 November. Within a week of his departure, he received a serious political reverse. Canadian voters on 21 September defeated the Liberal government of Sir Wilfred Laurier that had negotiated the reciprocity agreement with Taft. The initiative to which the president had devoted so much of his energy and political capital was now dead. The administration had suffered a substantial rebuke and still had the resentment of farmers along the Canadian border to deal with in 1912. Sereno Payne, the ranking Republican on the Ways and Means Committee, told a congressional colleague: "I am very much at sea about what the effect of the rejection of reciprocity will be as you can possibly be."[21]

Once Taft's trip got started on his fifty-fourth birthday, the president enjoyed receptive audiences for his set speeches and informal appearances

Taft's travels took him all over the country on his speaking junkets. This photograph was taken during an appearance at Bull Run, Virginia, during the summer of 1911. Library of Congress.

as he moved westward. Charles D. Hilles noted that at Kalamazoo, Michigan, the organizers of the event had arranged for five wagonloads of insane patients from a local asylum to greet the president. Newspaper correspondents said of these inmates that "they were madly enthusiastic." The president defended his policies on trusts, arbitration, and the tariff. In Kansas on 25 September, he gave seventeen speeches and spoke to thousands of spectators. He added stops to his itinerary until the journey exceeded 17,000 miles and became the longest such presidential tour up to that time.[22]

While the president gave speeches, Hilles met with Republican state leaders behind the scenes to crystallize sentiment for the renomination effort in 1912. He recorded his activities in memoranda for Taft that summarized the state of play in each of the states through which the presidential party passed. After talking with leaders in Missouri, Hilles reported that the state "will go solidly for Taft in the Convention." On the West Coast, Washington state was predicted to give Taft "eight delegates at large and at least four of the six district delegates." In Oregon, a "strong committee" was to be formed in favor of Taft to offset the opposition of Senator Jonathan Bourne. State by state, Taft and Hilles were building the organization that would carry the president to renomination in 1912.[23]

To the extent that the trip was designed to preempt both La Follette and a Roosevelt challenge, it functioned as the president desired. While he was out of Washington, however, the business of government continued. The long-building nationalist pressures within China against the Manchu regime erupted in October 1911. In messages to the traveling Taft, Knox expressed doubts about the ability of the Peking government to survive the "most serious" challenge it had faced in some time. The secretary of state questioned, therefore, whether recognition of any insurgent elements would be wise. For the moment, he advised Taft to withhold recognition and prepare the military to intervene if American lives were put at risk. Knox also sought to use the internal crisis in China to promote cooperation among the powers as a check on the ambitions of Russia and Japan. To that end, he held back from an endorsement of a loan to the Chinese government from the powers.[24]

Within the United States, the Chinese revolution enjoyed public sympathy as American politicians interpreted these events as evidence of democratic sentiments in the Far East. The end of the Manchu dynasty in February 1912 and the creation of a new provisional government raised anew the matter of recognition. In the House of Representatives, William Sulzer, a New York Democrat, offered a resolution asking the administration to extend recognition. Under pressure from the White House, which was concerned to protect Taft's executive prerogatives, the lawmakers accepted a watered-down statement of support for Chinese aspirations that stopped short of calling for recognition. There remained for the administration the question of a loan for China, which persisted throughout Taft's final year in office.[25]

More important for Taft's future than the news from China were the actions of the Department of Justice while the president was on tour. Deliberations about a possible antitrust case against United States Steel had been going on for some weeks. Those talks in turn touched on an area of intense sensitivity to Theodore Roosevelt and his relationship with William Howard Taft. As a result, by the end of October 1911, even before the president had returned to Washington, the prospect of a Roosevelt candidacy for the Republican nomination now seemed more of a genuine possibility.

The problem for Taft grew out of his policy toward large corporations and the enforcement of the Sherman Antitrust Act. He did not share Roosevelt's belief that an administration and a president could discern genuine differences between a "good trust" and a "bad trust." Rather, he believed "in the gentle but continuous prosecution of all these combinations until they learn better." Attorney General Wickersham echoed the president's position on the question of antitrust prosecutions. "The essence of monopoly is always the *power* or the exercise of the power to fix prices, control supply and exclude or admit competitors at will."[26]

The president and his attorney general proved to be vigorous enforcers of the antitrust laws. More cases were filed during the four years of Taft's presidency than in Roosevelt's seven years in office. High-profile actions were pursued against the "beef trust," the United Shoe Machinery Company, and the electrical trust. Even more significant were the prosecutions of Standard Oil and American Tobacco, begun under the Roosevelt Justice Department, but carried to the Supreme Court by Taft and Wickersham. The government achieved positive Supreme Court rulings against both of these large firms during the spring of 1911. The result was intense unhappiness within the business community about what the administration was doing. Some businessmen, forgetting their earlier discontent with Theodore Roosevelt on this same subject a few years earlier, regarded the regulatory ideas of the former president with more sympathy. "Wall Street is looking for a candidate for President and is much displeased with Taft," wrote one Iowa supporter of Taft.[27]

None of these prosecutions affected the relationship between Taft and Roosevelt except in the most indirect way. When it came to the question of an antitrust case against United States Steel, however, the decision focused on one of the most heated disputes of Roosevelt's presidency. In 1907, during the financial panic of the fall that threatened the stability of the banking system, financiers led by J. P. Morgan informed Roosevelt that it was necessary for United States Steel to purchase stock in Tennessee Coal and Iron to resolve the dangerous situation. The intent of the meetings that Roosevelt held with Morgan and later with steel company executives was to obtain White House assurances that no antitrust case would be filed against United States Steel if this purchase went forward. Roosevelt assured the businessmen that "I felt it no public duty of mine to interpose any objections."[28]

Almost as soon as the deal was announced, there were allegations that Roosevelt had been deceived. These assertions outraged him, and he defended his conduct in his usual vigorous manner. When the Democrats took over control of the House in 1911, they started an investigation of the subject and examined Roosevelt's actions in 1907. During the summer of 1911, Roosevelt appeared before the congressional panel, chaired by Augustus O. Stanley of Kentucky, and maintained that he had not been fooled. Instead, he had acted in the public interest during a moment

George W. Wickersham was Taft's partner in pursuing a
vigorous antitrust policy. Library of Congress.

of crisis. To question Roosevelt's probity on this subject thus meant not only impugning his record as president, but also doubting his personal honesty.

The truth was, of course, that Roosevelt had been deceived in 1907. Henry Clay Frick and Elbert H. Gary had not given him all the facts, and he had served their financial interests far more than the interests of the public. But for Roosevelt, the Tennessee Coal and Iron dispute had become more than an assessment of his policy performance as president. Roosevelt's judgment in the case had been "absolutely right," and in his mind, his testimony before the congressional panel had laid the subject to rest. To reopen the question of whether Roosevelt had been misled was to risk an explosion from an angry former president.[29]

While Roosevelt was making his position clear, the Justice Department was considering whether or not to file an antitrust suit against the steel giant. To help with framing the case, Wickersham asked Taft's former secretary of war, Jacob M. Dickinson, to be a special assistant who would act as a de facto prosecutor against United States Steel. Dickinson and the attorney general approached the case in the spirit of two lawyers intent on providing all the evidence that might demonstrate the illegal business practices of the steel company. If that strategy included a discussion of the Tennessee Coal and Iron episode, then the information should be included, no matter what its potential impact on Theodore Roosevelt. Dickinson, for his part, was convinced that the former president would understand that no imputation of wrongdoing on his part was being alleged. That was certainly a naive judgment on Dickinson's part. As a Democrat, he was insensitive to the political implications of his actions.[30]

Taft's presidential method of allowing his cabinet officers very wide discretion in the discharge of their duties now revealed the flaws in its practical operation. Neither Dickinson nor Wickersham were politicians, and they did not evaluate the possible implications for the volatile Roosevelt of the allegations in the proposed lawsuit. That these two subordinates did not think it was either necessary or appropriate to inform Taft of the substance of the charges being made in the government's statement deprived the president of a chance to examine the consequences of a negative reaction from Roosevelt. Taft's prolonged absence from Washington on his nationwide journey left him out of touch with current events in the Justice Department.[31]

The government's suit against United States Steel was filed on 26 October 1911. It contained language that said of Roosevelt in 1907, "the President was not made fully acquainted with the state of affairs in New York relevant to the transaction as they existed." Roosevelt had not been "fully advised." If he had been, he would have understood the motives of the steel company to buy up "a company that had recently assumed a position of potential competition of great significance." The plain thrust of the government's language was that Roosevelt had been fooled in the incident, and the steel company had gulled the president. Elihu Root understood what had happened. "It was a sin of omission rather than of commission, which mitigates it. Wickersham handled it as he would have handled any case in his office without considering the political relations between Taft and Roosevelt."[32]

By late 1911, relations between Roosevelt and Taft had frayed almost to the point of a rupture. For William Howard Taft and his renomination prospects, keeping Roosevelt docile and on the sidelines was a political imperative. This fact did not mean shaping policy to satisfy the former president. It did involve seeing to it that no unnecessary provocations of Roosevelt occurred. It would have been a simple matter, before he left on his trip, for the president to have informed his cabinet members not to take any action regarding Roosevelt without the express approval of the White House. The junketing president did not take that step. It is not clear that he ever even contemplated such an approach. Taft seems to have decided that he had no obligation to reach out to Roosevelt to forestall misunderstandings. After the Controller Bay and arbitration treaty cases, Taft may well have believed that Roosevelt did not deserve such indulgences. That was human and understandable. But the failure of Taft to go the extra mile would soon have large consequences, once Roosevelt read that the suit had been filed and what it said about his conduct in 1907.

The news of the suit against United States Steel and the comments about his conduct in 1907 outraged Theodore Roosevelt. The president and the attorney general were "playing small, mean and foolish politics in this matter." To his oldest son, he wrote that "Taft has fallen down at every point in the last six months." To answer the attack on his record, Roosevelt prepared an article for the *Outlook* in which he assailed the reasoning behind the government's indictment of United States Steel. He also proclaimed, "I was not misled," and any assertion that he was "is itself not in accordance with the truth." He then went on to argue that enforcing the Sherman act to break up big businesses was futile. "Such an effort represents not progressiveness but an unintelligent though doubtless entirely well-meaning toryism."[33]

Having thus come to the brink of an open break with Taft and the administration over antitrust policy, Roosevelt also now began to back away from his previous statements that he did not want to be a candidate in 1912. In a letter to a friend, he said in December 1911, after repeating all the reasons why he should not run, "of course circumstances might conceivably arise when I should feel that there was a duty to the people which

Mabel Boardman, head of the American Red Cross, was a close friend of
the president. She defended him to influential members of the press.
Library of Congress.

I could not shirk, and so would accept the nomination." Once Roosevelt
framed the matter in that way, his enthusiastic supporters set about establishing the circumstances that would lead him to decide it was his duty
to run. By mid-November 1911, the chances that Taft would face a serious challenge to his nomination from his predecessor had dramatically
risen.[34]

In fact, the whole political scene posed genuine problems for the Republicans in the presidential race. The Democrats had shown unexpected
discipline in Congress throughout 1911. As former vice president Charles
Fairbanks put it, should the Democrats "avoid any considerable schism
in their own ranks we will certainly be brought face to face with a serious
situation." There were problems with the morale of Taft supporters as
Roosevelt boomed and the president's chances worsened. His friend in
New York City, Otto Bannard, told the secretary of war, Henry L. Stimson, that "it is a good time for Taft's friends to be outspoken, so many
being weak-kneed just now."[35]

The president took these developments with surprising calm. There was no effort to reach out to Roosevelt and explain how the decision to file the indictment had been made. Nor did the White House issue a statement separating Roosevelt's actions from the other aspects of the United States Steel suit. Taft did not think that he owed his predecessor an explanation for the decision of the Justice Department, and none was forthcoming. The president was confident that he would win renomination even if Roosevelt entered some states where "an open preference presidential primary" would be held. "There are enough states without such a primary to give me the convention and the nomination, but a defeat in all the popular primaries might be depressing." So any explanation to Roosevelt about the circumstances of the United States Steel suit was not to be considered.[36]

On the face of things, Taft seemed to be in good shape to achieve the renomination. La Follette's candidacy was still treading water, though the senator now promised allies he would get out on the stump in the new year. Taft assured himself that Roosevelt would not get into the race for the GOP nomination after all. Once the president was renominated, an educational campaign would draw the Republicans back together and lift Taft to a second term. It was a reassuring scenario for a president who had gone through a difficult year in 1911.

Taft still confronted the long session of Congress that would convene in December 1911 with the Democrats in control of the House. The opposition would be anxious to maximize their chances to gain the White House in 1912. As Taft began to prepare his third annual message, a number of disputed questions pressed for answers. In foreign policy, there was a dispute with Russia over the treatment of American Jews holding passports when they visited that czarist country. The revolutionary ferment in Mexico continued, and in China, the Manchu regime was in its last throes. Central America remained a focus for the policy of dollar diplomacy. Taft had much to consider as he entered the fourth year of his administration. Yet he did so with an underlying confidence that he might win reelection despite his troubles. As he wrote to Mabel Boardman on Christmas Eve, "I am hopeful that after a campaign of education the people will conclude that I have given them a pretty good administration and that they would have less risk with me than with another."[37]

12

★ ★ ★ ★ ★

"ROOSEVELT WAS MY CLOSEST FRIEND"

Although the threat of a Theodore Roosevelt candidacy was the major political worry for William Howard Taft as 1912 began, the Democratic House of Representatives provided ample short-term problems for the beleaguered Republican administration. The likelihood of a victory for the opposition in the presidential race emboldened Champ Clark and his colleagues. As a result, they found numerous ways to make life more difficult for the White House during the first six months of the year. Investigations of administration actions, foreign policy initiatives from lawmakers, and dissent from the president's leadership all combined to force Taft to run at once a renomination campaign and a rearguard battle with Capitol Hill.[1]

Taft opened the political season with his annual messages to Congress in December 1911. The extensive nature of the issues to be addressed, Taft wrote to lawmakers, "make it impossible to include in one message of a reasonable length a discussion of the topics that ought to be brought to the attention of the National Legislature at its first regular session." In following this approach, Taft was diluting the impact of the annual message as an event. Instead of clearly setting priorities on a single date when the whole nation focused on the president's written words, he extended the process through the entire month of December in a way that reduced the effectiveness of his statements. It did not occur to Taft, any more than it had to Roosevelt, to deliver his message in person. That would take place under Woodrow Wilson, and so Taft's messages in 1911 and 1912 became the last of the century-old tradition of presidential communication at the opening of Congress.[2]

By this period in his presidency, Taft's political troubles had caused the public to tune out his annual messages. His policy proposals were going nowhere in the Democratic House in an election year. With a nomination contest against Theodore Roosevelt a growing possibility, the White House would have the distraction of a campaign to wage during the winter and spring. A weakened president encountered growing resistance to his legislative initiatives.

An example of Taft's predicament came early in December 1911. For some years, Jews in the United States had complained about the restrictive anti-Semitic policies of Russia toward American citizens of their religion traveling in that country. An American passport did not exempt an American Jew from the limits that the czar's regime put on the movement and activities of Russian Jews or the outright exclusion of American Jews from entering Russia at all. The treaty of 1832 between Russia and the United States specified that holders of American passports should be treated in Russia like all other citizens traveling abroad. The Russians responded that the regulation of Jewish citizens in their country or the exclusion of Jewish visitors was an internal matter over which the United States had no control. Because the United States imposed restrictions on the immigration of Chinese and Japanese into the United States, Washington, in the opinion of the Taft administration, had a weak legal case to protest Russian actions.[3]

These considerations did not dissuade the Jewish leaders from pressing their case in Congress that the 1832 treaty should be abrogated. Taft endeavored to buy time in his foreign policy annual message on 7 December 1911 with a statement about renegotiating the treaty. Nonetheless, the House voted 301 to 1 for a resolution asking Taft to abrogate the treaty. It was clear that the Senate was going to take similar action. Faced with an accomplished fact and with the Russians unwilling to change their anti-Semitic policies, Taft abrogated the treaty in mid-December.

"I took the only course that was open to me, after the negotiations had exhausted every resource of diplomacy," Taft wrote in response to a letter of congratulations from a Jewish spokesman in Washington. Although he gained some political capital from his decision, Taft had little choice but to do what he did with an election year impending and the tide of popular opinion against Russia as strong as it was in late 1911.[4]

In other areas of foreign policy, the presence of the Democrats in Congress produced reverses for the administration during these months. Taft asked the lawmakers to approve the conventions with Nicaragua and Honduras that had been worked out in 1911. "Their rejection here might destroy the progress made and consign the Republics concerned to still deeper submergence in bankruptcy, revolution, and national jeopardy."

When the conventions came up before the Senate Foreign Relations Committee, they were approved on a party line vote with the Democrats voting against them. There was thus no chance that the upper house could attain the two thirds needed for approval. The treaties, key parts of the Taft–Knox policy of dollar diplomacy, were in effect dead.[5]

Completing the string of foreign policy reverses was the difficulties that the president's arbitration treaties faced during the early part of 1912. Despite Taft's intense lobbying efforts during his fall 1911 tour of the country, he could not translate the broad popular support for the arbitration pacts into approval in the Senate. The failure of Taft and Knox to consult the Senate in advance created a climate of ill will that could not be overcome. Of course, had he told Senate leaders of the content of the proposed pacts during 1911, the difficulties inherent in Taft's broad view of arbitration would have at once been evident.[6]

During the debate in 1912, Henry Cabot Lodge, Elihu Root, and other influential legislators expressed their reservations about the extent to which the administration was, in their mind, putting the national interest at risk with the broad definition of what these pacts would cover. To assuage Senate criticism, the treaties were amended to the point that they had very little remaining substance. After the Senate had acted in March 1912, the president told reporters, "I don't know whether the treaties as they are now amended are worth putting through." In the end, the White House decided not to go forward with them, and this major initiative of Taft's presidency came to a quiet end.[7]

To bolster support for American diplomacy in Latin America, the president dispatched Secretary Knox on a tour of the region during the winter of 1912. Elihu Root had made a successful swing through Latin America for Theodore Roosevelt in 1906. Knox's visit to ten countries did not achieve that positive result because of persistent suspicion of the United States and dollar diplomacy. Nor did Knox's pleas for support of the Honduran and Nicaraguan treaties while he was away move Congress. It did have the effect of keeping the secretary of state away from the press during the start of the primary contest against Theodore Roosevelt.

Along with these rebuffs in foreign policy, the White House aroused scant interest in the president's reform initiatives. On 17 January 1912, he sent the Congress a message "on economy and efficiency in the Government service." He sought more funds to extend the work of his Commission on Economy and Efficiency. But the Democrats, sensing that they could control the White House and Congress within the next year, were not likely to implement Taft's policy changes. The two ends of Pennsylvania Avenue could offset each other during 1912. They could not achieve anything on their own in a substantive way.[8]

The major preoccupation for the president was his renomination and reelection. In late December 1911, he told his friend, Mabel Boardman, that "it is very difficult for me to escape the conclusion not only that I can be renominated but also that I can be reelected." Yet at the same time, he recognized that "my weakness is in Roosevelt allowing his name to go to the voters in California, Oregon, Washington, North & South Dakota and New Jersey and some possible inroads in Ohio, Texas and North Carolina." Should those developments take place, he added, that trend could cut into his delegate total. As far as Roosevelt actually getting into the race was concerned, "I think he expects me to be nominated and beaten, a result which he will bear with Christian fortitude."[9]

On the substance of a race for another nomination, Taft had good reason to be confident. The spadework that he and Hilles had done in 1911 led to administration control of the majority of states in the South where Republican delegates were chosen. The local and state conventions in February and March 1912 went in the president's favor, and all the Roosevelt partisans could do was to institute contests against the Taft slates for the Republican National Committee to rule on before the convention. During that controversial spring, the president retained the control of the Republican agenda that he had established throughout 1911. That process ensured his renomination at Chicago in mid-June.[10]

Taft was less successful in managing his personal struggle with Roosevelt. Although he tried not to descend into a contest of personalities with his predecessor, it proved impossible for the two men to focus on issues. In part this was Roosevelt's fault. Once he got into a political fight, he knew only how to go all out to win. For the first two months of the campaign, Taft tried an above-the-battle strategy. Once Roosevelt began to win primaries during April, however, it became imperative for Taft to strike back. The result was a rapid descent into mutual vituperation that eroded whatever lingered of Republican unity.

During January 1912, Taft watched as Roosevelt moved closer and closer to an outright declaration of a presidential candidacy. By the end of the month, it was evident that Roosevelt was only seeking the proper venue to announce his entry into the race. The disastrous address of Senator Robert M. La Follette at a newspaper publishers' banquet in early February seemed to eliminate the senator as a contender. That conclusion proved premature, but it allowed Roosevelt to step forward as the main progressive challenger to Taft. Taft himself assailed the former president by implication at a Lincoln Day speech in New York City. He denounced "extremists" who attacked the courts and other institutions. These individuals were not progressives. "They are political emotionalists or neurotics who have lost that sense of proportion, that clear and candid consideration of their own weakness as a whole, and that clear perception of the necessity for checks upon hasty popular action which made our people who fought the Revolution and who drafted the Federal Constitution the greatest self-governing people that the world ever knew."[11]

Roosevelt did not like being criticized in those terms, and the president's words accelerated his move toward a declared candidacy. The coming-out moment for Roosevelt occurred at the Ohio constitutional convention on 21 February. In his speech there, he announced his views on a number of issues. The sensation of his appearance was his endorsement of the recall of judicial decisions as a key element in his prospective candidacy. The usually shrewd Roosevelt presented Taft with a political gift. When Roosevelt identified with the radical notion of popular votes on judicial rulings about regulatory laws in the states, he frightened conservatives within the Grand Old Party who might otherwise have been sympathetic to his economic ideas. A surge of support came Taft's way. After all, he had denounced the recall in a New York speech in January. "Judicial recall! Judicial recall! The words themselves are so inconsistent that I hate to utter them." As Henry Cabot Lodge put it, the Columbus speech had turned Taft "from a man into a principle."[12]

Coupled with Taft's superior organization, Roosevelt's Columbus, Ohio, speech gave the president an initiative he maintained throughout March 1912. Hilles teamed with Congressman William B. McKinley (no relation to the deceased president) to develop an efficient process for gathering in delegates for the White House. On 21 February, Hilles sent a memo to Taft predicting that "the score at the end of March would be 234 for Taft, 2 for Cummins, 10 for La Follette, and 22 for Roosevelt." In Indiana, one operative told Taft, "The republicans you and I would be likely to meet socially are practically unanimous for your nomination. The republicans opposed are worthy of consideration only because of their number." Lawyers and business people favored Taft; farmers, veterans, and union members stood with Roosevelt. As Taft gathered in state delegations, there were predictions that the Roosevelt campaign might collapse.[13]

Throughout the spring of 1912, Taft made the tough political decisions that his nomination fight now required. After seeking to oust African American Republicans from federal offices in the South for three years, he now turned to these politicians for key delegates to sustain his cause. "In Texas and Louisiana," Hilles wrote to Booker T. Washington in early April, "it is our action that has made it possible for the colored people to have representation and recognition." Although black resentment at Taft lingered, the president was successful in finding enough support from this group of Republicans to establish winning coalitions against Roosevelt across the South.[14] Taft's ill-fated effort to reshape Republican politics in the South by excluding blacks had ended.

Roosevelt and his allies knew that the early states would be against them. They hoped that their candidate's fortunes would revive when the primaries began. To that end, Roosevelt made a personal tour at the end of March. His campaigning accounted for a decisive primary win in Illinois on 9 April that brought him fifty-six delegates to two for the president. Four days later, in Pennsylvania, Roosevelt scored another success and added sixty-seven delegates to his total. He still lagged far behind Taft, but the twin triumphs revived Roosevelt's challenge and disconcerted the White House. Taft wrote that Roosevelt "seems to have thrown all discretion to the winds and to seize upon any weapon which he thinks will help him in his mad chase."[15]

Amid these political reverses, Taft also suffered a personal loss. Archie Butt had gone to Europe during the spring and was returning to the United States on the *Titanic* when it went down in the Atlantic on 14 April. The military aide had been one of the few presidential confidants on whom Taft could rely in 1912, and the loss of his friend compounded the strain on the president during his confrontation with Roosevelt. As he said at the memorial service for Butt on 6 May 1912, "the life of the President is rather isolated, and those appointed to live with him come much closer to him than any one else. The bond is very close, and it is difficult to speak on such an occasion."[16]

As long as he was piling up committed delegates, Taft took the view that he should not assail Roosevelt personally. "I want to be consulted about every paragraph that goes out of a critical or hostile nature, and especially of a personal nature, with respect to Colonel Roosevelt or the canvass," he told McKinley on 12 March. However, with the Roosevelt victories in April, the president realized that he would have to speak out. His advisers had been urging him to do that for some time. His cabinet and prominent Republicans pressed him to go on the attack against his challenger. A newspaper story reported discontent with the president's passivity among his advisers. They shared "an impatience with their silent chief which is much more pronounced under cover than it appears in the open."[17]

The cabinet members who pushed Taft to take the stump were more reluctant to assume such surrogate duties themselves. Taft suffered because of the lack of strong political figures in his official family. Attorney General Wickersham had no partisan base, and his antitrust policies had made him unpopular among businessmen. The postmaster general, Frank Hitchcock, had alienated Republicans with his patronage policies.

Secretary of the Navy George von Lengerke Meyer talked about closing naval facilities until Taft pleaded with him: "Can't you stop this discussion about the Portsmouth yard? Our enemies seize everything you say on the subject and send it right down to Portsmouth and then there is the devil to pay." He also implored Secretary of War Henry Stimson to take to the hustings. "This is a time when workers in the vineyard are needed. Will you please let me know at once whether you can go?" Even old friends such as Elihu Root declined to go out and participate in a direct attack on Roosevelt, also an old friend.[18]

Taft realized that he had no choice about assailing Roosevelt in person. "I dislike to speak with directness about Theodore Roosevelt," he told Mabel Boardman, "but I can not longer refrain from refuting his false accusations." If he did not respond, Massachusetts could go for Roosevelt, and the resulting momentum for Taft's rival might sweep away delegates who had been pledged to the president. As Taft put it, "my friends have met with some reverses which might easily lead to a rout if they were not checked."[19]

The campaign thus heated up when the two rivals sought the votes of Republicans in Massachusetts. The White House on 24 April released documents indicating that Roosevelt had backed away from prosecuting the International Harvester Company in 1907. These revelations undercut Roosevelt's allegations that the president was a friend of corporate power. The next day in Boston, Taft took the offensive. Because of Roosevelt's ambition and drive for personal power, he "ought not to be selected as a candidate of any political party." The result might be one-man rule and a presidency for life. "One who so lightly regards constitutional principles, and especially the independence of the judiciary, one who is naturally impatient of legal restraints and of due legal procedure, and who has so misunderstood what liberty regulated by law is, could not safely be intrusted with successive Presidential terms. I say this sorrowfully, but I say it with the full conviction of its truth." According to a journalist who witnessed the scene, after he gave his main speeches in Boston, the president returned to his railroad car. There Taft said, "Roosevelt was my closest friend," and began to sob.[20]

Roosevelt, who relished public confrontation, fired back at Taft. He charged that the president had "not merely in thought, word, and deed been disloyal to our past friendship, but has been disloyal to every canon of ordinary decency and fair dealing such as should obtain even in dealing with a man's bitterest opponents." During the next several days, they argued about their positions on the International Harvester issue, Canadian reciprocity, which Roosevelt now opposed, and the question of Senator William Lorimer of Illinois. In Lowell, Massachusetts, Taft's pent-up anger boiled over. "I was a man of straw; but I have been a man of straw long enough; every man who has blood in his body, and who has been misrepresented as I have been is forced to fight. I appeal to my friends in Massachusetts, who, I think believe in a square deal."[21]

When the votes were tabulated, Taft eked out a narrow victory on 30 April. That success stemmed Roosevelt's momentum and prevented the president's campaign from going into a downward spiral. The two men then moved on to Ohio for a primary in Taft's backyard. For more than a week in the middle of May, the battle for popular support shook Ohio politics. Taft warned his listeners that Roosevelt was "in favor of innovations and changes that would make the Constitution worth little more than the paper it is written on." Amid his campaigning, the president informed Charles Hilles that "we are getting along fairly well, and most of the people with us are enthusiastic."[22]

The result in Ohio, however, produced another victory for Roosevelt, who won thirty-one delegates to Taft's eleven. On the bright side for the Taft forces who controlled the party apparatus, the ensuing state convention seemed likely to provide the president with another half-dozen delegates. Nonetheless, the defeat in his home state a month before the National Convention was a severe blow. Taft remained confident. "We have already enough votes to give us considerably more than a majority in the convention," he wrote to an old friend. "We don't propose to be defrauded or bulldozed out of it." Taft suffered another reverse when New Jersey went for Roosevelt in the final GOP primary. Attention turned to the preliminaries of the convention and the role of the Republican National Committee in settling the disputed delegates.[23]

When the primaries were over, the arithmetic for the impending convention tilted the delegate tally toward Taft. Press accounts gave Roosevelt 411 committed delegates to 201 for the president. The count understated Taft's strength. There were 166 uninstructed delegates, most of them from the large New York delegation, which was filled with pro-Taft supporters. Robert La Follette had 36 delegates from Wisconsin and North Dakota. Albert B. Cummins of Iowa controlled 10 delegates from his state.

Then there were 254 contested delegates, largely from the South, which the National Committee would address during the week before the convention proceedings opened. In deliberations of that panel, the outcome of the Republican nomination race would be decided. "The attitude of the National Committee is exceedingly improved," Taft wrote on 26 May. "If they take a firm stand, as I believe they will do, and throw out the flimsy contests trumped up by agents of the other side we shall readily control."[24]

PLATFORM AMENITIES.

President Taft (*conductor of the White House Express*). "YOU CAN'T GO ON THIS TRAIN."
Colonel Roosevelt. "WELL, IF I CAN'T, YOU SHAN'T!"

After Charles Keene.

A British take from *Punch* on the Taft–Roosevelt struggle during the spring of 1912.

The president's operatives had been looking to the composition of the national committee for some time, and they felt confident that they had a majority of the panel behind Taft. The men chosen for the committee in 1908 and the subsequent replacements during the Taft presidency had left the administration with as many as thirty-five votes on the fifty-three-member committee. The chair of the national committee, Victor Rosewater of Nebraska, was also a firm adherent of the Taft cause. The president's ability to control the party machinery meant Roosevelt operated at a definite disadvantage throughout these key procedural deliberations.[25]

For Roosevelt and his partisans, on the other hand, the former president's victories in the primaries illustrated his strength with the GOP rank and file. More important, the primary votes demonstrated his greater electability in the fall against the Democrats. If that candidate was Speaker of the House Champ Clark, Roosevelt could run as a true progressive. Should the Democrats pick New Jersey governor Woodrow Wilson, the race would be more difficult. In either event, Roosevelt seemed the Republican with the best chance to win. Because Roosevelt was the evident choice of the party faithful, any Taft victory would have to be the result of boss-driven conventions and caucuses that were unrepresentative and undemocratic. Should the nomination go to Taft as a result of such machinations, Roosevelt began thinking about bolting the ticket and running a third party of his own.

First came the deliberations of the National Committee during the week of 7–14 June in Chicago. Taking up the contests in alphabetical order, the members dismissed most of Roosevelt's challenges to the southern delegates. Even some of the pro-Roosevelt members recognized the weakness of these cases. As a Missouri Republican wrote, Roosevelt "put up a contest that his own men would not swallow."[26] By this time, however, Roosevelt had forgotten the tactical purpose that animated the filing of the contests months earlier. He and his aides concluded that the Republican National Committee, under the control of the White House, was engaged in stealing from Roosevelt delegates and therefore a nomination that he had honestly won.

Four cases came to symbolize for the Roosevelt side what was happening. Arizona, California, Texas, and Washington were the states in question where the Roosevelt men thought they had a compelling argument. In Texas, where a modern analysis of the forty-member delegation has been done, the outcome that gave Taft thirty-one delegates and Roosevelt only nine seems unduly tilted toward Taft. A fairer result would have been twenty-one for Roosevelt and nineteen for Taft. However, the methods of the national committee were not designed to dispense political justice. As one of the committee members told the leader of the Roosevelt slate in

Texas when he asked how many of his supporters might be seated, "he had not been able to learn how many of the Texas delegates we actually need in our business and that until then, he could not say."[27]

Writing to the chairman of the national committee, Taft had said, "I do not want any contest decided in my favor merely for the purpose of giving me the majority." The president added that it was important "that the public should know that there are no star chamber proceedings, and that they shall have access to the evidence upon which you act, through the newspapers." These pious sentiments were all very well for Taft to express in public. No doubt he meant them too. His hardened operatives on the ground also knew how many delegates he needed to be nominated. "Our fellows are in tip-top shape and working hard all along the line," wrote the head of Taft's literary bureau. "We are organized, united and everybody knows what is expected of them."[28]

Hilles, McKinley, and their colleagues would have been naive if they had treated the deliberations of the national committee as a forum for achieving true justice. Had the Roosevelt delegates been in the majority on the national committee, they would have decided the cases in their favor, as the national committee under Roosevelt's guidance had done for Taft in 1908.

When the national committee concluded its work on 14 June, it had awarded 235 of the contested delegates to Taft and 19 to Roosevelt. There were immediate cries of fraud from the Roosevelt camp. The candidate said that "a great moral issue" faced the Republican Party and that he was entitled to sixty to eighty more delegates than he had been awarded. By Roosevelt's calculations, that change would have been enough to have given his forces control of the national convention. Angry at the "theft" that he believed was being perpetrated on his hopes, Roosevelt broke with the precedent that kept presidential candidates away from the convention. He traveled to Chicago and addressed his supporters the night before the convention opened. That was the moment when he told them "we stand at Armageddon and we battle for the Lord."[29]

President Taft remained in Washington in telephone contact with Hilles and McKinley in Chicago. Republicans who sensed an imminent rupture in the party thought about the possibility of a compromise third choice instead of either Roosevelt or the president. One party member wrote the White House suggesting that Taft withdraw in favor of Justice Charles Evans Hughes. "The future of the United States Government is at stake," Taft was told, and if he stepped aside "you will have done a service to your country and your party which no man has ever had the opportunity of doing before." By the time the letter reached Taft, he had already shot down any talk of withdrawal in favor of another. "The report that I am in any way considering the possibility of [a] compromise candidate is wholly unfounded and you are authorized emphatically to deny the report. With confidence I abide the judgment of the convention."[30]

When the convention opened, the Taft forces had narrow control of the proceedings. The first test came on the selection of a temporary chairman. To forestall Roosevelt's action on this issue, the president had persuaded Elihu Root to be the administration's candidate. Root had been reluctant to campaign for Taft during the primary season, much to the displeasure of the candidate himself. After the selection was made, Roosevelt announced that he would propose his own choice and fight the Root selection. "Root is a man who would rather avoid a fight if he can," Taft told William A. Barnes Jr. of New York, "but when he is put to the issue he will fight as long as anybody; and that is what they have done to him now."[31]

As their candidate, the Roosevelt side put up Francis E. McGovern, the governor of Wisconsin. The hope was that Senator La Follette's supporters would have no choice but to vote for the leader of the state's delegation. Instead, La Follette's leader at the convention proclaimed, "we make no deals with Roosevelt. We make no trades with Taft." On the election of the temporary chairman, Root prevailed by a vote of 558 to 501. That confirmed the president's dominance of the convention. The following day, a motion to substitute Roosevelt delegates for the ones the national committee had seated also failed by a 567 to 507 tally. Roosevelt now believed he could not be nominated, and he also rejected any thought of a compromise candidate.[32]

After assuring himself that he had funding for a third-party race, Roosevelt sent a statement to the convention declaring that the gathering was "in no proper sense any longer a Republican convention."[33] Delegates pledged to him should abstain from the proceedings. When the balloting occurred, Taft won renomination easily, by a count of 561 votes for the president, 107 for Roosevelt, and 41 for La Follette. The Taft camp had not given much thought to the vice presidency and agreed to the renomination of Sherman even though he was seriously ill and added nothing to the ticket for the fall election. Few Republicans expected Taft to be really competitive in the general election. They saw abundant evidence that Roosevelt was going to make a third party try at the presidency.

In the immediate aftermath of the convention, Taft looked to winning back Republican votes that had gone to Roosevelt during the primary season. "Our campaign has got to be one of conciliation instead of alienation. We must educate rather than excoriate." When it came to Theodore Roosevelt, however, the president's mind was still on criticizing his defeated rival. "Whatever the outcome may be I feel that the party has escaped from a danger which seriously threatened its existence." As for the convention victory, "we have ended the menace that existed in the possibility of Theodore Roosevelt becoming again President of the United States." Roosevelt was such a menace because there had been no one "in our history so dangerous and so powerful because of his hold upon the less intelligent voters and the discontented."[34]

Taft believed that his title to the Republican nomination in 1912 was good, and he rejected Roosevelt's charges that his victory had been accomplished through fraud. The White House devoted much attention to the issue of the contested delegates over the summer of 1912 and prepared elaborate evidence to demonstrate that Roosevelt had not been cheated. It did not matter in the end. The president and his allies had the majority of the votes on the procedural questions that determined the outcome of the convention, and they used their advantage to the fullest to accomplish the defeat of Roosevelt and the progressives.

In gaining his triumph over the Roosevelt challenge, Taft had shown his ability as a party leader. Incumbent presidents can achieve renomination even in the face of likely defeat in the general election, as Benjamin Harrison had demonstrated twenty years earlier. Yet Harrison had to confront an aging and ill James G. Blaine, who could not make a real campaign for the Republican prize. Roosevelt, however, had the popularity attached to his personality, nationwide support within the party, and the talent to campaign as few other challengers before or after him did. Taft took Roosevelt's best punches and fought him on even terms throughout the primary and caucus season. Because Roosevelt started late and lacked a clear strategy for winning the nomination, the president in the end gained the narrow but decisive victory at the Chicago convention.

Historians are still debating what went wrong in the Taft–Roosevelt relationship that produced the events of 1912. There is plenty of blame to go around for both of the individuals involved. A friendship that arose out of a set of circumstances during the early 1890s when both were young men in Washington became something else during the Roosevelt presidency from 1904 to 1909. Taft fit easily into the role of cabinet subordinate as secretary of war, and the force of Roosevelt's charisma pulled the Ohioan in a progressive direction. Aware that Roosevelt could put him on the Supreme Court or open the road to the White House, Taft kept to himself his reservations about the president's working style and his constitutional views. If Roosevelt wanted to conclude that the two men thought exactly alike, there was no reason for Taft to disabuse the chief executive of that errant notion. Any deviation from the orthodoxy as Roosevelt enunciated it would have likely ended Taft's presidential ambitions.

Once the balance of power shifted from the summer of 1908 onward, Taft believed that he should receive the deference due a president, even from a previous occupant of the office. Roosevelt was willing to observe these constraints on the surface, but at bottom, he never accepted that the underlying nature of his friendship with Taft had changed forever. Roosevelt did not quite say that he wanted to be a kind of copresident, but he expected a degree of consultation and participation that moved in that direction.

When the two men differed over policy questions such as conservation and corporate regulation, there was little real regard on a personal level to keep them working together. The tensions between the Taft family members and the Roosevelt family did not help the situation, but these flare-ups were more of a reflection of a preexisting tension than a cause of disillusion. In retrospect, it is striking that Taft and Roosevelt collaborated for as long as they did in light of their very different approaches to politics and governing.

Both men were too stubborn to sit down and air their differences in private once Taft became president. It is striking how much they endeavored not to communicate in a frank and open way during the period after Roosevelt had returned from Africa and Europe. Perhaps such a session would only have added to the rancor between them by 1912. Taft often wondered what he had done to alienate Roosevelt. Had it been the 1908 comment about Charles P. Taft? Had the firing of Pinchot been the catalyst for unhappiness? In the end, it did not matter. Two proud individuals decided that their personal ambitions and grievances were more significant than finding common ground about what they had once believed. For Taft, it meant that during the summer of 1912, the sands were running out on his single term as president.

13

★ ★ ★ ★ ★

THE 1912 CAMPAIGN

After the Republican convention, William Howard Taft was not officially a lame-duck president. It was conceivable that he might win the election against Woodrow Wilson and Theodore Roosevelt. Yet the chance of such an outcome seemed improbable to most political observers during the summer of 1912. Once the Democrats selected Wilson at their convention in Baltimore that climaxed in early July, the odds on the opposition party winning the White House improved. The emergence of Roosevelt's Progressive Party and the deepening of the Republican split made a Democratic triumph almost a certainty unless Wilson made some serious mistake in the campaign.

Even going through the motions of a presidential race presented great challenges for Taft and his party. He had to assemble a different kind of campaign organization from the one he had used during the primary contests. The Republicans had to raise money in an unfriendly setting, set up campaigns in the major states, and also confront the problems that Roosevelt's third-party race posed. In many states, there came to be competing slates of pro- and anti-Taft electors vying for the Republican label. The White House had to become involved in resolving these arcane electoral disputes. Taft also had to write his acceptance speech for the Republican nomination that would serve as a keynote for the campaign ahead. At the same time, the echoes from the battle over the contested delegates at Chicago resounded. There was much for Taft to manage during the steamy Washington summer of 1912.

The policy problems of the United States did not take a holiday for the election campaign. Several issues demanded solutions during these months as the Democrats in Congress positioned themselves for the coming election. Reform of the army, tolls on the soon-to-be-finished Panama Canal, and the perennial argument over the tariff were on Taft's plate. In foreign affairs, Central America continued to be volatile. With Mrs. Taft away at Beverly, Massachusetts, for the season, the president went through his last summer by himself amid gloomy prospects for his political future.

One issue that arose from the Congress said more about its author than the merits of the case. In 1911, there had been press reports that the Japanese were trying to acquire land or fishing rights near Magdalena Bay in Baja California. These alleged sightings of Japanese business figures acting on behalf, it was presumed, of the Tokyo government, were always vague and insubstantial. Japan had no interest in a confrontation with Washington over such a facility because Tokyo knew that the United States would react with alacrity to such a threatening presence. Senator Henry Cabot Lodge, however, believed in the reality of the Japanese menace, and he raised the question in the debate over the arbitration treaties in February 1912.[1]

The press, led by William Randolph Hearst, wrote in ominous tones about the threat of a Japanese naval base near the western United States. On 2 April, the Senate asked Taft to send any information the government might possess about the interest of Japan in Magdalena Bay. In the days that followed, both Japan and Mexico denied that any such thing as a naval installation was contemplated. The report of the Department of State, sent to lawmakers on 30 April 1912, stated authoritatively that there was "no evidence" of any attempt on the part of Japan to purchase land in Mexico.[2]

Although the nonexistent threat of Japan had been put to rest, Lodge felt impelled to make a general point. Working with Elihu Root, he persuaded the Foreign Relations Committee to adopt a resolution that "when any harbor, or other place in the American continent" might prove a threat to the United States if it came under the control of "any corporation or association which has such a relation to another Government, not American, as to give that Government practical power to control for national purposes," then the American government "could not see" such a development "without grave concern." The Senate adopted the Lodge resolution 51 to 4 on 2 August 1912.[3]

The Lodge Corollary to the Monroe Doctrine was not a document that Taft or Philander Knox endorsed. "I don't regard the Lodge resolution as very important," Taft wrote. "He has had this bee in his bonnet for some time, and he started in on Magdalena Bay, having been fooled by a lawyer who was hunting a defunct client." Taft added, "I should not feel under any obligation to follow a resolution like this."[4]

Another foreign policy issue, however, received presidential approval even though it contradicted his endorsement of arbitration as a way of settling international disputes. The Panama Canal was nearing completion and would likely go into operation within a few years. Congress began work on legislation to set out the rules and regulations under which the waterway would function. In the Hay–Pauncefote treaty of 1901, which had cleared the way for the United States to build a canal in Central America, Washington and London had agreed that the path between the seas would be open to shipping of all countries. Moreover, the negotiators decided that any tolls involving the projected canal should be "equitable" for all the nations involved. The treaty seemed to rule out any financial favoritism for American shipping.

When it came time to write the legislation in 1912, however, Congress and the president looked to an exemption from the payment of tolls for some American ships engaged in what was known as the coastwise trade. These vessels would be subsidized; the practical effect would be that some American ships would be charged less than foreign vessels. To Great Britain and other countries, the proposed American action seemed in clear violation of the express terms of the Hay–Pauncefote pact. The British issued strong protests against the American action, much to the displeasure of the president and Congress.[5]

Taft became convinced, however, that the United States had the right "to discriminate in favor of our own ships." He told Congress that it could do so, and of course the lawmakers readily complied because this policy would benefit their constituents engaged in the shipping trade. The British government then made a formal complaint about what it claimed was a breach of the Hay–Pauncefote pact. To many in the Senate, including Elihu Root, the British had the better of the argument. Nonetheless, the measure passed the House and was headed for enactment in the Senate. Taft, as he told his wife on 15 August 1912, was "not clear what ought to be done." Great Britain and critics of the president contended that this debate was a natural subject for the kind of arbitration the president had so recently favored. There was a treaty signed in 1908 that could have been used to facilitate that process. But now Taft worried that the arbitration he favored might result in a decision adverse to American interests.[6]

To meet that difficulty, the president proposed that Congress write legislation enabling the matter to be taken to the United States Supreme Court. The lawmakers refused to do so. Taft concluded that he would sign the bill and provide a message indicating why he had not vetoed it. "I suppose I shall create enemies in signing the bill, but that is what one usually

REPUDIATION OF TREATY

ELECTION BAITS

TH TOWNSEND 1912.

A MERE MATTER OF HONOUR.

President Taft. "HERE, SWALLOW THIS!"
America. "THANKS, I'M AN EAGLE; I'M NOT A VULTURE."

The British took a dim view of Taft's position on tolls for
the Panama Canal. Author's collection.

does and makes no friends. However, that is what politics is." Throughout the rest of his presidency, Taft remained adamant against arbitration of the tolls question. Even the urging of Elihu Root could not shake Taft from his position.[7]

The protracted session of Congress during the summer of 1912 also confronted Taft with the unresolved issues surrounding Secretary of War Henry L. Stimson's efforts to assert greater civilian control of the United States Army. Stimson and the chief of staff, Leonard Wood, clashed with Adjutant General Fred C. Ainsworth, who had, through his mastery of the bureaucracy of the army, amassed institutional power without any increase in military efficiency. A dispute between Wood and Ainsworth in early 1912 led the secretary to threaten Ainsworth with a court-martial if he did not retire. The general did so, but the events caused resentment on Capitol Hill, where Ainsworth had many allies.

In the army appropriation bill that came before Congress in the summer, many of the provisions echoed recommendations that Ainsworth had made about the future of the army. These would have the effect of permitting bureau chiefs such as Ainsworth to remain in power. When the Senate got the measure from the House, these sections were deleted, and the bill went to conference. That panel added riders limiting Stimson's capacity to close army posts. More important, another rider would have made Leonard Wood ineligible to hold the post of chief of staff. Stimson and Root made the case to the president that he could not allow Congress to dictate to him the choices he made to head the army. It took some pressure to persuade Taft who, in Root's estimate, was not "very bright about some things."[8]

Congress pressed on with its anti-Stimson and anti-Wood campaign throughout the summer. A reluctant Taft had to be pushed into a veto threat in mid-August. If he did not do so, Leonard Wood, about whom Taft had rather tepid opinions, would be ousted as chief of staff. As he reported to his wife on 23 August, "Yesterday they tried to get my consent to sign the Army bill, with the same old restriction against Wood, but I would not do it. I told them I would veto it, so they changed it in conference, and now it is about as well as our friend Stimson would wish to have it." The president's action was grudging, but in the end, he had done the right thing.[9]

Taft confronted the Magdalena Bay question, the Panama Canal tolls fight, and the furor over the army bill as he endeavored to get his general election campaign under way during the summer. Debate dragged on through July and August over the tariff and other contentious matters. The president's vetoes saved the commerce court from extinction at the hands of the Democrats. Taft also rejected opposition efforts to enact bills

Henry L. Stimson entered the cabinet in 1911 and became an important member of the administration during its final year. Library of Congress.

lowering the tariff on wool, iron, and steel. "Looking back over the whole session," Taft wrote on 26 August 1912, "I feel as if I had come out about as well as I had reason to expect. Those who are free traders and revenue for tariff men will continue to criticise me."[10]

With Archie Butt dead on the *Titanic* and Charles Hilles having departed to run the Republican campaign, Taft had few close advisers during that concluding summer of his presidency. He approached the fall campaign with the consolation that he had defeated Roosevelt for the nomination. "I can look forward to any result now with very considerable satisfaction," he wrote, "whether it leads me out of the White House or keeps me there four years more."[11]

His first choice, of course, was another four-year term, but that prospect seemed ever more remote as the summer elapsed. Throughout July, Roosevelt worked toward the organization of a third-party convention early in August. As he did so, the former president diminished Republican chances of victory against Woodrow Wilson, whom the Democrats had nominated in early July. So the president had to rally his party, put together a campaign organization, and stave off the perception that he was a foregone loser. His inclination was to avoid any campaigning himself that involved speaking tours such as those he had made in 1908. The existing custom was that an incumbent president did not campaign for another four years in office. Taft declared that he would observe that tradition in 1912. "I do not expect to take any part in the campaign," the president observed in mid-August, "following in that respect the tradition of former Presidents."[12]

Beyond that act of political self-denial, Taft intended to wage as vigorous a campaign as the Republicans and his surrogates could mount against Roosevelt and Wilson. Hilles was the natural choice to oversee this effort. He had demonstrated organizing skill in the primary races and the nomination chase, and he was acceptable to the president and party regulars. As Taft told his wife, "Hilles was the only one who had no enemies and no objections to him, and while he was reluctant to accept, he soon concluded that he was the only man really whom we could take."[13] There were not many other members of the Grand Old Party clamoring to head what seemed to be a doomed Taft cause. Hilles would prove to be an adept leader in the face of obstacles that even his energy could not overcome.

Once the chairmanship of the campaign had been resolved, there arose questions of the advisory committee to assist Hilles, as well as the even more vexed issue of fund-raising through a campaign treasurer. The departure of Roosevelt and his progressive followers had left the conservatives in control. Many of the regulars, such as Boies Penrose of

Pennsylvania and William A. Barnes Jr. of New York, had unsavory public reputations. Putting them in charge of the Taft canvass would confirm the allegations that Roosevelt had made about a boss-ruled Grand Old Party. Taft allocated these men to advisory committees where he could get their advice without making them too prominent in public. The matter of the campaign treasurer was more difficult. Hilles ran through an array of candidates before George R. Sheldon, a previous treasurer, again agreed to seek out donors for the president's effort.[14]

Because Roosevelt had based his bolt on the purported theft of convention delegates, the president spent much time in July arranging for a public statement of rebuttal to the charges of fraud and deceit. The controversy was arcane and dry, but it was necessary to answer Roosevelt's denunciation of what had happened in Chicago. It took most of July before the White House could issue a detailed response, based on the work of Samuel J. Elder and the other attorneys involved, which denied what Roosevelt had charged. In the end, all the work defending Taft's title to the nomination proved unnecessary. By early August, most of the sting had gone out of the issue, and Roosevelt had turned to other matters as a rationale for his third-party race.[15]

More difficult was the problem of competing Republican electors in states that the party needed to carry. During July 1912, Roosevelt toyed with the idea of running as a kind of quasi-Republican who would have the Republican electors chosen in the spring primaries be on the ballot for him on the Republican line. Taft and the party leadership rejected any such arrangement which they called an "outrage" and an "injustice." They insisted that only genuine Republicans committed to the president should serve as electors. Fighting the battle in the courts to ensure that pro-Taft electors were on the ballot took up needed time. The same was true for internal battles in states such as Ohio, where Taft's men worked to expel Roosevelt supporters from their positions. Even though Taft was the nominee, he still had to fight to assert his control of the party as the campaign drew near.[16]

With all these obstacles to his candidacy, Taft realized that his speech of acceptance would be crucial to his fading hopes of reelection. This occasion would be the one time when he might expect to dominate the news coverage amid the clamor for Roosevelt and Wilson. He decided to use the White House as the natural site for the event. There would not be any potential embarrassment from drawing only a small crowd at another location, and the press in Washington could provide the needed reports on what the president said.

Throughout July, while arguing with Congress amid the heat, Taft pulled the speech together. He wrote the address by himself, without any assistance. At first he intended to deal with the question of the disputed delegates and provide an answer to Roosevelt's charges. As the issue receded in the public mind, he decided to leave the rebuttal to Roosevelt to others. With 1 August scheduled as the date for the speech, Taft told his wife on 28 July 1912 that he had fifty minutes in hand. "I don't know that that is too long, although I could wish to make it shorter. I am going over so much ground that I have covered before that it seems stale, and I don't care for it much at any rate, but I have got to get through the business and set my teeth."[17]

As he readied his speech, Taft mused about the impact of Roosevelt and his third-party candidacy. "The Bull Moose continues to roar as much as ever, but I don't think he frightens as many people. Sometimes I think I might as well give up so far as being a candidate is concerned. There are so many people in the country who don't like me." Contemplating his own record in a letter to his wife, Taft added: "I have strengthened the Supreme Bench, have given a good deal of new and valuable legislation, have not interfered with business, have kept the peace, and on the whole have led people to pursue their various occupations without interruption. It is a very humdrum, uninteresting administration, and does not attract the attention or enthusiasm of anybody, but after I am out, I think that you and I can look back with some pleasure in having done something for the benefit of the public weal."[18]

Before a gathering that included his wife, Elihu Root, who introduced him, and several hundred invited guests, the president delivered his acceptance speech on 1 August. He did not mention Roosevelt by name, referring to him only as "the leader of former Republicans who have left their party." He said that Roosevelt and Wilson, if not socialists themselves, followed policies that "lead directly toward the appropriation of what belongs to one man, to another." The Constitution "as it is" was "the supreme issue" in the campaign, and neither the Democrats nor the Progressives were "to be trusted on this subject." He praised the Payne–Aldrich tariff and warned that Democratic success would mean "a recurrence of the hard times that we had between 1890 and 1897." Taft defended his trust policies and opposed the strengthening of the antitrust law that the Democrats favored. Above all, "it is greatly in the interest of the people to maintain the solidarity of the Republican Party for future usefulness and to continue it and its policies in control of the destinies of the Nation."[19]

In the course of his remarks, the president took credit for the positive accomplishments of his administration. He praised the adoption of postal savings legislation, the creation of the Children's Bureau, the Mann–Elkins act, and the antitrust policy that he and Attorney General Wickersham had followed. In foreign affairs, he pointed to the arbitration treaties, the buildup of the navy, and the increase in foreign trade. Of the Mexican revolution, he warned against involvement in the internal affairs of that country. "I am very sure that the course of self-restraint the administration has pursued in respect to Mexico will vindicate itself in the pages of history."[20]

Taft gave a good, fighting speech, but his problem was that the country had ceased to accord him its attention. A Republican who went to the Taft campaign headquarters in New York in mid-August contrasted the scene there with a visit to the Wilson offices. The Democrats had "a corps of people hustling and bustling with every one confident that they were going to win and inspiring all visitors with the same belief." At the Taft rooms, "he found gloom on every floor and idleness in every room." The verdict was that "some ginger must be infused into this campaign or we will lose so much ground that he will not be able to regain it." Nothing Taft said did much to disturb the gloomy mood among the Republicans.[21]

During the week that followed, Wilson delivered his acceptance address. The president called it "milk and water." Nonetheless, the Democratic candidate had everything going his way in the electoral contest. At the same time, Roosevelt and his followers held their Progressive convention in Chicago. Amid scenes of revivalist enthusiasm, the third party took to the hustings. Roosevelt had a contagious magnetism that Taft lacked. Taft described his former friend as one of "the leaders of religious cults who promote things over their followers by any sort of physical manipulation and deception." As he began his campaign in mid-August in New England, Roosevelt dominated the headlines. Taft complained that "the campaign moves slowly" during the dull season in Washington. "Everybody is away and it is hard to collect money, and money is essential to the running of a campaign." Taft's lament well described the problems of the president's reelection effort in August 1912.[22]

After his speech, Taft made a brief visit to Ohio. While he was there, a foreign policy issue reappeared. In Nicaragua, even though the treaty with that country had been shelved, loans from American bankers and the government had continued. Unhappiness with those in power culminated in an insurrection at the end of July 1912, led by Luis Mena, the incumbent minister of war. Secretary of State Knox authorized a detachment of 100 marines to the capital at Managua. He passed responsibility for dealing further with the crisis to his second in command, Francis Huntington Wilson, and left for Japan, where he represented the United States at the funeral of the emperor.[23]

Huntington Wilson favored an aggressive approach to events in Nicaragua. He informed the White House that the United States needed to put more troops into the country to keep order and protect American interests.

By the end of August, he was requesting Taft to introduce enough American troops into the country to establish effective control of the situation. At that point, Secretary of War Henry Stimson argued to the vacationing Taft that putting an army regiment into Nicaragua would not sit well with public opinion in Latin America. The president concluded that Wilson had overstated the danger and was gratified that he had been able "to keep the army out of these disturbances in Central America."[24]

Despite Taft's prudence about introducing more troops into Nicaragua, this episode had lasting consequences for American foreign policy in Latin America. A small detachment of 130 Marines remained in the country, ostensibly to guard the legation. In fact, the force was a kind of warning to the warring factions in Nicaragua that they should not commence fighting with each other again, lest the Americans return in larger numbers. A long-term involvement with the political fortunes of the country was thus one of the legacies of the Taft administration's approach to Latin America.

Taft and the Democrats both wanted to end the 1912 congressional session. The president needed rest after the exertions of the nomination campaign. The opposition party wanted to be on the campaign trail to claim the victory in both the presidential contest and the congressional battle that seemed likely to occur. Throughout August, the two sides wrangled over the familiar issue of the tariff. The Democrats sent the White House bills they knew that Taft would veto. In so doing, they buttressed their argument that Republican protectionism was responsible for the high prices that consumers paid. Taft countered that voting Democratic would pose a threat to the economic prosperity the country enjoyed. With the two sides deadlocked, Congress adjourned without accomplishing much beyond the enactment of necessary appropriation measures. "Looking back over the whole session," the president wrote, "I feel as if I had come out about as well as I had reason to expect."[25]

True to his word, Taft did not in the weeks that followed take an active speaking part in the presidential campaign. He went to Beverly, Massachusetts, for a vacation, and spent his time traveling around New England during September. His appearances were ostensibly nonpartisan as he discussed the "common soldier of the civil war" before the Vermont legislature in October and the Maine Teachers Association later in the month. His vacation extended until almost the end of October. He entertained a delegation of Jews who came out for his reelection, and he praised the historical contributions of Poles in an address to the National Polish Alliance. These gestures toward key ethnic groups were an element in the president's reelection strategy, but not one that he pursued with great energy during his time away from Washington.[26]

The president issued frequent statements on the election and granted a series of interviews to put his views out before the voters. He doubted that dissident Republicans would in the end "commit hara-kiri" by voting for the Progressive candidate. In a public letter to the governor of Minnesota, he said that "the Democratic platform promises a change in our tariff system whose effect would be to halt manufacturing enterprise, throw out of employment thousands of wage earners, and destroy the home markets now enjoyed by the American farmer." The choice for Taft was simple: "On one side, prosperity and real progress, on the other, a leap in the dark."[27]

As the campaign wore on, Taft indulged in the hope that the voters might be turning his way. "The situation is foggy and not rosy," he told Vice President James Sherman on 24 August, "but I believe that the reaction toward sanity and regularity is beginning to manifest itself." By late September, he was arguing to his secretary of commerce that "the splendid headway that we have made in the last two or three weeks is so gratifying and the nearness of victory is so inspiring that it needs but a nerve-straining final effort to pull us through." On the eve of the contest, he told his brother Horace, "If we win we win by a very close margin, and whether we win or not, I sincerely hope that we shall beat Roosevelt in most of the States."[28]

More objective observers among the Republicans recognized that Taft's cause was almost certainly hopeless. "Political conditions are certainly in a chaotic state," wrote Secretary of the Navy George Meyer on 3 September 1912, "and the trend is towards a Democratic victory at the present moment." Chairman Hilles complained that "we are hard pressed for money. The fight has been carried on by the National Committee with only a minimum of assistance." There were complaints about Taft's passivity as a candidate. Only a few of the cabinet officers campaigned, and their presence on the stump did not match the drawing power of the president himself. The Republican effort in the autumn of 1912 was essentially leaderless as far as surrogate speakers for the president were concerned. There was even a Taft campaign song for the three-way race:

> Shout then for Taft, he is on the safest craft,
> Working for the right and for YOU,
> "Bull Moose" may blow, Woodrow Wilson he may row,
> But 'tis Billy puts the "Old Ship" through.[29]

In mid-October, with the optimism that losing campaigns often discover, Taft convinced himself that the tide was turning his way. The good economic conditions were supposed to portend a Republican victory.

The assassination attempt on Roosevelt on October 14 disrupted whatever momentum the president might have achieved. Some Republicans
decided that it would be better for Wilson to win if it ensured the defeat
of Roosevelt and the Progressives. "To my mind," wrote Elihu Root, "the
really important thing at stake in the election is the question whether the
Republican party shall be captured by Populism."[30]

Taft's bad luck continued right down to the eve of the election. Vice
President Sherman died on 31 October from the chronic heart disease that
had troubled him throughout the administration. The New Yorker had
not been close to Taft, who largely excluded Sherman from any serious
decision making.[31] It does not seem to have occurred to the president to
employ this former member of the House as a positive link with Capitol
Hill. The party selected the president of Columbia University, Nicholas
Murray Butler, as Sherman's replacement. It was an empty procedural
gesture because by early November 1912, no one expected Taft to win.
The question was whether he might finish second to Wilson and outpoll
Theodore Roosevelt. Taft held out hope that he might somehow pull off
a victory, though in his rational moments, he knew that the odds were
against such an outcome.

It did not take long on election night to determine that Taft was coming in a very distant third behind the other two candidates. The president
carried only Vermont and Utah. Wilson achieved a landslide electoral college triumph with 435 votes to Roosevelt's 88 and Taft's 8. Roosevelt ran
second in the popular vote, with more than 700,000 ballots ahead of Taft's
total. The Democrats swept the House of Representatives and regained
control of the Senate. Taft wired the victor: "I cordially congratulate you
on your election, and extend to you my best wishes for a successful administration." A few days later, Speaker of the House Champ Clark, whom
Wilson had defeated at the Democratic National Convention, came by to
see the president. With a wink to Taft, Clark observed: "Well, we are more
handsome than he is anyhow."[32]

It was as thorough a repudiation of Taft and his administration as
anyone could have predicted. Taft wrote a friend three days after the election: "The vote in favor of Mr. Roosevelt was greater than I expected, and
to that extent the result was a disappointment." He had hoped for victory,
"but in my heart was making preparations for the future to be lived outside the White House."[33] The president's fate had really been determined
once Roosevelt decided to bolt the party after the national convention. As
Hilles wrote a week after the voting, "with one or two exceptions, all of
the devoted friends of the President disappeared in the crisis, after they
saw no satisfaction in contemplating the outcome."[34]

In letters consoling Taft, some of the correspondents expressed anger

James S. "Sunny Jim" Sherman did not play a large role in the Taft administration. Library of Congress.

at what Roosevelt had done to the party and to Taft himself. The president took a calmer tone. "The defeat has its compensations, for I have a very great sense of relief. I shall be content to await history's taking of the trial balance of the administration." To an old friend and member of the Longworth family, Taft was even more expansive about his situation. "The people of the United States did not owe me another election. I hope I am properly grateful for the one term of the presidency which they gave me, and the fact that they withheld the second is no occasion for my resentment or feeling a sense of injustice." As he wrote this letter, Taft saw his sister-in-law's children playing on the White House lawn and the Washington Monument in the distance, looking down on the scene "with benignity and encouragement. It exercises the same office with me. This is the only country we have, my dear Nannie, and we have to make the best of it; and such popular manifestations as we had the other day are not to be taken as an evidence of governmental incapacity."[35]

The president's serenity did not extend to Theodore Roosevelt and the Republicans who had defected from the party. "I am concerned," he wrote, "lest there be a spirit of compromise which will give to Roosevelt some control over the party and some power to push his pernicious principles of fundamental constitutional changes and a destruction of our constitutional limitations." The president thought that "many of our universities are becoming the seed-plots of socialism." Accordingly, the Republicans "ought to begin a propaganda on the subject." The mild progressivism that had come with Taft into the White House had hardened into a much more conservative posture after his treatment at the hands of Roosevelt and the progressives in the Republicans' ranks.[36]

There remained for Taft four months of transition before he left the White House. He planned another trip to the Panama Canal Zone to inspect the work on the waterway. There were also the problems of what he would do to make a living after the presidency and where he and Mrs. Taft would live. And, of course, the lame-duck session of Congress would start in December 1912 with the victorious Democrats anxious to get the Wilson presidency off to a running start. For William Howard Taft, the transition to Woodrow Wilson and private life provided more substantive work for the defeated chief executive. His tenure in the White House would remain a controversial one right down to 4 March 1913.

14

★ ★ ★ ★ ★

LEAVING THE WHITE HOUSE

The last four months of William Howard Taft's administration proved more turbulent than most such transitions from one president to another. The relationship between Taft and the president-elect was amicable and smooth. Taft did all he could to ensure that the changeover of power to Woodrow Wilson was accomplished in a harmonious manner. Where trouble arose was with Congress and in foreign policy. The thorny issues that the country faced, including immigration, prohibition, and Mexico, kept Taft engaged right down to 4 March 1913. At the same time, the press and the country pondered what had been accomplished since 1909 and how the Taft presidency would be judged.

The recipient of an overwhelming defeat at the polls, Taft had little reason to examine what he might have done in a different way with the voters. He displayed no outward trace of anger at the verdict of the people. In fact, his sunny acceptance of the outcome and his lack of recrimination won popular applause for good sportsmanship. There was a sense that although he had been defeated for reelection, as president, Taft had done his best for the country. The press did not treat him as a "failed" president, but rather as a chief executive whose hopes for a second term had encountered Roosevelt's ambition and the country's desire for a change in leadership. As a result, there was a harmony and calm about Taft's departure that helped smooth his process of moving back to private life.

In the weeks after the voting, Taft assured Republicans and the public that he did not intend to be a candidate in 1916. "I am very glad to have had the opportunity to be President," he told a reporter from the New

York *World*. "My tastes had been and still are judicial, but there is a very wide field of usefulness for a President." He predicted that the Democrats would in time fall short with the public, and the Republicans must be "ready to prevent that disappointment from being used by the bull moose and socialist combination to get into power."[1]

Taft appeared at a dinner of the Lotos Club in New York City on 16 November with a speech responding to the toast "The President." In a reflective, philosophical mood, the retiring executive gave an address "which many of his hearers considered the most remarkable he has ever made." Taft came out for a six-year term for presidents and pooh-poohed the idea of William Jennings Bryan that former presidents should sit in the Senate, but did recommend that members of the cabinet should be participants in the deliberations of Congress. He regretted again the failure to achieve approval of his arbitration treaties.[2]

Of his own experience in the White House, he recalled the boundaries on what a president could accomplish that were inherent in the American system of government. "What chiefly stares him in the face," Taft said, "in carrying out any plan of his is the limitation upon the power and not its extent." He added that "in spite of the very emphatic verdict by which I leave the office, I cherish only the deepest gratitude to the American people for having given me the honor of having held office." Taft closed his remarks by proposing a toast that brought the audience to its feet: "Health and success to the able, distinguished and patriotic gentleman who is to be the next President of the United States."[3]

For the three and a half months that remained of his term, Taft settled back into his familiar White House routine. After managing the Republican campaign, Charles D. Hilles returned to his post as presidential secretary. The annual message had to be written and a lame-duck Congress confronted. With the Democrats ready to take control of both houses in March, little that Taft wanted would be accomplished. His appointees would be held up and his initiatives stalled. At the same time, several popular pieces of legislation would move forward, in hopes that the president would not veto them or that his disapproval could be overridden. A measure to restrict immigration gathered supporters. At the same time, the advocates of the prohibition of alcoholic beverages prepared to enact a law barring the shipment of liquor from wet states into ones that had voted dry.

Above all, Taft now had to decide how he was going to make a living once he left the presidency. He and Mrs. Taft had been very thrifty during their years in the White House and had saved as much as $2,000 per month from his salary. He had amassed savings of $100,000 since 1909. Taft would tell Woodrow Wilson that a chief executive could do well on the $75,000 per year that the American people provided to their president. Nonetheless, the Tafts could not live on the income from their investments. What was he to do after 4 March 1913 that would be dignified and suitable for a former president?[4]

An obvious choice was to take up the practice of law. He talked of going back to Cincinnati and pursuing his profession. A moment's thought, however, produced obstacles to such a career path. Taft had appointed many of the judges on the federal bench, and the question of an appearance of a conflict of interest could well arise if he took up cases involving federal questions. As he thought about it, the president decided that "I could not practice as an advocate."[5]

A workable solution emerged out of Taft's connection with Yale University, where he had been a fellow of the Yale Corporation since 1906. The administration of the university suggested to Taft in mid-November 1912 that he take up teaching duties as a professor in the law school. "The proposition has some very attractive features about it," the president wrote to his brothers. "I do not retire to the practice of law; I retire to the academic shades of Yale to teach it, and this very act takes me out of the maelstrom of politics. It is a dignified retirement, one which [Grover] Cleveland had at Princeton, and one which would approve itself to the general sense of propriety of the country."[6]

The arrangements went forward during December 1912 and January 1913. Taft became the Kent Professor of Law in Yale College on 20 January 1913 at a salary of $5,000 per year. He set about finding a house to rent in New Haven and preparing for his new academic duties. The ideological implications of the post added to the allure of the job. He wrote to the *Yale Daily News* in late February: "I am coming back to Yale" to teach law because of the need "that our young men shall appreciate the Constitution of the United States, under which we have enjoyed so many blessings and under which we must work out our political and economic salvation." The fundamental document needed defense from "a class of fanatical enthusiasts seeking short cuts to economic perfection" and "unscrupulous demagogues" who promoted "disrespect and even contempt for the Constitution and the laws enacted under it."[7]

With his professional future arranged, Taft then addressed the remaining obligations of his presidency. Mindful of what he did not know about the nation's highest office in March 1909, Taft reached out to Wilson with invitations to talk about how the White House worked. Taft asked the Wilsons to accompany the president and his wife on an inspection trip to Panama in December. Wilson declined and added "that it is doubtful whether I ought to give myself even the indulgence of a day off at Washington to enjoy your hospitality, so graciously offered." Newspapers noted that turning down a request from the president to visit the White House was an innovation for the New Jersey governor.[8]

As a result, Taft wrote Wilson at length to fill him in on how a president lived and what the costs of occupying the White House would be. Apparently, Taft and Theodore Roosevelt had not touched on such tangible matters in the 1908–1909 transition period. "Congress is very generous to the President," he informed Wilson. When all the incidentals were added up that the chief executive received, from the Marine Band to money for laundry, the upshot was that "the salary of $75,000, with $25,000 for traveling expenses," was "very much more than is generally supposed." The president-elect found Taft's candid advice very useful as he prepared to leave New Jersey for Washington.[9]

Taft had already broken all existing records for presidential travel, but there was one more trip he made before relinquishing his power. He wanted to inspect the work on the Panama Canal as the waterway neared completion. During the time that Congress was away over the Christmas holidays, Taft left Washington and spent a week examining the progress that had been made in the two years since his last tour. It was, as the newspapers noted, his third trip to the isthmus since his election to the presidency. During his stay, Taft had to leap from the tug that took him from the harbor at Colon to the battleship *Arkansas* as waves rocked the naval vessel. "As he jumped aboard," the ship's executive officer "grabbed him with both hands and welcomed him with a fervor begot of fear."[10]

The president also decided to name Colonel George Washington Goethals the governor of the Canal Zone and to reorganize the government of the zone as operation of the canal would get under way in 1914. Although the canal would not be opened during Taft's presidency, he had carried forward the work begun under Theodore Roosevelt. The trip to the canal also did not alter the president's conviction of the right of the United States to use Panama Canal tolls to favor American shipping. He refused to reconsider his position on that issue during the waning months of his administration. It would be left to Woodrow Wilson to push through repeal of the Panama Canal tolls legislation in 1914.[11]

By the time Taft left for Panama, he had been dealing with the final session of the Sixty-second Congress for two weeks. He went through the ritual of preparing his annual message without any illusions that his words would persuade Democratic legislators to implement his ideas. As now had become customary for Taft, he sent the message to Capitol Hill in three parts, the first on foreign policy, the second on judicial and fiscal matters, and the third on the work of the other departments. The transmission of the documents stretched over almost two weeks, and their impact, already lessened because of the result of the election, was further attenuated. Under Taft, the annual messages had lost a good deal of their power to attract public attention.

In his remarks about the tariff, the president recognized that "a new Congress has been elected on a platform of a tariff for revenue only rather than a protective tariff, and is to revise the tariff on this basis." He did not provide a sustained defense of his policies because "it is needless for me to occupy the time of this Congress with arguments or recommendations in favor of a protective tariff."[12] Taft, of course, did not know that the adoption of the Underwood tariff in 1913 and the inclusion of an income tax would further diminish the relevance of the protective tariff in American politics. In the same way that the annual message under Taft was becoming an anachronism, the generations of debate about the tariff issue as central to national politics were coming to a close by the end of 1912.

The second part of Taft's annual message on domestic issues touched on a subject that would dominate the deliberations of the incoming Wilson administration in 1913. After the Panic of 1907, Congress had created the National Monetary Commission, chaired by Senator Nelson Aldrich, to propose reforms in the banking system to prevent future disturbances and disruptions to the nation's finances. The commission issued its report in February 1912 recommending a central bank. In the political climate of that election year, the support of the banking community for the change was not enough to move lawmakers to take action.

The Democrats, their confidence in victory growing, did not want to hand the Republicans a success in Congress. The Republicans disliked the idea of being identified with the still unpopular former Rhode Island senator. Therefore, little was done in the way of actual legislation. Instead, the Democrats decided to conduct a probe of the "Money Trust," which began in the spring and then resumed in December when Congress reconvened. Led by Representative Arsene Pujo of Louisiana, the inquiry would produce sensational revelations about the extent of banker influence on the economy. When Taft told Congress that "there is no class in the community whose experience better qualifies them to make suggestions as to the sufficiency of a currency and banking system than the bankers and business men," he illustrated how out of touch he was about the attitudes and proposals of the incoming administration.[13]

A new issue that would shape domestic debate for the next two decades appeared during the Taft–Wilson transition. The Anti-Saloon League, founded in 1895, pushed for national prohibition for the manufacture and sale of alcoholic products. One problem this cultural crusade encountered was the interstate shipment of liquor from states where alcohol was legal into states that had adopted prohibition. To end this practice, prohibitionists (drys) in Congress introduced legislation to outlaw such sales. The bill, sponsored by Democrat E. Y. Webb of North Carolina in the House and Republican William S. Kenyon in the Senate, was very popular with lawmakers in the lame-duck session. The measure passed both houses with large majorities in mid-February 1913.

Taft had little sympathy for the prohibition cause. He did not drink, except on very rare occasions. Before taking office, he won praise from the drys when they concluded from his own temperate approach that he would not serve alcohol in the White House. The president soon disabused the Anti-Saloon League and others of their error. He planned to serve alcohol to his guests, especially because Mrs. Taft saw no reason to deprive visitors of beverages she regarded as civilized and sophisticated. There was also criticism when the president accepted a gift from a prominent brewer for his twenty-fifth wedding anniversary. This cultural tolerance in the White House grated on the prohibitionists during Taft's administration. Protestant leaders resented that he played cards on the Sabbath. Added to his Unitarian faith, the president's apparent insensitivity to these religious questions fed suspicions about his piety.[14]

When it came time to consider the Webb–Kenyon bill, Taft looked first to the constitutional issues. He decided that the measure violated "the interstate commerce clause of the Constitution, in that it is in substance and effect a delegation by Congress to the States of the power to regulate interstate commerce in liquors which is vested exclusively in Congress." Both houses brushed aside these arguments. The Senate spent only half an hour debating the veto message before it overrode the veto by a vote of 63 to 21. The next day the House took the same action with 246 voting to override and 85 against. A year later, the general secretary of the Temperance Society of the Methodist Church said that Taft's veto had been "true to his whole liquor record" as president.[15]

Another bill that Taft vetoed during this busy lame-duck session addressed the controversial issue of immigration. Restricting the flow of newcomers to the United States, especially those from southern and eastern Europe, had long been a goal of nativist sentiment within the Republican Party. The president and the administration had not invested much political capital in the immigration issue. He supported the continuation of the gentlemen's agreement with Japan and negotiated an extension of the commercial treaty between the two countries while dropping language that asserted an American right to bar Japanese workers. Instead, the exclusion policy toward the Japanese rested on the rights of the United States as a sovereign nation to regulate immigration.

On the larger matter of restricting immigration from Europe, the administration waited for the recommendations of the Dillingham Commission, created in 1907 to study immigration issues and recommend policy changes. The panel issued its findings in December 1910. One key proposal was a literacy test for prospective immigrants based on understanding words in the Constitution. Restrictionists favored this approach, which would have fallen hardest on new arrivals from southern and eastern Europe. Before the start of the presidential campaign, both the Senate and the House adopted bills limiting immigration. Further deliberations paused until the voters spoke. In the campaign, Taft appealed for the votes of immigrants in several speeches and appearances during the fall before Italian American and Polish American groups.[16]

Once Taft had lost, Congress sent him by large votes in both houses a bill with a literacy test and other restrictive language. The measure reached the president on 1 February 1913. Taft spent several days listening to proponents and critics of the legislation. On the basis of the advice of his secretary of commerce and labor, Charles Nagel, in the end he decided to veto the bill. Nagel, sympathetic to the immigrants, asserted in a letter to Taft that the literacy test "would embrace probably in large part undesirable but also a great many desirable people" and would cause "embarrassment, expense, and distress to those who seek to enter" that "would be out of all proportion to any good that can possibly be promised for this measure." Nagel argued that "we need labor in this country, and the natives are unwilling to do the work which the aliens come over to do." Moreover, "the character of the people who come to stay" in the United States belied the charges of the critics of immigration. Nagel advised a veto.[17]

Taft sent in the message with Nagel's letter in support. The Senate overrode the veto by a 72 to 18 count. In the House, the tally was 213 to 114, five votes shy of the two thirds required. One Republican told the president "it was deemed by everybody to be one of the most courageous and creditable things you ever did." In the end, the movement for immigration restriction would prevail in the early 1920s, but for the moment, Taft had delivered a setback to that cause. Just as in his treatment of Jews during his administration, Taft displayed a vein of tolerance and inclusion that did him credit in this area.[18]

The foreign policy problems that the Taft administration had confronted would now be passed on to the Democratic administration. In the case of China, which had formed such a large feature of the dollar diplomacy policy of the Taft years, the White House withheld recognition of the Chinese republic. Instead, the United States was, Taft told Congress in December 1912, "according to precedent, maintaining full and friendly *de facto* relations with the provisional Government." In his annual message, Taft reviewed the efforts of the powers in the Far East to work out a loan for the Chinese government. The prospective lenders had set forth conditions that the Chinese would have to accept. The government in China refused to do so, and the matter remained in limbo as the Taft administration wound down.[19]

In the final days of the administration, the question about what to do regarding the volatile situation in revolutionary Mexico imparted something of an air of crisis to the close of the Taft presidency. The government of Francisco Madero, created in 1911 after Porfirio Diaz was overthrown, had not established itself in power, and its enemies within Mexico looked for ways to oust the new president. Ambassador Henry Lane Wilson, long a critic of Madero and a friend to conservatives within Mexico, put his political influence and the prospect of American support behind the potential counterrevolutionaries. In mid-February, the insurgency, led by Victoriano Huerta, arrested Madero and imprisoned him. Four days later, on 22 February, Madero and an associate were shot. Wilson was privy to the plot and encouraged it.[20]

Wilson had urged Taft and the State Department to intervene in Mexico to protect American citizens when the uprising against Madero started. He fired off such requests to Washington in ways that would have committed the United States to political and military action. The administration took some steps to ready the army and navy for possible use in Mexico. The most immediate question was whether Washington would recognize the new government under Huerta, as Wilson wished them to do. Taft and Secretary of State Knox were cautious about that kind of commitment. Taft did not wish to tie the hands of the incoming president, whose "policy may be very different from mine."[21]

At a dinner of the American Peace and Arbitration League in New York City on 22 February 1913, the president said that he had no sympathy for a course "which would prompt us for purposes of exploitation and gain to invade another country and involve ourselves in a war the extent of which we could not realize, and sacrifice thousands of lives and millions of treasure." The Mexican problem, which would so trouble Woodrow Wilson, was also passed on to the new president on 4 March 1913.[22]

As Taft approached the end of his administration, newspapers and magazines summed up his record in office. Unlike the verdict of future historians, the theme was not of a failed presidency but rather of one that mixed political defeats with positive results. The dominant note was one of respect for Taft's human qualities. "Few Presidents," wrote the editors of the *Philadelphia Inquirer*, "have gone into retirement with so much personal good feeling following him as Taft." His serenity in the face of his overwhelming defeat made him "the worst licked, best liked, and least sore" of all presidents, concluded the Portland *Oregonian*.[23]

In analyzing Taft's record, the press followed the lead of the *New York*

Times, which called him "the victim of too much Roosevelt." The *Times* believed Taft was mistaken in submitting "so meekly to the Roosevelt dominance" at the outset of his administration. Other editors noted that Taft failed to emulate his predecessor. "The people had become accustomed to Mr. Roosevelt's constant series of sensations. The placid calm with which Mr. Taft went about his work fell upon them like a wet blanket." The *Outlook,* which still reflected the views of Theodore Roosevelt, concluded that "it is because the American people have resolved to secure a further development of democracy, both in government and in industry, that they have rejected the counsel and the leadership of Mr. Taft."[24]

The Payne–Aldrich tariff seemed to symbolize the drawbacks of the Taft presidency. He had failed to carry the fight to the standpatters in the Congress and had erred in endorsing Nelson Aldrich and other party leaders. Other writers decided that he had mishandled the Ballinger–Pinchot battle and had been too close to the conservative wing of the party. As for Canadian reciprocity, his aims were noble, but his public statements contributed to the defeat of the agreement. Few writers mentioned dollar diplomacy. Taft's call for international arbitration and his desire for world peace drew much praise. The impression of ineptitude was mixed with admiration for his values. His enemies called him "that good, honest, well-meaning, likable but blundering Taft."[25]

When Taft departed, no president had served two full elected terms since Ulysses S. Grant between 1869 and 1877. Thus Taft's failure to achieve a second term did not connote to contemporary writers the verdict of presidential ineptitude that would become so common during the rest of the twentieth century. He was defeated and repudiated, but not consigned to historical obscurity. His genial human qualities outweighed political disagreements. Ellen Maury Slayden, the wife of a Texas Democratic member of the House, observed a few months later that "of all presidents I have known, Taft is the most perfect everyday gentleman." The *Wilkes-Barre Times Leader* caught something of the popular mood in March 1913 when it said that "President Taft has made as good a President as conditions would allow and history will be kind to him. He leaves tomorrow with the best wishes of his countrymen."[26]

The outgoing president retained his sunny disposition as 4 March 1913 approached. He spoke at the National Press Club on 1 March 1913, where he told the audience of newspaper reporters that "my sin is an indisposition to labor as hard as I might; a disposition to procrastinate and a disposition to enjoy the fellowship of others more than I ought." Taft exaggerated his own tendencies in these areas, but historians have taken this statement as literal fact. He added that he had been in public life since the age of twenty-one and had little about which to complain in how his career had unfolded. "Now, gentlemen, after that record, still in health, do you suppose that I have an occasion for kicking and squealing? What kind of man would I be if I did, with the measure all on my side?"[27]

Three days later, the inauguration occurred. The weather was pleasant, and the outgoing president remained in a genial mood. He gave the Wilsons an informal luncheon before leaving the White House at around three o'clock to catch his train for Augusta, Georgia, and a golf vacation. As the Tafts drove through the streets of Washington, they could hear the bands playing for the new president. Spectators cheered the couple, and a small crowd at Union Station clapped for them as they boarded the train.[28]

Taft settled into his teaching routine at Yale and fended off questions about Wilson's performance as president. "I wish to keep as far in the background as I can," he told Mabel Boardman in April 1913. "I have grown fully used to reading the papers without my name in them, and it is not an unpleasant change."[29]

The eight years of Wilson's administration were a productive time for the former president. He lost the weight he had gained in the White House, and he never went back over 300 pounds for the rest of his life. He wrote several books on the presidency in which he took issue with Theodore Roosevelt's expansive view of the powers of the office. The idea, expressed by Roosevelt, he wrote in 1916, that there existed "an undefined residuum of power to the President" was "an unsafe doctrine that . . . might lead under emergencies to results of an arbitrary character, doing irremediable injustice to private right."[30]

He presided over the League to Enforce Peace, which sought an international organization to maintain the peace once World War I ended. During the conflict, he served on the War Labor Board at President Wilson's request. From late 1917 until he became chief justice of the United States, Taft wrote a newspaper column in which he analyzed the news of the day and drew on his own experiences as a chief executive.[31]

Despite occasional flurries about another race for the White House, Taft knew that his office-seeking days were over. He became a critic of Wilson's domestic policies and supported Charles Evans Hughes in 1916. Two years later, a reconciliation with Theodore Roosevelt was arranged to help the Republican cause in the election of 1918. "I don't know that he has changed his opinion on the issues of the past, but I think we were both glad to come into friendly relation again. Life is too short to cherish these resentments, and while one should not in future action ignore the lessons of the past, one may well forgive and forget so far as associations are concerned." In the next sentence, however, Taft spoke of Roosevelt's "absorbing egotism" that "makes him very unjust in dealing with those

The outgoing president posed with his successor on 4 March 1913 looking glad to be putting down the burdens of office. Library of Congress.

whom fortune has put on a level with him, and who independently mark out a policy for themselves to meet their responsibilities."[32]

Taft's return to public life came with the election of Warren G. Harding to the presidency in 1920. When Chief Justice Edward Douglass White died in May 1921, a lobbying campaign for Taft culminated in his nomination several weeks later. The Senate acted to confirm him, with only four dissenting votes. William Howard Taft was now where he had always wanted most to be: the chief justice of the United States. Four years after taking his seat on the Court, he wrote to a friend: "The truth is that in my present life I don't remember that I ever was president."[33]

During his years as chief justice, Taft reorganized the lower court system and secured the construction of the present Supreme Court building. In his decisions and judicial conferences, he guided a conservative majority toward rulings that buttressed business and limited the rights of unions. He was a successful leader and a hard worker as a jurist. The tales of procrastination and allegations of laziness that had marked his presidency were no longer current. By the late 1920s, however, the aging Taft was in increasingly poor health. He resigned from the Supreme Court in February 1930 and died on 8 March.[34]

Taft forged ahead of Roosevelt at first in the biographical sweepstakes. After depicting Roosevelt as a perennial adolescent in his 1931 life, Henry F. Pringle wrote a thorough, well-received two-volume study of Taft that appeared in 1939. It argued that Taft had been justified in the removal of Gifford Pinchot in 1910 and that Richard A. Ballinger had been wrongly accused of corruption. The book soon became and has remained the standard work on Taft's life. It also set the pattern for subsequent Taft biographies in its use of sources. Confronted with the extensive Taft papers, Pringle relied on the easily available letter books that his subject maintained. Incoming correspondence received less attention, and the collections of Taft's friends and colleagues were for the most part ignored.

After World War II, the historical reputations of Theodore Roosevelt and Woodrow Wilson ascended among historians. The writings of George E. Mowry and John Morton Blum on Roosevelt and the masterful biographical volumes on Wilson of Arthur Link put Taft in the shadow of these two significant chief executives. When Arthur M. Schlesinger Sr. first conducted a poll of historians about ranking the presidents in 1948, Taft came in sixteenth of the thirty-two chief executives being appraised. In the six decades that followed, his place among the presidents changed little. He rose as high as nineteenth in one 1982 survey and fell to twenty-fourth in another. When such a poll was taken in 2005, he stood at twentieth out of the forty-three presidents. On the eve of the 2008 election, the London *Times* had Taft in twenty-ninth place, tied with Benjamin Harrison, and behind such predecessors as Andrew Johnson and Chester Alan Arthur. The main criticism of Taft was that he had such a sweeping defeat in his reelection bid.[35]

During the recent half century, there has not been a genuine surge of interest in Taft's performance in the White House among biographers and scholars. In 1973, Paolo Coletta wrote *The Presidency of William Howard Taft* for the then-new University Press of Kansas series on the presidents. Although he stressed Taft's conservative philosophy, Coletta found more positive aspects to his subject's performance in office. Nonetheless, Coletta's verdict did little to raise Taft's stature with political scientists and historians.

Donald F. Anderson used Taft's outgoing letters to trace his conservative approach to the presidency in a volume that appeared the same year as Coletta's study. In 1981, Judith Icke Anderson, a student of Fawn Brodie, explored Taft's "intimate history" in a biography that concentrated on the psychological aspects of Taft's weight and his marriage in assessing his problems in the White House.[36]

Twenty-two years later, Michael L. Bromley's *William Howard Taft and the First Motoring Presidency* (2003) used the theme of the president's interaction with cars to provide a favorable and informed assessment of his record in the White House. There is no evidence, however, that these books did anything to disrupt the scholarly consensus about Taft as a lackluster chief executive.

Taft also had some biographical bad luck. During the early 1960s, Stanley Solvick published several articles, based on his dissertation, that formed part of a projected biography of the president. That project did not appear.[37] Ralph Eldon Minger achieved a similar record with an investigation of the origins of Taft's foreign policy views and published a volume that collected those articles. Minger's work did not reach the presidential period or the battle over the League of Nations.[38]

Compared with the biographical outpouring on Roosevelt and Wilson, however, the record of Taft's life and career remains full of gaps. There is no good study of the 1908 election, no careful recent analysis of his foreign policy accomplishments, and only sporadic treatments of such issues as the tariff, antitrust policy, and his performance on conservation matters. His efforts at promoting governmental efficiency and a budget system have been scrutinized in recent years, but less attention has been devoted to his work as head of the armed forces, his campaign to improve the civil service, and his role as leader of the Republican Party.

The verdict that Taft was an average president seems correct. He was not an important chief executive, though of course significant things happened during his term of office: the adoption of the income tax amendment to the Constitution, and the approval of the amendment for the direct election of senators. The Payne–Aldrich tariff, the Mann–Elkins act, and the struggle for Canadian reciprocity were legislative battles with enduring consequences for tariffs, railroads, and American trade. His capacity to reshape the Supreme Court helped delay and deflect the progressive movement for several decades. Elected to extend the programs of Theodore Roosevelt, Taft did so on one level, but the turn to the right in the Republicans that he promoted proved a long-range asset to the conservative cause.[39]

Taft's part in moving the Grand Old Party rightward in 1911–1912 was one of the most persistent consequences of his presidency. The ascendancy of the conservatives among Republicans owed much to Taft's intense commitment to defeating Roosevelt and purging progressivism from the party. These sentiments shaped the views of his oldest son, who became known as "Mr. Republican" during the 1930s and 1940s when Robert A. Taft extended his father's suspicion of presidential power, big government, and labor unions.

The Supreme Court appointments of which Taft was so proud also benefitted conservatism in the 1920s and 1930s. For Taft to have so many vacancies come open during his four years was one of those accidents of history and timing that produce undue importance for some chief executives and frustration for others. Taft had a large part in making the high court an effective barrier to the economic and social change bubbling up within society during the first three decades of the twentieth century. Taft's narrow vision of what a judge should be and what role law should play in politics did not serve the nation well.

In foreign policy, Taft's dollar diplomacy approach remains fascinating to students of international affairs. There are continuities between Taft and Wilson over the issue of world peace and its promotion that could use more scrutiny. Taft's leadership of the League to Enforce Peace and his general sympathy for the League of Nations reflect this empathy. At the same time, the paternalism and cultural condescension that animated Taft and Philander Knox in Latin America continue to draw scorn from recent writers in this area. Taft's readiness to observe the constitutional limits on a president in foreign policy seems refreshing a century after his term in office. He insisted that the United States would not intervene in revolutionary Mexico without the approval of Congress, which he knew would not be forthcoming.

There is in the presidency of William Howard Taft a pervasive sense of a lost opportunity. An intelligent, hardworking public servant came into power with the good wishes of his fellow citizens in March 1909. He labored with great diligence at his job and provided an honest, efficient administration. Yet somehow Taft never connected with the American people until after he had been defeated for reelection. By then, it was too late to change the impression of political mediocrity that surrounded his White House career. There are aspects of his record as a chief executive that might assist in an upward revision of his standing among other presidents. These elements would include his call for a governmental budget and his concern for greater administrative efficiency. Yet in light of his lapses in other areas, such as the tariff and conservation, there are inherent limits to what can be said in mitigation of the negative verdict on his performance at the time and in history. William Howard Taft and the presidency were not well matched, and it showed. Only with the Supreme Court a decade later did his judicial temperament and political conservatism find a suitable outlet for his talents.

NOTES

CHAPTER 1: "THE MAN OF THE HOUR" IN 1908

1. Lawrence F. Abbott, ed., *The Letters of Archie Butt* (Garden City, N.Y.: Doubleday, Page & Co., 1924), 377–381, captures some of the tension that accompanied the event.

2. James Bryce to Edward Grey, 6 November 1908, Edward Grey Papers, F0800/81, British National Archives.

3. Helen Herron Taft, *Recollections of Full Years* (New York: Dodd, Mead, 1914), 327.

4. Henry F. Pringle, *The Life and Times of William Howard Taft*, 2 vols. (New York: Farrar & Rinehart, 1939), remains the best biography of the president.

5. Ibid., 1:45–46. Ulysses G. B. Pierce, *The Religious Faith of William Howard Taft* (Boston, Mass.: Unitarian Laymen's League, 1930), is a brief introduction to Taft's religious views.

6. Pringle, *Taft*, 1:44; "Yale College," Chicago *Inter Ocean*, 26 June 1878; "Yale College," *New York Times*, 28 June 1878.

7. Taft to William Allen White, 26 February 1908, William Howard Taft Papers, Manuscript Division, LC. Melvyn Dubofsky, "William Howard Taft: Mr. Chief Justice," in Norman Gross, ed., *America's Lawyer Presidents: From Law Office to Oval Office* (Evanston, Ill.: Northwestern University Press, 2004), 218–229, is the most recent examination of Taft as an attorney and judge. William Allen White, "Taft: A Hewer of Wood," *American Magazine* 66 (May 1908): 19–32. Brian Balogh, *A Government Out of Sight: The Mystery of National Authority in Nineteenth-Century America* (New York: Cambridge University Press, 2009), 327–330, is interesting on the role judges such as Taft played in the field of labor relations.

8. Carl Sferrazza Anthony, *Nellie Taft: The Unconventional First Lady of the Ragtime Era* (New York: William Morrow, 2005), is the only biography of Mrs. Taft.

9. Lewis L. Gould, *The Presidency of William McKinley* (Lawrence: University Press of Kansas, 1980), 186.

10. Ibid., 187.

11. Rene R. Escalante, *The Bearer of Pax Americana: The Philippine Career of William H. Taft, 1900–1903* (Quezon City: New Day Publishers, 2007), looks at Taft's performance from a Philippine perspective.

12. Roosevelt to William Howard Taft, 14 February 1903, in Elting E. Morison et al., eds., *The Letters of Theodore Roosevelt,* 8 vols. (Cambridge: Harvard University Press, 1951–1954), 3:425–426.

13. The *New York Times,* 4 April 1905, quotes Roosevelt about Taft.

14. Walter E. Clark to Erastus Brainerd, 27 March 1908, Erastus Brainerd Papers, University of Washington Library, Seattle.

15. Taft to C. M. Heald, 25 December 1907, Taft Papers; Roosevelt to George O. Trevelyan, 19 June 1908, Morison et al., *Letters of Theodore Roosevelt,* 6:1085.

16. Taft to Henry W. Taft, 21 October 1901, Taft to Louise Taft, 21 October 1901, Taft to Helen Taft, 18 April 1902, Taft Papers.

17. Mabel Boardman to Winthrop Murray Crane, 20 July 1907, Taft to Boardman, 11 September 1907, Mabel Boardman Papers.

18. Conference between Secretary Taft, Mr. Burton, and Mr. Vorys, 8 June 1907, Taft Papers, quotes Taft on Iowa.

19. Helen Taft to Taft, 27 October 1906, Taft Papers. Alfred D. Sumberg, "William Howard Taft and the Ohio Endorsement Issue," in Daniel R. Beaver, ed., *Some Pathways in Twentieth Century History* (Detroit: Wayne State University Press, 1969), 77.

20. For this episode in the relations of Roosevelt and Foraker, see Lewis L. Gould, *The Presidency of Theodore Roosevelt* (Lawrence: University Press of Kansas, 1991), 240–243.

21. Taft to Howard C. Hollister, 11 March 1907, Taft Papers.

22. William Loeb Jr. to Taft, 25 March 1907, Taft Papers, conveyed the clipping from the *Kansas City Times* with the lines of verse. Roosevelt to George von Lengerke Meyer, 16 March 1907, Morison et al., *Letters of Theodore Roosevelt,* 5:625.

23. Conference, 18 June 1907, Taft Papers; Taft to Charles D. Hilles, 21 July 1907, Charles D. Hilles Papers, Sterling Memorial Library, Yale University.

24. Taft to William Rockhill Nelson, 25 December 1907, Taft Papers.

25. Mark Sullivan, *Our Times, 1900–1925. Vol. IV: The War Begins, 1909–1914* (New York: Scribner's, 1936), 304.

26. Taft to Roosevelt, 28 August 1906, Taft Papers. Joseph W. Blythe to John F. Lacey, 7 January 1908, Box 258, John F. Lacey Papers, Iowa Department of History and Archives, Des Moines. For Taft's comments, see Pringle, *Taft,* 1:289. See also William F. Draper to Joseph B. Foraker, 10 February 1908, Joseph B. Foraker Papers, Cincinnati Historical Society, for more anti-Taft sentiment based on his tariff views.

27. William H. Taft, *Present Day Problems: A Collection of Addresses Delivered on Various Occasions* (New York: Dodd, Mead, 1908), 66; George von Lengerke Meyer Diary, 2 June 1908, Manuscript Division, LC.

28. James S. Sherman to H. B. McQueen, 6 June 1908, James S. Sherman Papers, New York Public Library, Astor, Lenox, and Tilden Foundations.

29. Taft to Dallas Boudeman, 14 June 1908, Taft Papers. Albert J. Beveridge to John C. Shaffer, July 1908, Albert J. Beveridge Papers, Manuscript Division, LC. For Dolliver, see Jonathan P. Dolliver to Grenville M. Dodge, 12 June 1908, Grenville M. Dodge Papers, Box 43, Iowa State Department of History and Archives, Des Moines. For Hughes's declination, see Elbert F. Baldwin to Theodore Roosevelt, 19 June 1908, Theodore Roosevelt Papers, Manuscript Division, LC.

30. DeSilva S. Alexander to Theodore E. Burton, 20 June 1908, Theodore E. Burton Papers, Western Reserve Historical Society, Cleveland. "James Schoolcraft Sherman," in Mark O. Hatfield et al., eds., *Vice Presidents of the United States, 1789–1993* (Washington, D.C.: Government Printing Office, 1997), 325–333.

31. Milton W. Blumenberg, comp., *Official Report of the Proceedings of the Fourteenth Republican National Convention* (Columbus, Ohio: Press of F. J. Heer, 1908), 117.

32. Ibid., 119. Taft to Frank B. Kellogg, 16 June 1908, Frank B. Kellogg Papers, Minnesota Historical Society, St. Paul.

33. Taft to Roosevelt, 19 June 1908, with Roosevelt's response, Roosevelt Papers.

34. See Henry L. Stoddard, *As I Knew Them: Presidents and Politics from Grant to Coolidge* (New York: Harper & Bros., 1927), 386, and *Taft and Roosevelt: The Intimate Letters of Archie Butt Military Aide,* 2 vols. (Garden City, N.Y.: Doubleday, Doran, 1930), 2:551, for the contrasting versions of this episode.

35. Taft to Roosevelt, 17 July 1908, Taft Papers.

36. Taft to Roosevelt, 18 July 1908, Roosevelt Papers.

37. *Presidential Addresses and State Papers of William Howard Taft from March 4, 1909, to March 4, 1910* (New York: Doubleday, Page, 1910), 6.

38. Ibid., 34.

39. Taft to Roosevelt, 31 July 1908, Taft Papers; "Taft Is Notified, Cincinnati Joyful," *New York Times,* 29 July 1908. The quotations from the *New York Press* and the *New York Post* also appeared in the *New York Times,* 29 July 1908.

40. Oscar King Davis, *William Howard Taft: The Man of the Hour* (St. Louis, Mo.: Thompson Publishing, 1908). For the writing of the book, see Oscar King Davis, *Released for Publication: Some Inside Political History of Theodore Roosevelt and His Times, 1898–1918* (Boston, Mass.: Houghton Mifflin, 1925), 96–97.

CHAPTER 2: BEING HIS OWN KING

1. Mark H. Salt, ed., *Candidates and the Issues: An Official History of the Campaign of 1908* (Charles B. Ayer, 1908), 86.

2. "Bryan on Prosperity," *New York Times,* 3 October 1908. William Jennings Bryan to Edward M. House, 7 October 1908, Edward M. House Papers, Sterling Memorial Library, Yale University, New Haven, Conn.

3. George R. Sheldon to Theodore Roosevelt, 22 September 1908, Theodore Roosevelt Papers, Manuscript Division, Library of Congress (hereafter LC); Julius Whiting Jr. to William C. Beer, 7 October 1908, Beer Family Papers, Sterling Memorial Library, Yale University, New Haven, Conn.

4. Robert Bolt, "William Howard Taft: A Frustrated and Fretful Unitarian in the White House," *Queen City Heritage* 42 (Spring 1984): 39, 47; Edgar A. Hornig, "The Religious Issue in the Taft–Bryan Duel of 1908," *Proceedings of the American Philosophical Society* 105, no. 161 (December 1961): 530–537, covers the matter in detail.

5. *Chicago Tribune,* 7 September 1908; Taft to Theodore Roosevelt, 21 September 1908, William Howard Taft Papers, Manuscript Division, LC.

6. Taft to Roosevelt, 13 July 1908, Roosevelt Papers. On the Hughes nomination, see Taft to Roosevelt, 10 August 1908, Taft Papers.

7. Taft to Roosevelt, 11 September 1908, Taft Papers.

8. Taft, *The Collected Works of William Howard Taft: Volume II, Political Issues and Outlooks: Speeches Delivered between August 1908 and February 1909,* ed. David H. Burton (Athens: Ohio University Press, 2001), 36, 41, 76–77.

9. *Chicago Tribune,* 7 October 1908, quotes Taft. Fred W. Upham to William Kent, 19 October 1908, William Kent Papers. Sterling Memorial Library, Yale University, New Haven, Conn.

10. Mark Sullivan to Theodore Roosevelt, 11 September 1908, Roosevelt Papers.

11. Henry F. Pringle, *The Life and Times of William Howard Taft,* 2 vols. (New York: Farrar & Rinehart, 1939), 1:377 (first two quotations); Jean Adrien Antoine Jules Jusserand, *What Me Befell: The Reminiscences of Jules Jusserand* (Boston, Mass.: Houghton Mifflin, 1933), 337.

12. Taft to Roosevelt, 7 November 1908, Taft Papers; Lucius B. Swift to Mrs. Swift, 8 July 1910, Lucius B. Swift Papers, Indiana State Library, Indianapolis.

13. Taft to Philander Knox, 23 December 1908, Taft Papers. On Newberry, see Henry Cabot Lodge to Henry L. Higginson, 8 March 1909, Henry Cabot Lodge Papers, Massachusetts Historical Society, Boston.

14. Entry for 24 November 1908, Oscar Straus Diary, Oscar Straus Papers, LC; Diary of Mrs. Truman Newberry, 26 January 1909, Truman Newberry Papers, Detroit Public Library. Entry for 4 January 1909, George von Lengerke Meyer Diary, LC.

15. Taft to J. C. Shaffer, 21 December 1908, Taft Papers; John C. O'Laughlin to James A. Irons, 26 January 1909, James C. O'Laughlin Papers, Manuscript Division, LC; entry for 4 January 1909, James R. Garfield Diaries, Box 8, James R. Garfield Papers, Manuscript Division, LC.

16. Lodge Journal, 9 December 1908, Lodge Papers.

17. F. M. Huntington Wilson, *Memoirs of an Ex-Diplomat* (Boston, Mass.: Bruce Humphries, 1945), 175; Walter V. Scholes and Marie V. Scholes, *The Foreign Policies of the Taft Administration* (Columbia: University of Missouri Press, 1970), 8. Paige Elliott Mulhollan, "Philander C. Knox and Dollar Diplomacy, 1909–1913" (Ph.D. diss., University of Texas, 1966), is a good study of Knox as secretary of state.

18. "Knox Seems Barred from the Cabinet," *New York Times,* 10 February 1909; "Way Clear for Knox to Enter Cabinet," *New York Times,* 16 February 1909. Henry Adams to Whitelaw Reid, 15 February 1909, in J. C. Levenson et al., eds., *The Letters of Henry Adams, Volume VI: 1906–1918* (Cambridge: Belknap Press of Harvard University Press, 1988), 223.

19. James Bryce to Edward Grey, 28 March 1910, Edward Grey Papers, F0800/82, British National Archives, London.

20. Mulhollan, "Philander C. Knox," 33.

21. Taft to Elbert F. Baldwin, 24 December 1908, Taft Papers. For Wickersham, see Thomas Roger Wessel, "Republican Justice: The Department of Justice under Roosevelt and Taft, 1901–1913," (Ph.D. diss., University of Maryland, 1972), 306–307, and James Clifford German Jr., "Taft's Attorney General: George W. Wickersham" (Ph.D. diss., New York University, 1969).

22. Clayton Coppin, "James Wilson and Harvey Wiley: The Dilemma of Bureaucratic Entrepreneurship," *Agricultural History* 64 (Spring 1990): 169–172, is incisive on Wilson's administrative style. Taft to Helen Taft, 26 July 1911, Taft Papers.

23. Wayne Wiegand, *Patrician in the Progressive Era: A Biography of George von Lengerke Meyer* (New York: Garland, 1988), is an excellent examination of Meyer's career.

24. Hitchcock remains a shadowy figure in the Taft presidency. "Cabinet Photographs—Mr. Hitchcock," *New York Times,* 4 April 1909, is a sketch of his life. "Motor Trucks for Mail," *New York Times,* 25 September 1910.

25. J. M. Dickinson to the members of the American Bar Association, 12 April 1913, pamphlet in author's collection. Elbert F. Baldwin, "New Secretary of War," *Outlook* 92 (22 May 1909): 167–170.

26. Henry Adams to Whitelaw Reid, 13 February 1909, in Levenson et al., *Letters of Henry Adams,* 223.

27. Frank Kellogg to Taft, 22 February 1909, Frank B. Kellogg Papers, Minnesota Historical Society, St. Paul; Herbert S. Duffy, *William Howard Taft* (New York: Minton, Balch, 1930), 328.

28. Elbert F. Baldwin to Taft, 13 January 1909, Taft Papers. Ballinger thought at first that Garfield would be reappointed. Richard A. Ballinger to M. D. McEnery, 9 November 1908, Ballinger to Ormsby McHarg, 25 November 1908, Richard A. Ballinger Papers, University of Washington Library, Seattle.

29. James L. Penick Jr., *Progressive Politics and Conservation: The Ballinger Pinchot Affair* (Chicago: University of Chicago Press, 1968), 26 (first quotation); James R. Garfield Diary, 25 January 1909, James R. Garfield Papers, Box 8 LC, (second quotation).

30. Oscar Straus Diary, 23 January 1909, Straus Papers, LC; Lawrence F. Abbott, ed., *The Letters of Archie Butt: Personal Aide to President Roosevelt* (Garden City, N.Y.: Doubleday, Page, 1924), 338.

31. Taft to Charles Phelps Taft, 5 January 1909, Taft Papers.

32. Taft to Elihu Root, 25 November 1908, Elihu Root Papers, Manuscript Division, LC; Taft to Joseph L. Bristow, 5 December 1908, Taft Papers.

33. Roosevelt to Henry Beach Needham, 15 March 1909, Theodore Roosevelt Papers, William L. Clements Library, University of Michigan, Ann Arbor.

34. Helen Herron Taft, *Recollections of Full Years* (New York: Dodd, Mead, 1914), 347.

35. Taft to Knox, 23 December 1908, Taft Papers.

36. Taft to Roosevelt, 25 February 1909, Taft Papers.

37. Pringle, *Life and Times*, 1:394.

38. Washington *Star*, 4 March 1909, quoted in Mark Sullivan, *Our Times: The United States, 1900–1925, IV. The War Begins, 1909–1914* (New York: Charles Scribner's Sons, 1932), 344.

39. *Supplement to the Messages and Papers of the Presidents Covering the Administration of William Howard Taft, March 4, 1909, to March 4, 1913* (Washington, D.C.: Bureau of National Literature, 1914), 7368.

40. Ibid., 7369, 7370.

41. Ibid., 7372, 7373–7374.

42. Ibid., 7376.

43. Ibid., 7377.

44. Ibid., 7378, 7379.

45. Pringle, *Life and Times*, 1:396.

46. "A Review of the World," *Current Literature* 46 (April 1909): 347 (third quotation), 352 (*Times*), 357 (Springfield *Republican*).

CHAPTER 3: THE NEW PRESIDENT AND HIS COUNTRY

1. Charles Willis Thompson, "'Undesirables' Again Seen at the White House," *New York Times*, 25 April 1909.

2. Judith Icke Anderson, *William Howard Taft: An Intimate History* (New York: Norton, 1981), 27–30, discusses Taft's weight issue while he was president.

3. Taft to Horace Taft, 29 May 1912, William Howard Taft Papers, Manuscript Division, Library of Congress. For the concerns about Bright's disease, see Patricia O'Toole, *When Trumpets Call: Theodore Roosevelt after the White House* (New York: Simon and Schuster, 2005), 113–115.

4. John G. Sotos, "Taft and Pickwick: Sleep Apnea in the White House," *Chest* 124 (September 2003): 1133–1142.

5. For Taft's schedule, see William Bayard Hale, "The President at Work," *World's Work* 20 (June 1910): 13006, and Charles D. Hilles to D. B. Randolph Keim, 4 August 1911, Charles D. Hilles Papers, Sterling Memorial Library, Yale University, New Haven, Conn.

6. John Hays Hammond, *The Autobiography of John Hays Hammond*, 2 vols. (New York: Farrar & Rinehart, 1935), 2:561.

7. Leroy Vernon to Charles M. Faye, 21 March 1911, Leroy Vernon Papers, Center for American History, University of Texas at Austin.

8. William Howard Taft to Frank H. Shaffer, 26 March 1910, Taft Papers.

9. "Society at Variance, Westerners Sanction Plans of Mrs. Taft for the Capital," *Washington Post*, 14 March 1909 (first quotation); "Mrs. Taft Lays Plans,"

Washington Post, 9 March 1909 (second quotation). Elise K. Kirk, *Music at the White House: A History of the American Spirit* (Urbana: University of Illinois Press, 1986), 188–192.

10. Henry L. Stimson, "1913 Recollections, summer of 1911," Henry L. Stimson Papers, Sterling Memorial Library, Yale University, New Haven, Conn. *Taft and Roosevelt: The Intimate Letters of Archie Butt Military Aide,* 2 vols. (Garden City, N.Y.: Doubleday, Doran, 1930), 1:88.

11. "Robert Taft in Auto Runs over Laborer," *New York Times,* 28 June 1910; "Robert Taft Exonerated," *New York Times,* 28 June 1910. On the impostor, see William Howard Taft to Helen Herron Taft, 10 July 1912, Taft Papers.

12. Horace Dutton Taft, *Memories and Opinions* (New York: Macmillan, 1942), 120–121.

13. Two attempts to describe a Taft inner circle were "The 'Kitchen Cabinet' of the President," *New York Times,* 8 August 1909, and E. J. Edwards, "The Most Intimate Friends of President Taft," *New York Times,* 29 May 1910.

14. "How Taft Keeps Cool," *New York Times,* 21 May 1911.

15. "Taft Cow Worth $80 a Day," *New York Times,* 10 August 1911. The button honoring Pauline was on sale on eBay during the autumn of 2007.

16. See *Index to the William Howard Taft Papers,* 5 vols. (Washington, D.C.: Library of Congress, 1972), 1:xi–xii, for the Taft filing system. Ira T. Smith with Joe Alex Morris, *"Dear Mr. President . . . ": The Story of Fifty Years in the White House Mail Room* (New York: Julian Messner, 1949), 82–84.

17. Michael L. Bromley, *William Howard Taft and the First Motoring Presidency* (Jefferson, N.C.: McFarland, 2003), focuses on Taft and automobiles but also provides much useful information about the president's performance in office.

18. Jacob H. Gallinger to James O. Lyford, 6 May 1910, James O. Lyford Papers, New Hampshire Historical Society, Concord. "Taft's Journeying," *Washington Post,* 10 May 1910, reprinting an editorial from the Philadelphia *Public Ledger.*

19. Taft to Roosevelt, 21 March 1909, Taft Papers.

20. Taft to Helen Taft, 31 October 1906, Taft Papers.

21. Hammond, *Autobiography,* 2:541; Charles Willis Thompson, *Presidents I've Know and Two Near Presidents* (Indianapolis, Ind.: Bobbs-Merrill, 1929), 247.

22. "Lincoln" in the Boston, Mass., *Evening Transcript,* quoted in *Springfield Daily Republican,* 17 August 1909. *Taft and Roosevelt,* 1:38.

23. Charles Hardinge to James Bryce, 26 March 1909, Embassy Papers, James Bryce Papers, Bodleian Library, Oxford; Henry White to Henry Cabot Lodge, 4 May 1909, Henry Cabot Lodge Papers, Massachusetts Historical Society, Boston; Henry White to Joseph Hodges Choate, 22 July 1909, Joseph Hodges Choate Papers, Manuscript Division, Library of Congress. Taft to Charles Phelps Taft, 10 September 1910, Taft Papers. Allan Nevins, *Henry White: Thirty Years of American Diplomacy* (New York: Harper & Bros., 1930), 299.

24. "Secretary Works Hard," *Washington Post,* 4 March 1909; "Pity the Sorrows of the President's Secretary," *New York Times,* 5 June 1910.

25. Oscar King Davis, *Released for Publication: Some Inside Political History of Theodore Roosevelt and His Times, 1898–1918* (Boston, Mass.: Houghton Mifflin, 1925), 94, 157.

26. Boston, Mass., *Evening Transcript*, 18 March 1910.

27. Taft to William Allen White, 20 March 1909, Taft Papers.

28. William Bayard Hale, "The President at Work," *World's Work* 20 (June 1910): 13008, 13011.

29. Taft to William Kent, 29 June 1909, Taft Papers.

30. For Taft's coolness toward Pinchot and the forester's relations with Roosevelt, see Taft to Helen Taft, 31 October 1906, 1 November 1906, Taft Papers.

31. Taft to Knox, 27 January 1909, Taft Papers.

32. Taft to Helen Taft, 3 October 1909, Taft Papers.

33. Taft to W. H. Phipps, 1 July 1909, Taft Papers.

34. Taft to Charles Nagel, 14 August 1909, Taft Papers.

35. Booker T. Washington to William Howard Taft, 23 April 1909, 18 June 1909, Taft to Washington, 24 June 1909, Washington to Charles William Anderson, 20 August 1909, Emmett Jay Scott to Washington, 6 November 1909, in Louis R. Harlan, ed., *The Booker T. Washington Papers* (Urbana: University of Illinois Press, 1981, 2000), 91–92, 138–140, 157, 191.

36. Jacob H. Gallinger to George H. Moses, 15 April 1909, George H. Moses Papers, New Hampshire Historical Society, Concord.

CHAPTER 4: SEEKING DOWNWARD REVISION: THE PAYNE–ALDRICH TARIFF

1. Scott William Rager, "The Fall of the House of Cannon: Uncle Joe and His Enemies, 1903–1910," (Ph.D. diss., University of Illinois at Urbana–Champaign, 1991), 129–137.

2. Taft to William Allen White, 12 March 1909, William Howard Taft Papers, Manuscript Division, Library of Congress (hereafter LC).

3. Stanley D. Solvick, "William Howard Taft and Cannonism," *Wisconsin Magazine of History* 48 (Autumn 1964): 56–57; Claude E. Barfield, "The Democratic Party in Congress, 1909–1913," (Ph.D. diss., Northwestern University, 1965), 24–26.

4. "Message Convening Congress in Extra Session," 16 March 1909, in *Presidential Addresses and State Papers of William Howard Taft from March 4, 1909, to March 4, 1910* (New York: Doubleday, Page, 1910), 69.

5. "Happy over Message," *Washington Post*, 17 March 1909.

6. "Aldrich, the Master of Details," *Current Literature* 46 (August 1909): 48.

7. A. H. Lockwood to Charles H. Jones, 30 April 1909, Commonwealth Shoe and Leather Company Papers, Baker Library, Harvard Business School, Boston, Mass.

8. F. E. Stevens to Eugene Gano Hay, 19 March 1909, Eugene Gano Hay Papers, Manuscript Division, LC. Taft to Frank L. Dingley, 21 March 1909, Taft Papers.

9. Stevens to Hay, 10 April 1909, Hay Papers, LC; Taft to Horace Taft, 27 June 1909, Taft Papers.

10. *Washington Post*, 11 April 1909.

11. Barfield, "Democratic Party," 80–81, summarizes what Aldrich did. See also Richard Cleveland Baker, *The Tariff under Roosevelt and Taft* (Hastings, Neb.: Democrat Printing, 1941), 80–81. The only biography of Aldrich is Nathaniel Wright Stephenson, *Nelson W. Aldrich: A Leader in American Politics* (New York: Scribner's, 1930), 348–351.

12. U.S. Senate, *Congressional Record,* 61st Cong., 1st Sess. (22 April 1909): 1460.

13. Taft to J. D. Brannan, 29 June 1909, Taft Papers.

14. Joseph L. Bristow to Harold T. Chase, 27 May 1909, Joseph Little Bristow Papers, Kansas State Historical Society, Topeka.

15. L. Ethan Ellis, *Newsprint: Producers, Publishers, Political Pressures Including the Text of Print Paper Pendulum: Group Pressures and the Price of Newsprint* (New Brunswick, N.J.: Rutgers University Press, 1948, 1960), 57–67, discusses the issue in the context of the tariff battle in 1909.

16. Taft to Horace White, 25 March 1909, Taft Papers.

17. Taft to Therese McCagg, 26 June 1909, Taft Papers. The case in question was *Pollock v. Farmers' Loan and Trust Company,* 157 U.S., 429 (1895).

18. *Presidential Addresses and State Papers of William Howard Taft from March 4, 1909, to March 4, 1910,* 167, 168, 169.

19. Taft to Horace Taft, 27 June 1909, Taft Papers. This letter was a long discussion by the president about his role in the tariff battle. In it he quotes Senator Aldrich.

20. Barfield, "Democratic Party," 121–132, is an excellent analysis of the income tax/corporation tax issue during the debate in the Senate.

21. Thomas J. Akins to Charles Nagel, 19 June 1909, Charles Nagel Papers, Sterling Memorial Library, Yale University, New Haven, Conn. Bristow to Harold T. Chase, 19 June 1909, Bristow Papers.

22. Taft to W. H. H. Miller, 13 July 1909, Taft Papers.

23. *Springfield Daily Republican,* 14 July 1909.

24. Robert M. La Follette to Taft, 13 July 1909, La Follette Family Papers, Box B103, Manuscript Division, LC.

25. Taft to Helen Taft, 11 July 1909, Taft Papers.

26. For the work of the boot and shoe manufacturers, see A. H. Lockwood to Charles H. Jones, 12 June 1909, Commonwealth Shoe and Leather Company Papers; for Francis E. Warren and the strategy of the Western range senators, see Warren to George S. Walker, 10 July 1909, Francis E. Warren Papers, American Heritage Center, University of Wyoming, Laramie.

27. Thomas H. Carter to Mrs. Carter, 18 July 1909, Thomas H. Carter Papers, Manuscript Division, LC.

28. Taft to Helen Taft, 17 July 1909, Taft Papers (first quotation); *Washington Post,* 17 July 1909 (second quotation).

29. T. J. Akins to Nagel, 17 July 1909, Nagel Papers; Reed Smoot Diary, 24 July 1909, Brigham Young University.

30. Taft to Helen Taft, 27 July 1909, Taft Papers.

31. Boston, Mass., *Evening Transcript,* 26 July 1909.

32. Taft to Aldrich, 29 July 1909, Taft to Helen Taft, 30 July 1909, Taft Papers.

33. Taft to Helen Taft, 1 August 1909, Taft Papers. Albert J. Beveridge to Albert Shaw, 7 August 1909, Albert Shaw Papers, New York Public Library, Astor, Lenox and Tilden Foundations.

34. *Kansas City Star,* quoted in *Springfield Republican,* 6 August 1909; *Washington Post,* 6 August 1909; *Wall Street Journal,* 31 July 1909.

35. Albert B. Cummins to Albert J. Beveridge, 17 August 1909, Albert J. Beveridge Papers, Manuscript Division, LC.

36. Oscar King Davis to James T. Williams, 11 October 1909, James T. Williams Papers, Duke University, Durham, N.C. Taft to Bristow, 18 August 1909, Bristow Papers; Taft to Nagel, 23 August 1909, Nagel Papers.

37. Taft to Frederic H. Gillett, 13 September 1909, Taft Papers.

38. *Washington Post,* 23 August 1909 (first quotation); John F. Lacey to Taft, 28 August 1909, John F. Lacey Papers, Iowa State Department of History and Archives, Des Moines.

39. James A. Tawney to Taft, 18 August 1909, Taft Papers. James A. Tawney to the editor, *Republican-Gazette,* Wilmar, Minn., 18 August 1909, James A. Tawney Papers, Minnesota Historical Society, St. Paul.

40. Taft to Helen Taft, 16 September 1909 (telegram), Taft Papers. "Taft Defends Payne Tariff," *Grand Forks* [North Dakota] *Herald,* 18 September 1909.

41. "Taft Defends Payne Tariff," *Grand Forks Herald,* 18 September 1909; *Presidential Addresses and State Papers of William Howard Taft from March 4, 1909, to March 4, 1910* (New York: Doubleday, Page, 1910), 211, 222.

42. *Presidential Addresses,* 222.

43. Ibid., 224–226.

44. Porter J. McCumber to Nelson Aldrich, 20 September 1909, Nelson W. Aldrich Papers, Manuscript Division, LC. James A. Tawney to John J. Esch, 22 September 1909 (quotation), William B. McKinley to Esch, 27 September 1909, Box 20, John J. Esch Papers, Wisconsin Historical Society, Madison.

45. Albert J. Cummins to Bristow, 25 September 1909, Bristow Papers; Albert J. Beveridge to Albert Shaw, 4 October 1909, Albert Shaw Papers; "Western Republican Opinions on the Winona Speech," *Harper's Weekly* 53 (2 October, 1909): 5, San Francisco *Call.* Francis E. Warren to Theodore Justice, 27 September 1909, Warren Papers.

46. Henry F. Pringle, *The Life and Times of William Howard Taft,* 2 vols. (New York: Farrar & Rinehart, 1939), 1:456.

47. William Kent to W. C. Boyden, 28 July 1909, William Kent Papers, Sterling Memorial Library, Yale University, New Haven, Conn.

CHAPTER 5: THE BALLINGER–PINCHOT CONTROVERSY

1. Elihu Root to Henry L. Stimson, 18 November 1909, Henry L. Stimson Papers, Sterling Memorial Library, Yale University, New Haven, Conn.

2. Taft to Horace Taft, 18 October 1909, William Howard Taft Papers, Manuscript Division, Library of Congress (hereafter LC).

3. There is no biography of Ballinger. "Man Who Does Things," *Washington Post*, 18 April 1909, is a brief biographical sketch. Willard French, "Richard A. Ballinger: Secretary of the Interior," *Independent* 67 (28 October 1909): 965 (quotation). After Ballinger left the government, Henry Cabot Lodge wrote that "Ballinger was a perfectly honest man but he was also a mediocre man and not up to the place." Lodge to Henry L. Higginson, 10 March 1911, Henry L. Higginson Papers, Baker Library, Harvard Business School, Boston, Mass.

4. The best study of the Ballinger–Pinchot controversy remains James Penick Jr., *Progressive Politics and Conservation: The Ballinger–Pinchot Affair* (Chicago: University of Chicago Press, 1968), 43–47.

5. Gifford Pinchot, *Breaking New Ground* (New York: Harcourt Brace, 1947; Washington, D.C.: Island Press, 1974), 395.

6. "May Replace Newell," *Washington Post*, 17 June 1909. James R. Garfield Diary, 3 April 1909, James R. Garfield Papers, Manuscript Division, LC.

7. James R. Garfield Diary, 11 June 1909, Garfield Papers; Taft to Hulbert Taft, 12 May 1909, Taft Papers; "Pinchot on Warpath," *Washington Post*, 18 July 1909.

8. Taft to Elbert F. Baldwin, 13 August 1909, Taft Papers.

9. Taft to Helen Taft, 3 October 1909, Taft Papers.

10. Taft to Roosevelt, 26 May 1910, Taft Papers, offered that explanation for why Taft had not written Roosevelt.

11. "Ballinger on Trail," *Washington Post*, 23 July 1909, quotes Taft.

12. Penick, *Progressive Politics*, 107–136, looks at Glavis and his part in the controversy.

13. Pinchot, *Breaking New Ground*, 427; Taft to Ira E. Bennett, 27 August 1909, Taft Papers.

14. Taft explained his role in a letter to Senator Knute Nelson, 15 May 1910, Taft Papers. The text of the letter was released to the newspapers. See "Taft Told Lawler to Prepare Report," *New York Times*, 16 May 1910.

15. "Taft Told Lawler to Prepare Report."

16. Taft to Richard A. Ballinger, 16 September 1909, in "Taft Takes Stand with Ballinger," *New York Times*, 16 September 1909.

17. Taft to Pinchot, 13 September 1909, Taft Papers.

18. Taft to George W. Wickersham, 7 October 1909, Taft to Horace Taft, 18 October 1909, Taft Papers; Pinchot, *Breaking New Ground*, 434.

19. Taft to Helen Taft, 3 October 1909, Taft to Carpenter, 24 October 1909, Taft Papers.

20. Ida Tarbell to William Allen White, 29 September 1909, William Allen White Papers, Manuscript Division, LC.

21. The Indiana paper is quoted in Albert J. Beveridge to Albert Shaw, 15 November 1909, Albert Shaw Papers, New York Public Library, Astor, Lenox and Tilden Foundations. Oscar King Davis to James T. Williams Jr., 11 October 1909, James T. Williams Jr. Papers, Duke University Library, Durham, N.C.

22. Penick, *Progressive Politics*, 129–130.

23. Pinchot, *Breaking New Ground*, 438.

24. William Allen White, *The Autobiography of William Allen White* (New York: Macmillan, 1946), 426.

25. Victor Murdock to William Allen White, 9 December 1909, White Papers, LC.

26. Taft to Lafayette Young, 15 November 1909, Taft Papers.

27. Pinchot, *Breaking New Ground*, 449–451. Pinchot to Dolliver, 5 January 1910, quoted in Penick, *Progressive Politics*, 141.

28. Taft to Clarence H. Kelsey, 10 January 1910, Taft Papers.

29. *Taft and Roosevelt: The Intimate Letters of Archie Butt Military Aide*, 2 vols. (Garden City, N.Y.: Doubleday, Doran, 1930), 1:256; Taft to Pinchot, 7 January 1910, Taft Papers.

30. Theodore Roosevelt Jr. to Francis Warrington Dawson, 8 January 1910, Francis Warrington Dawson Papers, Duke University; Henry Cabot Lodge to Roosevelt, 8 January 1910, Henry Cabot Lodge, ed., *Selections from the Correspondence of Theodore Roosevelt and Henry Cabot Lodge, 1884–1918*, 2 vols. (New York: Charles Scribner's Sons, 1925), 2:356; Roosevelt to Lodge, 17 January 1910, in Elting E. Morison et al., eds., *The Letters of Theodore Roosevelt*, 8 vols. (Cambridge: Harvard University Press, 1954), 7:46.

31. Taft to Roosevelt, 26 May 1910, Taft Papers.

32. "Says Ballinger Wrote Taft Letter," *New York Times*, 15 May 1910.

33. "Taft Told Lawler to Prepare Report."

34. Pinchot to Roosevelt, 18 May 1910, quoted in Penick, *Progressive Politics*, 162.

CHAPTER 6: TAFT, KNOX, AND DOLLAR DIPLOMACY

1. Frank Ninkovich, *The Wilsonian Century: U.S. Foreign Policy since 1900* (Chicago: University of Chicago Press, 1999), 28–29.

2. Francis M. Huntington Wilson, *Memoirs of an Ex-Diplomat* (Boston, Mass.: Bruce Humphries, 1945), 199.

3. Walter V. Scholes and Marie V. Scholes, *The Foreign Policies of the Taft Administration* (Columbia: University of Missouri Press, 1970), 6–15, presents a negative portrayal of Knox as secretary of state. Paige Mulhollan, "Philander C. Knox and Dollar Diplomacy" (Ph.D. diss., University of Texas at Austin, 1966), is a more sympathetic interpretation of Knox at work.

4. John Callan O'Laughlin to Elihu Root, 5 September 1908, Elihu Root Papers, Box 56, Manuscript Division, Library of Congress (hereafter LC).

5. William H. Taft, *Present Day Problems: A Collection of Addresses Delivered on Various Occasions* (New York: Dodd, Mead, 1908), 44. For general background on Taft and Asia, see James Randolph Roebuck Jr., "The United States and East Asia, 1909–1913: A Study of the Far Eastern Diplomacy of William Howard Taft" (Ph.D. diss., University of Virginia, 1977), 25–46.

6. Taft to Rollo Ogden, 21 April 1909, William Howard Taft Papers, Manuscript Division, LC.

7. Taft to Ogden, 21 April 1909, Taft Papers.

8. Jerry Israel, *Progressivism and the Open Door: America and China, 1905–1921* (Pittsburgh: University of Pittsburgh Press, 1971), 64–65, reviews Taft's choices.

9. Knox is quoted in James Randolph Roebuck, "United States and East Asia," 58.

10. Taft to Prince Chun, 15 July 1909, Taft Papers.

11. "Crane Takes Post as Envoy to China," *New York Times,* 17 July 1909; Taft to Helen Taft, 14 July 1909, Taft Papers; William Kent to Theodore Roosevelt, 14 June 1910, Theodore Roosevelt Papers, Manuscript Division, LC. Crane's selection is examined in Jacob J. Sulzbach, "Charles R. Crane, Woodrow Wilson and Progressive Reform, 1909–1921" (Ph.D. diss., Texas A&M University, 1994), 58–60.

12. Crane's utterances are discussed in Roebuck, "United States and East Asia," 82–85, and Israel, *Progressivism and the Open Door,* 70–72. Taft to Knox, 24 October 1909, Taft Papers, referred to Crane's statements about Jews.

13. Israel, *Progressivism and the Open Door,* 71–72.

14. Philander Knox to J. C. Hemphill, 21 November 1909, Hemphill Family Papers, Duke University Library, Durham, N.C.

15. Knox to Taft, 4 December 1909, Taft Papers. "Calhoun Has China Post," *New York Times,* 7 December 1909.

16. Charles Chia-Wei Chu, "The China Policy of the Taft–Knox Administration" (Ph.D. diss., University of Chicago, 1956), 156, quotes Knox.

17. Taft's remark to the Chinese minister appears in *Taft and Roosevelt: The Intimate Letters of Archie Butt, Military Aide,* 2 vols. (Garden City, N.Y.: Doubleday, Doran, 1930), 1:215.

18. Roebuck, "United States and East Asia," 112.

19. Britannicus, "American Policy in the Far East," *North American Review* 192 (September 1910): 415–424, quoted in Roebuck, "United States and East Asia," 140.

20. Knox to Taft, 14 March 1911, Taft Papers.

21. Seward Livermore, "Battleship Diplomacy in South America: 1905–1925," *Journal of Modern History* 16 (March 1944): 34–39, recounts the sale of battleships to Argentina.

22. William H. Taft, *Presidential Addresses and State Papers of William Howard Taft from March 4, 1909, to March 4, 1910* (New York: Doubleday, Page, 1910), 456.

23. "Taft Breaks with Zelaya," *New York Times,* 2 December 1909, printed Knox's letter to the Nicaraguan charge d'affaires in Washington. John Ellis Findling, "The United States and Zelaya: A Study in the Diplomacy of Expedience" (Ph.D. diss, University of Texas at Austin, 1971), explores the shifts in the American relationship with the Nicaraguan leader.

24. The secretary of the navy, George von Lengerke Meyer, recorded the statements of Knox and the president in his diary. See Mark A. DeWolfe Howe, *George von Lengerke Meyer: His Life and Public Services* (New York: Dodd, Mead,

1919), 428–429. For Mexico's attitude, see Jurgen Buchenau, "Counter-Intervention against Uncle Sam: Mexico's Support for Nicaraguan Nationalism, 1903–1910," *Americas* 50 (October 1993): 207–232.

25. Knox to Taft, 28 September 1909, Taft Papers.

26. Taft, *Presidential Addresses and State Papers,* 459; Taft to Knox, 22 December 1909, Taft Papers.

27. Taft's message is contained in *Papers Relating to the Foreign Relations of the United States, 1912* (Washington, D.C.: Government Printing Office, 1919), 1073.

28. Dana G. Munro, *Intervention and Dollar Diplomacy in the Caribbean, 1900–1921* (Princeton, N.J.: Princeton University Press, 1964), 217–223.

29. Wilson is quoted in ibid., 224. For the Knox letter, see Knox to the Chairman of the Senate Committee on Foreign Relations, 13 February 1911, in *Papers Relating to the Foreign Relations of the United States, 1912* (Washington: Government Printing Office, 1919), 568–572.

30. "Knox May Prove Critics Wrong," *New York Times,* 13 February 1910; Elihu Root to Henry Stimson, 7 September 1927, quoted in Phillip Jessup, *Elihu Root,* 2 vols. (New York: Dodd, Mead, 1937), 2:250–251; Henry Cabot Lodge to Theodore Roosevelt, 27 December 1909, Henry Cabot Lodge Papers, Massachusetts Historical Society, Boston.

31. "Carnegie in Speech Takes Knox to Task," *New York Times,* 21 December 1909.

32. "Harrison Criticizes Knox as a Bungler," *New York Times,* 12 February 1910.

33. "Taft Praises Knox; Defends His Policy," *New York Times,* 3 May 1910.

34. Alfred Henry George Grey to James Bryce, 4 March 1910, the Papers of the Fourth Earl Grey, Durham University, Durham, England.

35. L. Ethan Ellis, *Reciprocity 1911: A Study in Canadian–American Relations* (New Haven: Yale University Press, 1939), 45, is the definitive study of this episode.

36. Taft to Guy Mallon, 13 January 1910, Taft Papers.

CHAPTER 7: TAFT AND CONGRESS, 1910

1. Henry Cabot Lodge to George von Lengerke Meyer, 7 November 1909, George von Lengerke Meyer Papers, Massachusetts Historical Society, Boston.

2. James R. Garfield to William Allen White, 18 November 1909, William Allen White Papers, Manuscript Division, Library of Congress (hereafter LC). Hugh Wallace to Judson Harmon, 26 November 1909, Judson Harmon Papers, Cincinnati Historical Society, quoted in John Bailes Wiseman, "Dilemmas of a Party Out of Power: The Democrats, 1904–1912" (Ph.D. diss., University of Maryland, 1967), 156.

3. Henry Cabot Lodge to Theodore Roosevelt, 27 December 1909, Henry Cabot Lodge Papers, Massachusetts Historical Society, Boston. Lodge did not include this important letter in his published correspondence with Roosevelt, perhaps because Taft was still alive.

4. Taft to Otto Bannard, 20 December 1909, Taft Papers.

5. Taft to Lucius B. Swift, 19 February 1910, Taft Papers.

6. "Message Is Heard," *Washington Post*, 8 December 1909.

7. *Presidential Addresses and State Papers of William Howard Taft from March 4, 1909, to March 4, 1910* (New York: Doubleday, Page, 1910), 456.

8. "Message Is Heard," *Washington Post*, 8 December 1909. Lodge to Roosevelt, 27 December 1909, Lodge Papers.

9. *Presidential Addresses and State Papers*, 481.

10. "The Message Mirrored," *Washington Post*, 9 December 1909; Belleville *News Democrat*, 8 December 1909; "The President's Message," *Washington Post*, 8 December 1909.

11. "Taft Lauds Tariff," *Washington Post*, 22 March 1910; "Presidency No Joke," *Washington Post*, 23 March 1910 (second quotation).

12. Taft to Horace Taft, 5 March 1910, Taft Papers.

13. "A Review of the World," *Current Literature* 48 (March 1910): 239.

14. James Bryce to Edward Grey, 21 February 1910, F0371/1020, British National Archives, London.

15. Jacob H. Gallinger to James O. Lyford, 24 March 1910, James O. Lyford Papers, New Hampshire Historical Society, Concord.

16. *Presidential Addresses and State Papers*, 515; George Wickersham to Henry L. Higginson, 23 November 1909, Henry L. Higginson Papers, Baker Library, Harvard Business School.

17. Lewis L. Gould, ed., *Bull Moose on the Stump: The 1912 Campaign Speeches of Theodore Roosevelt* (Lawrence: University Press of Kansas, 2008), 42–43.

18. Joseph L. Bristow to Harold T. Chase, 12 February 1910, both quotations, Bristow to Henry J. Allen, December 16, 1909, for Taft's request, Joseph L. Bristow Papers, Kansas State Historical Society, Topeka.

19. *Presidential Addresses and State Papers*, 531.

20. Wickersham to Higginson, 8 February 1910, Higginson Papers.

21. "Taft Bills Will Pass," *Washington Post*, 21 February 1910.

22. Taft to Helen Taft, 19 March 1910, Taft Papers.

23. Scott William Rager, "Uncle Joe Cannon: The Brakeman of the House of Representatives, 1903–1911," in Roger H. Davidson, Susan Webb Hammmond, and Raymind W. Smock, eds., *Masters of the House: Congressional Leadership over Two Centuries* (Boulder, Colo.: Westview Press, 1998), 77–81, discusses the revolt against the Speaker.

24. *Taft and Roosevelt: The Intimate Letters of Archie Butt Military Aide*, 2 vols. (Garden City, N.Y.: Doubleday, Doran, 1930), 1:316.

25. Charles P. Taft to Taft, 18 April 1910, Taft Papers.

26. Jacob H. Gallinger to James O. Lyford, 24 March 1910, James O. Lyford Papers, New Hampshire Historical Society, Concord.

27. *Taft and Roosevelt*, 1:297.

28. *Presidential Addresses and State Papers*, 583, 584.

29. James C. German, "Taft's Attorney General: George W. Wickersham" (Ph.D. diss., New York University, 1969), 221. The attorney general was paraphrasing from Shakespeare's *Henry V*, act 4, scene 3, "that he which hath no stomach to this fight, let him depart."

30. Ibid., 221 (La Follette quotation); Beveridge to Albert Shaw, 11 April 1910, Albert J. Beveridge Papers, Manuscript Division, LC.

31. Taft to Otto Bannard, 11 June 1910, Taft Papers.

32. "Pledges Kept, Says Taft," *New York Times,* 24 June 1910; "President Taft's Achievement," *Washington Post,* 21 June 1910.

33. James S. Clarkson to Greenville M. Dodge, 11 April 1910, Grenville M. Dodge Papers, Iowa State Department of History and Archives, Des Moines.

34. "One Year of Taft," *Literary Digest* 40 (19 March 1910): 524.

35. Taft to Roosevelt, 21 March 1909, Taft Papers.

36. Roosevelt to Taft, 23 March 1909, in Elting E. Morison et al., eds., *The Letters of Theodore Roosevelt,* 8 vols. (Cambridge: Harvard University Press, 1951–1954), 7:3–4.

37. Pinchot to Roosevelt, 31 December 1909, in Gifford Pinchot, *Breaking New Ground* (New York: Harcourt Brace, 1947), 500.

38. Lodge to Roosevelt, 27 December 1909, Lodge Papers.

39. Lodge to Roosevelt, 10 March 1910, William L. Ward to Roosevelt, 21 April 1910, Lodge Papers. William R. Nelson to Roosevelt, 7 April 1910, Theodore Roosevelt Papers, Manuscript Division, LC.

40. Pinchot, *Breaking New Ground,* 502; Roosevelt to Lodge, 5 May 1910, in Morison et al., *Letters of Theodore Roosevelt,* 7:80.

41. On Norton, see "Persons in the Foreground: The Assistant President of the United States," *Current Literature* 49 (August 1910): 4.

42. Taft to Roosevelt, 26 May 1910, Taft Papers.

43. Roosevelt to Taft, 8 June 1910, Morison et al., *Letters of Theodore Roosevelt,* 7:88–89.

44. Lodge to William Sturgis Bigelow, 21 June 1910, Lodge Papers.

45. "Meeting of Taft and Roosevelt," *Washington Post,* 30 June 1910.

46. Taft to Hulbert Taft, 30 June 1910, Taft Papers. *Taft and Roosevelt,* 1:431.

CHAPTER 8: TAFT, ROOSEVELT, AND THE 1910 ELECTION

1. Henry J. Haskell to William Allen White, 21 July 1910, William Allen White Papers, Manuscript Division, Library of Congress (hereafter LC).

2. George Kibbe Turner, "How Taft Views His Own Administration: An Interview with the President," *McClure's Magazine* 35 (June 1910): 211, 221.

3. *Taft and Roosevelt: The Intimate Letters of Archie Butt Military Aide,* 2 vols. (Garden City, N.Y.: Doubleday, Doran, 1930), 1:414.

4. Taft to Charles P. Taft, 19 April 1910, Taft Papers.

5. Jonathan Dolliver to Albert J. Beveridge, 2 April 1910, Albert J. Beveridge Papers, Manuscript Division, LC.

6. Frank D. Jackson to George D. Perkins, 18 April 1910, George D. Perkins Papers, Iowa State Department of History and Archives, Des Moines. The Perkins Papers have several letters on the development of his program.

7. Henry Wallace to Jonathan Dolliver, 13 June 1910, Jonathan Dolliver Papers, Iowa State Historical Society, Iowa City. Thomas Richard Ross, *Jonathan*

Prentiss Dolliver: A Study in Political Integrity and Independence (Iowa City: State Historical Society of Iowa, 1958), 279.

8. Lafayette Young to Taft, 10 June 1910, Charles D. Hilles Papers, Sterling Memorial Library, Yale University, New Haven, Conn.; Cummins to Dolliver, 6 July 1910, Dolliver Papers.

9. "Rout for Taft Men in Iowa Convention," *New York Times,* 4 August 1910.

10. Taft to Clarence Edwards, 27 July 1910 (first quotation), Taft Papers; Taft to Charles Nagel, 7 July 1910, Charles Nagel Papers, Sterling Memorial Library, Yale University, New Haven, Conn. Haskell to White, 19 July 1910, White Papers, quotes Norton.

11. Ashmun Brown to Erastus Brainerd, 15 August 1910, Erastus Brainerd Papers, University of Washington Library, Seattle.

12. "Big Party Upset; Taft Its Leader," *New York Times,* 13 August 1910.

13. Brown to Brainerd, 15 August 1910, Brainerd Papers; Taft to Nelson W. Aldrich, 15 August 1910, Nelson W. Aldrich Papers, Manuscript Division, LC.

14. John A. Stewart to Theodore Roosevelt, 29 April 1910, Theodore Roosevelt Papers, Manuscript Division, LC.

15. On the Hughes nomination, see Alexander M. Bickel, "Mr. Taft Rehabilitates the Court," *Yale Law Journal* 79 (November 1969): 7–13.

16. Roosevelt to Lloyd C. Griscom, 29 June 1910, in Elting E. Morison et al., eds., *The Letters of Theodore Roosevelt,* 8 vols. (Cambridge, Mass.: Harvard University Press, 1951–1954), 7:97. There is a memorandum, dated June–July 1910, about these events in the Charles Evans Hughes Papers, Box 1, New York Public Library, Astor, Lenox, and Tilden Foundations.

17. See Taft to Timothy L. Woodruff, 30 June 1910, Taft Papers, for one example of several letters that the president sent out.

18. James S. Sherman to Timothy L. Woodruff, 25 July 1910, James S. Sherman Papers, New York Public Library, Astor, Lenox, and Tilden Foundations.

19. Roosevelt is quoted in *Minneapolis Journal,* 13 July 1910; the Barnes quotation is in Lloyd Griscom, *Diplomatically Speaking* (New York: Literary Guild, 1940), 343.

20. William L. Ward to Sherman, 23 July 1910, Sherman Papers; "Roosevelt Asked to Strike Keynote," *New York Times,* 13 August 1910.

21. Taft to Sherman, 14 August 1910, in "Taft Denies He Aided Sherman," *New York Times,* 23 August 1910. *Taft and Roosevelt,* 2:480.

22. "T. R. Meets Defeat," *Washington Post,* 17 August 1910; *Taft and Roosevelt,* 2:481.

23. "T. R. Meets Defeat"; Roosevelt to Lodge, 17 August 1910, Morison et al., *Letters of Theodore Roosevelt,* 7:115–116.

24. Timothy L. Woodruff to Sherman, 17 August 1910, Sherman Papers; Taft to Griscom, 20 August 1910, in "Taft Denies He Aided Sherman," *New York Times,* 23 August 1910.

25. "Taft Denies Hand in Roosevelt Turn-Down," *Washington Post,* 23 August 1910; J. Kent Hamilton to William Howard Taft, 30 August 1910, Charles D. Hilles Papers.

26. Roosevelt to William Rockhill Nelson, 24 August 1910, Theodore Roosevelt Papers, William L. Clements Library, University of Michigan, Ann Arbor. Charles D. Norton to Mabel Boardman, 28 August 1910, Mabel Boardman Papers, Manuscript Division, LC.

27. *Taft and Roosevelt,* 2:496–497; Taft to Charles P. Taft, 10 September 1910, Taft Papers. The president had apparently forgotten about his postelection letter in 1908.

28. Taft to William B. McKinley, 20 August 1910, in Republican Congressional Committee, *Republican Text-Book for the Congressional Campaign, 1910* (Philadelphia, Pa.: Press of Dunlap Printing, 1910), 6, 17.

29. Theodore Roosevelt, *The New Nationalism* (New York: Outlook, 1910), 5.

30. Taft to Charles P. Taft, 9 September 1910 (first quotation), Taft to Horace D. Taft, 16 September 1910 (third and fourth quotations), Taft Papers; Taft to Elihu Root, 15 October 1910 (third quotation), Elihu Root Papers, Manuscript Division, LC.

31. Roosevelt, *New Nationalism,* 77 (on Taft); Henry F. Pringle, *The Life and Times of William Howard Taft,* 2 vols. (New York: Farrar & Rinehart, 1939), 2:575.

32. Herbert H. Rosenthal, "The Cruise of the Tarpon," *New York History* 39 (1958): 302–320, is the most thorough account of these events.

33. "President and Roosevelt in New York Pact," *Duluth News-Tribune,* 20 September 1910 (first quotation); "Talk with Taft Suits Roosevelt," Portland *Oregonian,* 20 September 1910 (second quotation).

34. "President and Roosevelt in New York Pact," *Duluth News-Tribune,* 20 September 1910.

35. "Roosevelt Didn't Seek Taft Meeting," *New York Times,* 21 September 1910; Taft to Helen Taft, 24 September 1910, Taft Papers.

36. Robert F. Wesser, *A Response to Progressivism: The Democratic Party and New York Politics, 1902–1918* (New York: New York University Press, 1986), 19–20, summarizes these events.

37. Entry of 6 November 1910, James R. Garfield Diary, Box 9, James R. Garfield Papers, Manuscript Division, LC.

38. Taft to Charles P. Taft, 11 October 1910, Taft Papers.

39. The Norton letter is in "Taft Willing to Step Aside," *New York Time,* 16 September 1910; Norton to Frank D. Jackson, 24 September 1910, Taft Papers (quotation).

40. "Personal Recollections of the Convention and Campaign of 1910," Henry L. Stimson Papers, Sterling Memorial Library, Yale University.

41. *New York Tribune,* 10 November 1910; Henry Cabot Lodge to J. T. Wilson, 16 December 1910, Lodge Papers.

42. Taft to Mrs. Aaron F. Perry, 3 November 1910, Taft Papers. Roosevelt to Theodore Roosevelt Jr., 11 November 1910, Roosevelt to Arthur Hamilton Lee, 11 November 1910, in Morison et al., *Letters of Theodore Roosevelt,* 7:159, 163.

43. Taft to Lafayette Young, 25 November 1910, Taft Papers.

44. "The Progress of the World," *American Review of Reviews* 42 (October 1910): 387.

CHAPTER 9: TAFT AS ADMINISTRATOR

1. *Presidential Messages and State Papers of William Howard Taft from March 4, 1909, to March 4, 1910* (New York: Doubleday, Page, 1910), 465, 466.

2. Peri E. Arnold, *Making the Managerial Presidency: Comprehensive Reorganization Planning, 1905–1996*, 2nd rev. ed. (Lawrence: University Press of Kansas, 1998), 26–30.

3. "Hit Taft Travel Bill," *Washington Post,* 27 May 1910; "Taft's Journeyings," *Washington Post,* 10 May 1910; Richard J. Ellis, *Presidential Travel: The Journey from George Washington to George W. Bush* (Lawrence: University Press of Kansas, 2008), 149–155.

4. Taft to Charles D. Norton, 8 March 1911, William Howard Taft Papers, Manuscript Division, Library of Congress. On the confidential nature of the commission, see Norton to M. C. Latta, 7 October 1910, Taft Papers.

5. "The Administration on Trial: Spending the People's Money," *Metropolitan Magazine* (September 1912): 771–774, copy in Case File 215, Series 6, Taft Papers.

6. *The Need for a National Budget: Message from the President of the United States Transmitting Report of the Commission on Economy and Efficiency on the Subject of the Need for a National Budget.* U.S. House, 62nd Cong., 2nd Sess., House Document 854 (Washington, D.C.: Government Printing Office, 1912).

7. "Copy of a Letter Sent by the President to the Secretary of the Treasury Relating to the Submission of a Budget to Congress," with Franklin MacVeagh to Taft, 24 October 1912, Taft Papers.

8. Wayne A. Wiegand, *Patrician in the Progressive Era: A Biography of George von Lengerke Meyer* (New York: Garland Publishing, 1988), 150–155, is excellent on the problems of the navy. Mark A. Dewolfe Howe, *George von Lengerke Meyer: His Life and Public Services* (New York: Dodd, Mead, 1920), is useful for the diary entries and letters it printed.

9. Henry Cabot Lodge to Henry L. Higginson, 8 March 1909, Henry Cabot Lodge Papers, Massachusetts Historical Society, Boston.

10. Howe, *Meyer,* 447.

11. Park Benjamin, "The Reorganization of the Navy Department," *Independent,* 16 December 1909.

12. Wiegand, *Patrician,* 189.

13. Elting E. Morison, *Turmoil and Tradition: A Study of the Life and Times of Henry L. Stimson* (Boston, Mass.: Houghton Mifflin, 1960), 146–154, is excellent on the problems of the army during the Taft years.

14. "Dickinson Out; Stimson Chosen," *New York Times,* 13 May 1911.

15. *Taft and Roosevelt: The Intimate Letters of Archie Butt Military Aide,* 2 vols. (Garden City, N.Y.: Doubleday, Doran, 1930), 1:386.

16. Taft to Don A. Pardee, 21 March 1909, Taft Papers.

17. Taft to Horace Lurton, 22 May 1909, Taft Papers.

18. Taft to Jacob M. Dickinson, 6 December 1909 (first quotation), Taft to Simeon Johnson, 25 July 1910 (second quotation), Taft Papers.

19. Alexander M. Bickel, "Mr. Taft Rehabilitates the Court," *Yale Law Journal* 79 (November 1969): 1–45, is an excellent account of White's selection and Taft's other court nominees.

20. Taft to Helen Taft, 9 November 1909, Taft Papers.

21. Henry F. Pringle, *The Life and Times of William Howard Taft,* 2 vols. (New York: Farrar & Rinehart, 1939), 2:854.

22. William Howard Taft, *Political Issues and Outlooks: Speeches Delivered between August 1908 and February 1910* (New York: Doubleday, Page, 1910), 33.

23. David Charles Needham, "William Howard Taft, the Negro, and the White South, 1909–1912" (Ph.D. diss., University of Georgia, 1970), 38–39.

24. Walter Hines Page, "Mr. Taft and the South," *World's Work* 17 (February 1909): 11187–11188, quoted in Needham, "Taft," 72.

25. Needham, "Taft," 132; Taft to Robert H. Terrell, 2 March 1910, Taft Papers.

26. "Taft Tribute to Jews," *New York Times,* 1 March 1910.

27. "Club Officers Quit after Taft Speech," *New York Times,* 18 May 1911.

28. Ibid.

29. Taft to Jacob M. Dickinson, 8 May 1911, Taft Papers; "Rebuke by President," *Washington Post,* 6 June 1911.

30. "Rebuke by President," *Washington Post,* 6 June 1911. Simon Wolf, *Presidents I Have Known* (Washington, D.C.: Press of Byron S. Adams, 1918), 389. Edward Coffman, *The Regulars: The American Army, 1898–1941* (Cambridge, Mass.: Belknap Press of Harvard University Press, 2004), 125–126, has a good summary of the case. Bloom continued to face prejudice during his ten-year career while Taft withdrew the reprimand against Colonel Garrard on 4 March 1913.

31. "Suffragettes Hiss Taft, Their Guest," *New York Times,* 15 April 1910.

32. Ibid., "Women Thank Taft, Condemn His Views," *New York Times,* 16 April 1910.

33. Kriste Lindenmeyer, *"A Right to Childhood": The U.S. Children's Bureau and Child Welfare, 1912–1946* (Urbana: University of Illinois Press, 1997), 15–26, is excellent on the background of the bureau and the legislative struggle to establish it.

34. Ibid., 28.

35. James N. Giglio, *H. M. Daugherty and the Politics of Expediency* (Kent, Ohio: Kent State University Press, 1978), 52–54, has a good summary of the Morse case.

36. "50,000 Sign Morse Petition," *New York Times,* 16 December 1910; "Taft Denies Pardon to Walsh and Morse," *New York Times,* 25 May 1911. Walsh was a Chicago banker convicted of a crime similar to what Morse had done.

37. Harry Daugherty to Charles D. Hilles, 29 August 1911, Taft Papers, Wickersham to Taft, 22 December 1911, Taft Papers.

38. Taft Statement on Morse, 18 January 1912, Taft Papers; "Taft Is Chagrined over Morse Pardon," *New York Times,* 16 November 1913. Taft had reason to know even while he was president what Morse had done. "Morse Fooled the Army Examiners," *New York Times,* 6 September 1912.

39. Giglio, *H. M. Daugherty,* 49–54, describes the aftermath of the Morse pardon.

40. Lewis L. Gould, *The Presidency of Theodore Roosevelt* (Lawrence: University Press of Kansas, 1991), 219.

41. Oscar E. Anderson Jr., "The Pure-Food Issue: A Republican Dilemma, 1906–1912," *American Historical Review* 61 (April 1956): 560–563, and Clayton A. Coppin and Jack High, *The Politics of Purity: Harvey Washington Wiley and the Origins of Federal Food Policy* (Ann Arbor: University of Michigan Press, 1999), 153–157, look at Wiley's role under Taft.

42. "Taft Is Advised by Wickersham to Oust Wiley," *New York Times*, 13 July 1911; "Taft Upholds Wiley but Reproves Aids," *New York Times*, 16 September 1911.

CHAPTER 10: RECIPROCITY, REVOLUTION, AND ARBITRATION

1. "Think Taft Will Be the Nominee of 1912," *New York Times*, 10 November 1910.

2. Joel Arthur Tarr, *A Study in Boss Politics: William Lorimer of Chicago* (Urbana: University of Illinois Press, 1971), 252–265, is an excellent study of the Lorimer case.

3. *Supplement to the Messages and Papers of the Presidents Covering the Administration of William Howard Taft, March 4, 1909, to March 4, 1913* (New York: Bureau of National Literature, 1913), 7502.

4. James Bryce to Edward Grey, 26 January 1911, FO 368/491, British National Archives, London.

5. *Canadian Reciprocity: Special Message of the President of the United States Transmitted to the Two House of Congress January 26, 1911*, Senate Document No. 787, 61st Cong., 2nd Sess. (Washington, D.C.: Government Printing Office, 1911), vi.

6. Ibid., ix–x.

7. Taft to Roosevelt, 10 January 1911, in "Taft's Reciprocity Letter," *New York Times*, 3 May 1912. The letter was published during the course of the Taft–Roosevelt battle in 1912.

8. Roosevelt to Taft, 12 January 1911, in Elting E. Morison et al., eds., *The Letters of Theodore Roosevelt*, 8 vols. (Cambridge: Harvard University Press, 1951–1954), 7:206.

9. James Bryce to Sir Edward Grey, 31 January 1911, FO 368/491, British National Archives, London.

10. Taft to Horace Taft, 30 January 1911, Taft Papers, Manuscript Division, LC.

11. Joseph R. Grundy to J. Hampton Moore, 13 February 1911, J. Hampton Moore Papers, Box 16, Pennsylvania Historical Society, Philadelphia; Albert Clarke to James Swank, 13 March 1911, copy in Joseph B. Foraker Papers, Cincinnati Historical Society, Ohio.

12. Knute Nelson to Ole O. Canestorp, 9 March 1911, Knute Nelson Papers, Box 44, Minnesota Historical Society, St. Paul.

13. Moses E. Clapp to Joseph Alfred Arner Burnquist, 2 March 1911, Joseph Alfred Arner Burnquist Papers, Minnesota Historical Society, St. Paul.

14. A good discussion of these events is in Claude E. Barfield, "The Democratic Party in Congress, 1909–1913" (Ph.D. diss., Northwestern, 1965), 303–305. Clark is quoted on 305. Taft to Samuel W. McCall, 15 February 1911, Taft Papers.

15. Winthrop Murray Crane to Nelson Aldrich, 17 February 1911, Nelson Aldrich Papers, Manuscript Division, Library of Congress (hereafter LC).

16. James S. Sherman to Lucius N. Littauer, 18 February 1911, James S. Sherman Papers, New York Public Library, Astor, Lenox, and Tilden Foundations.

17. Taft to Helen Taft, 15 October 1909, Taft Papers.

18. Henry Lane Wilson, *Diplomatic Episodes in Mexico, Belgium and Chile* (Garden City, N.Y.: Doubleday, Page, 1927), 229–230, makes clear the ambassador's dislike of Madero.

19. P. Edward Haley, *Revolution and Intervention: The Diplomacy of Taft and Wilson with Mexico, 1910–1917* (Cambridge, Mass.: MIT Press, 1970), 21, 25; *Papers Relating to the Foreign Relations of the United States with the Annual Message of the President Transmitted to Congress December 7, 1911* (Washington, D.C.: Government Printing Office, 1918), xi.

20. Taft to Knox, 11 March 1911, Taft Papers.

21. Ibid.

22. Taft to George von Lengerke Meyer, 14 March 1911, Taft Papers.

23. Taft to Oscar Straus, 6 May 1911, Taft Papers; James Bryce to Edward Grey, 18 March 1911, Foreign Office 800/334, British National Archives.

24. Sherman to Charles W. Fairbanks, 3 April 1911, Sherman Papers.

25. *Taft and Roosevelt: The Intimate Letters of Archie Butt Military Aide,* 2 vols. (Garden City, N.Y.: Doubleday, Doran, 1930), 2:607.

26. Taft to Ballinger, 7 March 1911, Taft Papers.

27. James R. Garfield to Gifford Pinchot, 5 April 1911, Gifford Pinchot Papers, Manuscript Division, LC. On Fisher, see Alan B. Gould, "'Trouble Portfolio' to Constructive Conservation: Secretary of the Interior Walter L. Fisher, 1911–1913," *Forest History* 16 (January 1973): 4–12.

28. Memorandum, 13 May 1911, Charles D. Hilles Papers, Sterling Memorial Library, Yale University, New Haven, Conn.

29. "Speech of President Taft on the Reciprocal Tariff Agreement with Canada," in *Supplement to the Messages and Papers of the Presidents,* 7594, 7595.

30. "Speech of President Taft," 7592; James Bryce to Sir Edward Grey, 1 May 1911, Papers of Sir Edward Grey, FO 800/83, British National Archives, London.

31. John J. Esch to Gustav Kustermann, 5 April 1911, John J. Esch Papers, Wisconsin Historical Society, Madison; William Allen White to Mark Sullivan, 5 June 1911, William Allen White Papers, Manuscript Division, LC.

32. Chauncey Depew to E. H. Butler, 6 March 1911, Chauncey Depew Papers, Sterling Memorial Library, Yale University, New Haven, Conn.

33. Alfred Henry George Grey to James Bryce, 21 July 1911, in Embassy Papers, Vol. 32, James Bryce Papers, Bodleian Library, Oxford.

34. The diplomat is quoted in Michael H. Hunt, *The Making of a Special Relationship: The United States and China to 1914* (New York: Columbia University Press, 1983), 210.

35. "Pith of American Diplomacy," *New York Observer and Chronicle*, 30 June 1910, 828, quoted Knox. Knox to Francis Huntington Wilson, 20 May 1910, Box 28, Philander Knox Papers, Manuscript Division, LC.

36. "Remarks of President Taft at a Banquet Given in His Honor by the American Peace and Arbitration League," 23 March 1910, and "Address of President Taft at the Banquet of the American Society for the Judicial Settlement of International Disputes," 17 December 1910, in *Peace, Patriotic and Religious Addresses by President Taft* (New York: International Peace Forum, 1912), 5, 7. David S. Patterson, *Toward a Warless World: The Travail of the American Peace Movement, 1887–1914* (Bloomington: Indiana University Press, 1976), 165–170, provides background on Taft's thinking.

37. Theodore Roosevelt, "The Arbitration Treaty with Great Britain," *Outlook* 98 (20 May 1911): 97–98.

38. "No Pledge to Taft," *Washington Post,* 8 June 1911. See also Roosevelt to James R. Garfield, 8 June 1911, Theodore Roosevelt Papers, Manuscript Division, LC.

39. Roosevelt to Arthur Hamilton Lee, 27 June 1911, 22 August 1911, Morison et al., *Letters of Theodore Roosevelt*, 7:297, 337.

CHAPTER 11: TOWARD A BREAK WITH ROOSEVELT

1. Walter Prescott Webb and Terrell Webb, eds., *Washington Wife: Journal of Ellen Maury Slayden from 1897–1919* (New York: Harper & Row, 1963), 156.

2. "Kin of Presidents Invited by Tafts," *New York Times,* 17 June 1911.

3. Roosevelt to Oscar King Davis, 31 May 1911, in Elting E. Morison et al., eds., *The Letters of Theodore Roosevelt*, 8 vols. (Cambridge: Harvard University Press, 1951–1954), 7:273.

4. Charles D. Hilles to R. I. Gammell, 6 June 1911, Charles D. Hilles Papers, Sterling Memorial Library, Yale University, New Haven, Conn.

5. Hilles to Charles P. Taft, 14 September 1911, Hilles Papers.

6. Verse from Denver *Republican*, 6 April 1911, Arthur Chapman, "Center Shots," in Francis E. Warren Letterbook, Francis E. Warren Papers, American Heritage Center, University of Wyoming, Laramie.

7. Taft to Helen Taft, 7 August 1911, Taft Papers, Manuscript Division, Library of Congress (hereafter LC).

8. Taft to Helen Taft, 20 July 1911, Taft Papers.

9. Taft to Helen Taft, 6 July 1911, Taft Papers. For background on the Ray case, see Beecher B. Ray to Charles D. Norton, 8 August 1910, Ray to Taft, 17 June 1911, 18 June 1911, Taft Papers.

10. The executive order of 28 October 1910 can be found in *Supplement to the Messages and Papers of the Presidents Covering the Administration of William Howard Taft, March 4, 1909, to March 4, 1913* (New York: Bureau of National Literature, 1913), 7600.

11. Theodore Roosevelt, "Alaska—It Must Be Developed," *Outlook* 98 (22 July 1911): 612–614; Taft to Helen Taft, 20 July 1911, Taft Papers.

12. *Supplement to the Messages and Papers of the Presidents,* 7617.

13. "The Pending Arbitration Treaties: Address by Hon. Philander C. Knox before the American Society of Judicial Settlement of International Disputes, Cincinnati, Ohio, November 8, 1911," U.S. Senate, Senate Document 298, 62nd Cong., 2nd Sess. (Washington, D.C.: Government Printing Office, 1912), 2.

14. Roosevelt to Arthur Lee, 22 August 1911 (first quotation), Roosevelt to Cecil Arthur Spring Rice, 22 August 1911 (second quotation), in Morison et al., *Letters of Theodore Roosevelt,* 7:334, 338; "Roosevelt Assails the Taft Treaties," *New York Times,* 8 September 1911.

15. Taft to Knox, 9 September 1911, Philander Knox Papers, Manuscript Division, LC.

16. "Nothing to Stop Taft Renomination," *New York Times,* 20 August 1911.

17. Roosevelt to Theodore Roosevelt Jr., 22 August 1911, in Morison et al., *Letters of Theodore Roosevelt,* 7:336.

18. Taft to Helen Taft, 16 August 1911, Taft Papers.

19. "Taft Denounces Tariff-for-Politics," *New York Times,* 27 August 1911.

20. Taft to George von Lengerke Meyer, 28 August 1911, George von Lengerke Meyer Papers, Massachusetts Historical Society, Boston.

21. Sereno E. Payne to Ebenezer J. Hill, 26 September 1911, Ebenezer J. Hill Papers, Sterling Memorial Library, Yale.

22. Hilles to Arthur I. Vorys, 26 September 1911, Hilles Papers.

23. Hilles to Charles Nagel, 26 September 1911 (Missouri), "Memorandum on Oregon," 12 October 1911, "Memorandum on Washington," 15 October 1911, Hilles Papers.

24. Knox to Taft, 13 October 1911, Taft Papers.

25. Daniel M. Crane and Thomas A. Breslin, *An Ordinary Relationship: American Opposition to Republican Revolution in China* (Miami: Florida International University Press, 1986), 110–116.

26. Taft and Wickersham are quoted in James Clifford German Jr., "Taft's Attorney General: George W. Wickersham" (Ph.D. diss., New York University, 1969), 110 (Taft), 115 (Wickersham).

27. Lafayette Young to John F. Lacey, 28 October 1911, John F. Lacey Papers, Box 263, Iowa State Department of History and Archives, Des Moines.

28. James C. German Jr., "Taft, Roosevelt and United States Steel," *Historian* 34 (August 1972): 599, quotes Roosevelt.

29. Roosevelt to Theodore Roosevelt Jr., 9 August 1911, Morison et al., *Letters of Theodore Roosevelt,* 7:322.

30. German, "Taft's Attorney General," 276–277, discusses Dickinson's actions in 1911.

31. Felix Frankfurter explored the contradictions in Taft's handling of the trust issue in general in his diaries at this time. See Joseph Lash, ed., *From the Diaries of Felix Frankfurter* (New York: Norton, 1975), 106–107.

32. German, "Taft, Roosevelt, and United States Steel," 605, 610.

33. Roosevelt to James R. Garfield, 31 October 1911, Roosevelt to Theodore

Roosevelt Jr., 9 November 1911, in Morison et al., *Letters of Theodore Roosevelt*, 7:431, 432; Theodore Roosevelt, "The Trusts, the People and the Square Deal," *Outlook* 99 (1911): 655.

34. Roosevelt to Benjamin Barr Lindsey, 5 December 1911, in Morison et al., *Letters of Theodore Roosevelt*, 7:451.

35. Charles W. Fairbanks to Joseph B. Foraker, 23 November 1911, Joseph B. Foraker Papers, Cincinnati Historical Society, Ohio; Otto Bannard to Henry L. Stimson, 11 December 1911, Henry L. Stimson Papers, Sterling Memorial Library, Yale University, New Haven, Conn.

36. Taft to Charles D. Norton, 26 December 1911, Hilles Papers.

37. Taft to Mabel Boardman, 24 December 1911, Mabel Boardman Papers, Box 5, Manuscript Division, LC.

CHAPTER 12: "ROOSEVELT WAS MY CLOSEST FRIEND"

1. For examples of Democratic probing, see "Knox Defies Committee," *New York Times*, 23 January 1912, questioning expenses for the Lake Champlain centennial in 1909, "Investigate Knox's Valet," *New York Times*, 21 March 1912; and "Dollar Diplomacy Hit by Democrats," *New York Times*, 12 May 1912.

2. *Supplement to the Messages and Papers of the Presidents Covering the Administration of William Howard Taft, March 4, 1909, to March 4, 1913* (New York: Bureau of National Literature, 1913), 7644.

3. Clifford L. Egan, "Pressure Groups, the Department of State, and the Abrogation of the Russian–American Treaty of 1832," *Proceedings of the American Philosophical Society* 115 (20 August 1971): 328–334.

4. Taft to Simon Wolf, 21 December 1911, in Simon Wolf, *The Presidents I Have Known from 1860 to 1918* (Washington: Press of Byron S. Adams, 1918), 320. "Taft Abrogates Russian Treaty," *New York Times*, 19 December 1911.

5. *Supplement to the Messages and Papers of the Presidents*, 7664. Emily S. Rosenberg, *Financial Missionaries to the World: The Politics and Culture of Dollar Diplomacy, 1900–1930* (Durham, N.C.: Duke University Press, 2003), 68–69.

6. David H. Burton, *William Howard Taft: Confident Peacemaker* (Philadelphia, Pa.: Saint Joseph's University Press, 2004), 82.

7. "Treaties May Be Useless, Says Taft," *New York Times*, 9 March 1912.

8. *Supplement to the Messages and Papers of the Presidents*, 7698–7719.

9. Taft to Mabel Boardman, 24 December 1911, Mabel Boardman Papers, Manuscript Division, Library of Congress (hereafter LC).

10. See, for example, "Only 202 Delegates Now Needed by Taft," *New York Times*, 14 April 1912.

11. "Taft Fires on His Opponents," *New York Times*, 17 February 1912.

12. "Taft Denounces Recall of Judges," *New York Times*, 21 January 1912; Lodge to Brooks Adams, 5 March 1912, Henry Cabot Lodge Papers, Massachusetts Historical Society, Boston.

13. Hilles to Taft, 21 February 1912, Merrill Moores to Taft, 9 March 1912,

Charles D. Hilles Papers, Sterling Memorial Library, Yale University, New Haven, Conn.

14. David Charles Needham, "William Howard Taft, the Negro, and the White House, 1908, 1912" (Ph.D. diss., University of Georgia, 1970), 228–288; Hilles to Booker T. Washington, 5 April 1912, Hilles Papers.

15. Taft to James W. Wadsworth, 12 April 1912, Hilles Papers.

16. "Taft in Tears as He Lauds Major Butt," *New York Times,* 6 May 1912.

17. Taft to William B. McKinley, 12 March 1912, Hilles Papers. "Taft to Hit Back at Roosevelt Soon," *New York Times,* 23 April 1912.

18. Taft to George von Lengerke Meyer, 28 March 1912, Taft Papers, Manuscript Division, LC; Taft to Henry L. Stimson, 16 April 1912, Henry L. Stimson Papers, Sterling Memorial Library, Yale University, New Haven, Conn. Elihu Root to Taft, 15 May 1912, Elihu Root Papers, Manuscript Division, LC.

19. Taft to Mabel Boardman, 23 April 1912, Boardman Papers; Taft to Louis E. Payn, 23 April 1912, Hilles Papers.

20. "Taft Opens Fire on Roosevelt," *New York Times,* 26 April 1912; Henry F. Pringle, *The Life and Times of William Howard Taft,* 2 vols. (New York: Farrar & Rinehart, 1939), 2:782.

21. "Colonel Says Taft Is the Disloyal One," *New York Times,* 27 April 1912; "500,000 Turn Out to Cheer Taft On," *New York Times,* 30 April 1912.

22. "Roosevelt Unsafe, Taft Tells Ohioans," *New York Times,* 14 May 1912; Taft to Hilles, 16 May 1912, Hilles Papers.

23. Taft to Clarence H. Kelsey et al., 22 May 1912, Hilles Papers.

24. Taft to Marshall Bullitt, 26 May 1912, Hilles Papers.

25. Victor Rosewater, *Backstage in 1912: The Inside Story of the Split Republican Convention* (Philadelphia, Pa.: Dorrance, 1932), 80–94.

26. Reuben Roy to Margaret Roy, 11 June 1912, author's collection. Roy was a commissioner of the Missouri Supreme Court.

27. Hilles to Taft, 9 June 1912, Hilles Papers.

28. Taft to Victor Rosewater, 31 May 1912, Hilles Papers. Leroy Vernon to Mrs. Vernon, 12 June 1912, Leroy Vernon Papers, Center for American History, University of Texas, Austin.

29. "The Case against the Reactionaries," in *Social Justice and Popular Rule: The Works of Theodore Roosevelt,* 20 vols. (New York: Charles Scribner's Sons, 1926), 17:204, 17:221, 17:231.

30. Taft to Hilles, 14 June 1912, Frederick C. Stevens to Taft, 16 June 1912, Hilles Papers.

31. Taft to William A. Barnes Jr., 29 May 1912, Taft Papers.

32. Robert M. La Follette, *La Follette's Autobiography: A Personal Narrative of Political Experiences* (Madison, Wis.: Robert M. La Follette, 1913), 655.

33. Theodore Roosevelt to the Republican National Convention, 22 June 1912, in Elting E. Morison et al., eds., *The Letters of Theodore Roosevelt,* 8 vols. (Cambridge, Mass.: Harvard University Press, 1951–1954), 7:562.

34. Taft to C. A. Ricks, 26 June 1912, Taft to George H. Earle Jr., 9 July 1912, Hilles Papers; Taft to Mrs. Buckner R. Wallingford, 14 July 1912, Taft Papers.

CHAPTER 13: THE 1912 CAMPAIGN

1. Thomas A. Bailey, "The Lodge Corollary to the Monroe Doctrine," *Political Science Quarterly* 48 (June 1933): 220–239, discusses Lodge's motives in this episode. Also see William C. Widenor, *Henry Cabot Lodge and the Search for an American Foreign Policy* (Berkeley: University of California Press, 1980), 135–136.

2. Bailey, "Lodge Corollary," 222; "Warning to Japan on Magdalena Bay," *New York Times*, 5 April 1912.

3. "Warning to Powers Adopted by Senate," *New York Times*, 3 August 1912.

4. Taft to David Starr Jordan, 5 August 1912, Taft Papers, Manuscript Division, Library of Congress.

5. The best source for the background of this dispute is Philip C. Jessup, *Elihu Root*, 2 vols. (New York: Dodd, Mead, 1938), 2:262–269. The American reaction to British protests is well set forth in "England a Meddler Is Washington View," *New York Times*, 12 July 1912.

6. Taft to Henry S. Drinker, 27 July 1912, Taft to Helen Taft, 15 August 1912, Taft Papers.

7. Taft to Helen Taft, 21 August 1912, Taft Papers.

8. Elting E. Morison, *Turmoil and Tradition: A Study of the Life and Times of Henry L. Stimson* (Boston, Mass.: Houghton Mifflin, 1960), 164.

9. Taft to Helen Taft, 23 August 1912, Taft Papers.

10. Taft to Helen Taft, 26 August 1912, Taft Papers. Taft probably meant those who were for a tariff only to raise revenue, a classic Democratic position.

11. Taft to George H. Earle, 9 July 1912, Charles D. Hilles Papers, Sterling Memorial Library, Yale University, New Haven, Conn.

12. Taft to Joseph Gaffney, 12 August 1912, Taft Papers.

13. Taft to Helen Taft, 9 July 1912, Taft Papers.

14. Hilles to Taft, 31 July 1912, 1 August 1912, 12 August 1912, Hilles Papers, for the problems about the treasurer and organizing the Taft campaign.

15. For these developments, see Lewis L. Gould, "Theodore Roosevelt, William Howard Taft and the Disputed Delegates in 1912: Texas as a Test Case," *Southwestern Historical Quarterly* 80 (July 1976): 33–34.

16. Taft to Helen Taft, 26 July 1912, Taft Papers.

17. Taft to Helen Taft, 28 July 1912, Taft Papers.

18. Taft to Helen Taft, 23 July 1912, Taft Papers.

19. "Speech of William Howard Taft Accepting the Nomination for the Presidency of the Republican National Convention," in Republican National Committee, *Republican Campaign Text-Book 1912* (Philadelphia: Press of Dunlap Printing, 1912), 8, 10, 16, 21.

20. Ibid., 13.

21. Francis Curtis to James S. Sherman, 13 August 1912, James S. Sherman Papers, New York Public Library, Astor, Lenox, and Tilden Foundations.

22. Taft to Helen Taft, 9 August 1912, 13 August 1912, 26 August 1912, Taft Papers.

23. Lars Schoultz, *Beneath the United States: A History of U.S. Policy toward Latin America* (Cambridge, Mass.: Harvard University Press, 1998), 218–219. Walter V. Scholes and Marie V. Scholes, *The Foreign Policies of the Taft Administration* (Columbia: University of Missouri Press, 1970), 65–67.

24. Taft to Henry L. Stimson, 2 September 1912, Taft Papers.

25. Taft to Helen Taft, 26 August 1912, Taft Papers.

26. "Asks for More Reserves," *Washington Post,* 10 October 1912; "Taft Talks to Jews," *Washington Post,* 19 October 1912; "Taft Tours in Rain," *Washington Post,* 24 October 1912.

27. "No G.O.P. Hara-Kiri," *Washington Post,* 21 October 1912; "Taft Warns Farmer," *Washington Post,* 25 October 1912; "Points Way to Voters," *Washington Post,* 29 October 1912.

28. Taft to Sherman, 24 August 1912, James S. Sherman Papers; Taft to Charles Nagel, 30 September 1912, Charles Nagel Papers, Box 22, Sterling Memorial Library, Yale University, New Haven, Conn., Taft to Horace Taft, 1 November 1912, copy in Charles D. Hilles Papers.

29. George von Lengerke Meyer to George D. Ayers, 3 September 1912, George von Lengerke Meyer Papers, Massachusetts Historical Society, Boston; Hilles to C. Sidney Shepard, 15 October 1912, Hilles Papers. Isabel Anderson, *Presidents and Pies: Life in Washington, 1897–1919* (Boston, Mass.: Houghton Mifflin, 1920), 157.

30. Elihu Root to Grenville M. Dodge, 16 October 1912, Grenville M. Dodge Papers, Box 56, Iowa State Department of History and Archives, Des Moines.

31. Sherman to Taft, 23 August 1912, Taft Papers, makes clear the vice president's limited role in the administration.

32. Taft to Woodrow Wilson, 5 November 1912, Taft Papers; Anderson, *Presidents and Pies,* 164.

33. Taft to Charles Hopkins Clark, 8 November 1912, Hilles Papers.

34. Hilles to Winthrop Murray Crane, 12 November 1912, Hilles Papers.

35. Taft to Myron T. Herrick, 7 November 1912, Taft to Mrs. Buckner A. Wallingford, 9 November 1912, Taft Papers.

36. Taft to Charles Hopkins Clark, 8 November 1912, Hilles Papers.

CHAPTER 14: LEAVING THE WHITE HOUSE

1. "Taft's Task Not Done," *Washington Post,* 14 November 1912.

2. "Taft Swan Song Plea for Change," *Washington Post,* 17 November 1912.

3. Ibid.

4. Taft to Woodrow Wilson, 6 January 1913, Taft Papers.

5. Frederick C. Hicks, *William Howard Taft: Yale Professor of Law and New Haven Citizen* (New Haven: Yale University Press, 1945), 1.

6. Taft to Charles P. Taft, 20 November 1912, Taft Papers, Manuscript Division, Library of Congress (hereafter LC).

7. Hicks, *Taft,* 6–7.

8. Wilson to Taft, 2 December 1912, in Arthur S. Link et al., eds., *The Papers*

of Woodrow Wilson, Volume 25, 1912 (Princeton, N.J.: Princeton University Press, 1978), 574; "Wilson Upsets Tradition," *Washington Post,* 26 December 1912.

9. Taft to Wilson, 6 January 1912, Taft Papers; Wilson to Taft, 8 January 1913, in Arthur S. Link et al., eds., *The Papers of Woodrow Wilson, Volume 26, 1913* (Princeton, N.J.: Princeton University Press, 1978), 18–19.

10. "Taft Is Sure of Canal on Time," *Washington Post,* 30 December 1912.

11. Taft to Robert Underwood Johnson, 15 January 1913, Taft Papers.

12. "Annual Message Part II," 6 December 1912, in *Supplement to the Messages and Papers of the Presidents Covering the Administration of William Howard Taft, March 4, 1909, to March 4, 1913* (New York: Bureau of National Literature, 1913).

13. *Supplement to the Messages and Papers of the Presidents,* 7795; Richard T. McCulley, *Banks and Politics during the Progressive Era: The Origins of the Federal Reserve System, 1897–1913* (New York: Garland, 1992), 256–260.

14. For Taft's difficulties with the Methodist church over these temperance issues, see Charles H. Grosvenor to Earl M. Cranston, 6 May 1912, Cranston to Charles H. Grosvenor, 11 May 1912, Grosvenor to Cranston, 20 May 1912, Taft Papers. John Hays Hammond, *The Autobiography of John Hays Hammond,* 2 vols. (New York: Farrar & Rinehart, 1935), 2:546, mentions Taft's attitude toward wine and liquor.

15. "Taft's Veto Is Vain," *Washington Post,* 1 March 1913; "Methodist Assails Taft," *New York Times,* 14 March 1914.

16. "Taft Talks to Jews," *Washington Post,* 19 October 1912; "Taft Due Home Today," *Washington Post,* 27 October 1912, a speech to the National Polish Alliance.

17. Charles Nagel to Taft, 12 February 1913, in "Veto Message," 14 February 1913, *Supplement to the Messages and Papers of the Presidents,* 7850–7851.

18. Hans Vought, *The Bully Pulpit and the Melting Pot: American Presidents and the Immigrant, 1897–1933* (Macon, Ga.: Mercer University Press, 2004), 92.

19. "Annual Message—Part I," 3 December 1912, in *Supplement to the Messages and Papers of the Presidents,* 7772, 7783–7784.

20. P. Edward Healy, *Revolution and Intervention: The Diplomacy of Taft and Wilson with Mexico, 1910–1917* (Cambridge: MIT Press, 1970), 53–64.

21. Walter Webb and Terrell Webb, eds., *Washington Wife: Journal of Ellen Maury Slayden from 1897–1919* (New York: Harper & Row, 1962, 1963), 194.

22. "No Intervention Is Taft's Decision," *New York Times,* 22 February 1913.

23. "Exit Taft: Enter Wilson," *Philadelphia Inquirer,* 5 March 1913; "Popular Verdict on Taft," Portland *Oregonian,* 4 March 1913.

24. "William H. Taft," *New York Times,* 4 March 1913; "The Retiring President," *Outlook,* 8 March 1913, 520.

25. "Popular Verdict on Taft," Portland *Morning Oregonian,* 4 March 1913.

26. Webb and Webb, *Washington Wife,* 207. *Wilkes-Barre Times Leader,* 3 March 1913.

27. "Taft Is Grateful for All He Has Had," *New York Times,* 2 March 1913.

28. "Crowds Cheer Taft as He Leaves City," *New York Times,* 5 March 1913.

29. Taft to Mabel Boardman, 16 April 1913, Mabel Boardman Papers, Manuscript Division, LC.

30. William Howard Taft, *The President and His Powers,* in W. Carey McWilliams and Frank X. Gerrity, eds., *The Collected Works of William Howard Taft* (Athens: Ohio University Press, 2003), 6:108.

31. James F. Vivian, ed., *William Howard Taft: Collected Editorials, 1917–1921* (New York: Praeger, 1990).

32. Taft to Katherine Wulsin, 4 July 1918, Taft Papers. Taft did not go into his differences with Roosevelt in his writings at the time of Roosevelt's death. "Brilliant Personality Gone (T.R.)," in Vivian, *William Howard Taft,* 153–156.

33. Taft to W. K. Hutchinson, 29 December 1925, in Henry F. Pringle, *The Life and Times of William Howard Taft,* 2 vols. (New York: Farrar & Rinehart, 1939), 2:960.

34. Alpheus Thomas Mason, *William Howard Taft: Chief Justice* (New York: Simon and Schuster, 1965), remains the standard source on Taft's years on the Supreme Court.

35. "The Times Presidential Rankings—Numbers 32 to 22," *Times Online,* 29 October 2008, http://www.timesonline.co.uk/tol/news/world/us_and_americas/us_elections/article 505540.

36. Judith Anderson's book, *William Howard Taft: An Intimate History* (New York: Norton, 1981), presented her psychological thesis. She has updated her views in "William Howard Taft," in Philip Weeks, ed., *Buckeye Presidents: Ohioans in the White House* (Kent, Ohio: Kent State University Press, 2003), 212–242. Donald F. Anderson, *William Howard Taft: A Conservative's Conception of the Presidency* (Ithaca, N.Y.: Cornell University Press, 1973).

37. Stanley D. Solvick, "William Howard Taft and the Progressive Movement: A Study in Conservative Thought and Politics" (Ph.D. diss., University of Michigan, 1963).

38. Ralph Eldon Minger, *William Howard Taft and United States Foreign Policy: The Apprenticeship Years, 1900–1908* (Urbana: University of Illinois Press, 1975).

39. For other assessments of Taft's record, see David W. Levy, "William Howard Taft, 1909–1913," in Melvin I. Urofsky, ed., *The American Presidents* (New York: Garland, 2000), 278–287; Alan Brinkley, "William Howard Taft, 1909–1913," in Alan Brinkley and Davis Dyer, eds., *The Reader's Companion to the American Presidency* (Boston, Mass.: Houghton Mifflin, 2000), 304–315; and Michael Harwood, revised by John Milton Cooper, "William Howard Taft: Reluctant Leader," in Michael Beschloss, ed., *American Heritage Illustrated History of the Presidents* (New York: Crown Publishers, 2000), 328–335.

BIBLIOGRAPHICAL ESSAY

The most important manuscript source for the presidency of William Howard Taft are the William Howard Taft Papers at the Manuscript Division, Library of Congress (hereafter LC). The Taft Papers were microfilmed and indexed in 1972. They consist of 658 reels, of which reels 323 to 461 provide the case files of the White House and reels 495 to 516 cover the presidential letter books. The *Index to the William Howard Taft Papers* (6 vols., Washington, D.C.: Library of Congress, 1972) is easy to use. Only in a very few instances did the indexers miss a document or fail to list one in the index.

For the political aspects of the Taft years, the Charles D. Hilles Papers, Sterling Memorial Library, Yale University, New Haven, Conn., rival the larger Taft collection. When he left the White House in 1913, Hilles retained the Series 6, Case File 300, political files for 1910–1912 that had once been part of the larger Taft collection. The Hilles Papers are indispensable for the story of Taft's renomination campaign and his reelection effort.

The papers of the members of Taft's cabinet vary in quality. The Richard A. Ballinger Papers, University of Washington, Seattle, have been microfilmed and are important for conservation policy. The papers of his successor, Walter L. Fisher, are at the Library of Congress. The Philander Knox Papers (LC) are significant for the foreign policy of the Taft years but do not shed much light on Knox as a person. The Charles Nagel Papers, Sterling Memorial Library, Yale University, have much on politics and the workings of the presidency from the perspective of the secretary of commerce. The Henry L. Stimson Papers, also at Yale, have a good deal of interesting material on the events of 1911–1912. The Jacob M. Dickinson Papers at the Tennessee Historical Society cover his tenure as secretary of war. The George von Lengerke Meyer Papers at the Massachusetts Historical Society and the Meyer Diaries (LC) are important for his career at the Navy Department.

The Franklin MacVeagh Papers (LC) are disappointing. The George Wickersham Papers are in the custody of the Wickersham family. The papers of James Wilson are at Iowa State University. The papers of James S. Sherman at the New York Public Library illustrate that the vice president was not close to Taft, but they are useful for New York politics and some aspects of Taft's relations with Congress. The Papers of Archie Butt are at Emory University.

For Congress, the important manuscripts in Washington are the Nelson Aldrich Papers (LC), the Albert J. Beveridge Papers (LC), the Thomas H. Carter Papers (LC), and the Robert M. La Follette Family Papers (LC). In Iowa, the Albert B. Cummins Papers, Iowa State Department of History and Archives, and the Jonathan P. Dolliver Papers, Iowa State Historical Society, were helpful. The Joseph L. Bristow Papers, Kansas State Historical Society, were illuminating on many legislative topics. The Bristow Papers have been microfilmed. The Henry Cabot Lodge Papers, Massachusetts Historical Society, were significant both for relations with Theodore Roosevelt and for Lodge's comments on Taft's policies. The Commonwealth Shoe and Leather Company Papers, Baker Library, Harvard Business School, provided new insights about the framing of the Payne–Aldrich tariff. The Henry L. Higginson Papers, also at the Baker Library, have some interesting letters on antitrust policy from George W. Wickersham.

The Francis E. Warren Papers, American Heritage Center, University of Wyoming, have much on tariff and conservation policy from the perspective of a conservative and cynical Republican lawmaker. The Elihu Root Papers (LC) reveal the views of a politician who liked Taft and was unfriendly to Philander Knox and his policies. The Chauncey Depew Papers, Yale University, have a number of interesting documents about the Payne–Aldrich tariff and the related question of Canadian reciprocity. The Jacob H. Gallinger Papers, New Hampshire Historical Society, have some revealing comments on Taft's propensity for travel. The Jonathan Bourne Papers at the University of Oregon are disappointing for the Taft years. The Wesley L. Jones Papers, University of Washington Library, are interesting for Taft's relations with Republicans in that state.

The Theodore Roosevelt Papers (LC) are crucial for the relationship with Taft and the former president's run for the White House in 1912. The Gifford Pinchot (LC), Amos Pinchot (LC), and James R. Garfield Papers (LC) often shed light on Roosevelt and Taft in constructive ways. For positive reactions to Taft's policies, the Mabel Boardman Papers (LC) are very helpful. I am indebted to Stacy Cordery for providing me with copies of these documents. The James Bryce Papers, Bodleian Library, Oxford, have some interesting insights about Taft from a British perspective. The same is true for the Lord Grey Papers at the University of Durham. The diplomatic records at the British National Archives, London, supplemented the Bryce and Lord Grey Papers.

Useful collections from prominent reporters and publishers of the Taft era included the Erastus Brainerd Papers at the University of Washington, the James T. Williams Jr. Papers at Duke University, and the Leroy T. Vernon Papers at the Center for American History, University of Texas, Austin. The William Allen White Papers (LC) have much on the attitudes of a Kansas editor and his correspondents to Taft's performance in office.

Other collections of value for Taft are the Nicholas Murray Butler Papers, Butler Library, Columbia University, Charles W. Fairbanks Papers, Lilly Library, Indiana University, Joseph B. Foraker Papers, Cincinnati Historical Society, William B. McKinley Papers, Syracuse University, and the Albert Shaw Papers, New York Public Library. The George A. Myers Papers at the Ohio Historical Society illuminate the responses of black Americans to Taft and are easy to use online.

DOCUMENTS, PERIODICALS, AND
SECONDARY WORKS

Paolo Coletta, ed., *William Howard Taft: A Bibliography* (Westport, Conn.: Mecker, 1989), is very thorough for the period it covers.

The published diplomatic documents of the United States for 1909–1913 are now readily available online as *Foreign Relations of the United States* through the Web site of the University of Wisconsin. *The Need for a National Budget: Message from the President of the United States Transmitting Report of the Commission on Economy and Efficiency on the Subject of the Need for a National Budget,* U.S. House of Representatives, 62nd Cong., 2nd Sess., Document 851 (Washington, D.C.: Government Printing Office, 1912), discusses Taft's proposed budgetary reforms. *Investigation of the Department of the Interior and of the Bureau of Forestry,* U.S. Senate, 61st Cong., 3rd Sess., Document 719 (13 vols., Washington, D.C.: Government Printing Office, 1910), is a mine of information about the conservation issues of the Taft era.

The major newspapers used in this book were the *New York Times* and the *Washington Post,* both of which are now indexed and available online. The online collection of "America's Historical Newspapers" includes a number of indexed newspapers around the country. The online source, "Chronicling America," provides access to the *New-York Tribune* through 1910. The *Tribune* was a key source for Republican opinion in this period. The same project has the *Washington Herald* and the *Washington Times* for 1909–1910, and they are instructive sources. In the case of periodicals for 1909–1913, the online collection of "American Nineteenth Century Periodicals" extends its coverage into the Taft period.

Useful contemporary periodical articles for Taft's presidency are William Bayard Hale, "President at Work," *World's Work* 20 (June 1910): 13005–13018; George Kibbe Turner, "An Interview with the President," *McClure's Magazine* 35 (June 1910): 220–221, Francis E. Leupp, "President Taft's Own View: An Authorized Interview," *Outlook* 99 (2 December 1911): 811–818, William Howard Taft, "What I Am Trying to Do," *World's Work* 24 (June 1912): 173–175, and Charles D. Hilles, "Socialism and Its Menace; Why Government Ownership Would Not Help the Wage-Earner—The Views of President Taft," *Century Illustrated Monthly Magazine* 34 (October 1912): 943–948.

There is no published collection of Taft's letters similar to what exists for Theodore Roosevelt and Woodrow Wilson. A few articles have appeared in which Taft letters are printed. Philip R. Shriver, ed., "William Howard Taft and Myron T. Herrick: Selected Letters, 1912–1916," *Historical and Philosophical Society of Ohio Bulletin* 14 (October 1956): 221–231; Willard B. Gatewood, ed., "The President and the

'Deacon' in the Campaign of 1912: The Correspondence of William Howard Taft and James Calvin Hemphill, 1911–1912," *Ohio History Quarterly* 74 (Winter 1965): 35–54; Gary Ness, "Proving Ground for a President: William Howard Taft and the Philippines, 1900–1905," *Cincinnati Historical Society Bulletin*, 34 (1976): 204–223; Gary Ness, "William Howard Taft and the Great War," *Cincinnati Historical Society Bulletin* 34 (1976): 6–23; Lloyd P. Gartner, "The Correspondence of Mayer Sulzberger and William Howard Taft," *Proceedings of the American Academy for Jewish Research* 46–47 (1979): 121–140. Simon Wolf, *Presidents I Have Known* (Washington, D.C.: Press of Byron S. Adams, 1918), prints some interesting Taft letters on issues involving immigration, the treatment of Jews in Russia, and the case of Frank Bloom. William Howard Taft, "A Letter to Nellie: President Taft Describing His El Paso Visit," *Password* 37 (1992): 189–192, reprints a letter from the president to his wife about his meeting with Porfirio Diaz in 1909. Searching on eBay and Google will reveal a number of individual Taft letters for sale from manuscript dealers.

For the presidency, there are three indispensable volumes. *Presidential Addresses and State Papers of William Howard Taft from March 4, 1909, to March 4, 1910* (New York: Doubleday, Page, 1910), is comprehensive on Taft's public statements during his first year. *Peace, Patriotic and Religious Addresses by President Taft Delivered during His Administration* (New York: International Peace Forum, 1912), brings together Taft's views on war and international arbitration. *Supplement to the Messages and Papers of the Presidents Covering the Administration of William Howard Taft, March 4, 1909, to March 4, 1913* (New York: Bureau of National Literature, 1913), contains his messages to Congress and selected speeches. The Ohio University Press is publishing *The Collected Works of William Howard Taft*, a series that has now reached eight volumes. The third volume on *Presidential Addresses and State Papers* (2004) and the fourth *Presidential Messages to Congress* (2002) deal with the presidency.

The standard biography of Taft is Henry F. Pringle, *The Life and Times of William Howard Taft* (2 vols., New York: Farrar & Rinehart, 1939). Pringle had access to the Taft papers first and used them in shaping a narrative sympathetic to his subject. On matters of politics, however, Pringle is a less than reliable guide. Herbert S. Duffy, *William Howard Taft* (New York: Minton, Balch, 1930), was an early biography that Pringle superseded. Judith Icke Anderson, *William Howard Taft: An Intimate History* (New York: Norton, 1981), assumes that Taft was a political failure in the White House and uses his obesity and sexual frustration as keys to understanding his problems. Jonathan Lurie is at work on a new biography of President Taft.

Ishbel Ross, *An American Family: The Tafts, 1678 to 1964* (Cleveland, Ohio: World Publishing, 1964), has useful information on the president's family and his background. Carl Sferrazza Anthony, *Nellie Taft: The Unconventional First Lady of the Ragtime Era* (New York: William Morrow, 2005), is a well-researched study of the president's wife and her impact on his career.

General works on Taft's presidency are Paolo E. Coletta, *The Presidency of William Howard Taft* (Lawrence: University Press of Kansas, 1973), which is balanced and fair about Taft's record in general while being critical of his conservatism. Donald F. Anderson, *William Howard Taft: A Conservative's Conception of the*

Presidency (Ithaca, N.Y.: Cornell University Press, 1973), explores the argument in its title through a survey of the president's outgoing letters. Michael L. Bromley, *William Howard Taft and the First Motoring Presidency* (Jefferson, N.C.: McFarland, 2003), emphasizes the automotive aspects of Taft's tenure but also says a good deal about his performance as the chief executive.

Several doctoral dissertations are informative about Taft and the presidency: John L. Withers, "The Administrative Theories and Practices of William Howard Taft" (Ph.D. diss., University of Chicago, 1957), Martin Harr Lease, "William Howard Taft and the Powers of the President" (Ph.D. diss., Indiana University, 1961), Stanley D. Solvick, "William Howard Taft and the Progressive Movement: A Study in Conservative Thought and Politics" (Ph.D. diss., University of Michigan, 1963), and Louis Peter Schultz, "William Howard Taft: A Constitutionalist's View of the Presidency" (Ph.D. diss., Northern Illinois University, 1979).

Rene N. Ballard, "The Administrative Theory of William Howard Taft," *Western Political Quarterly* 7 (1954): 65–74, is a brief survey of Taft's thinking on administration.

Memoirs about Taft's tenure in the White House include Helen Herron Taft, *Recollections of Full Years* (New York: Dodd, Mead, 1914), written by her daughter, which has much of interest about the Taft marriage and her role as first lady. *Taft and Roosevelt: The Intimate Letters of Archie Butt* (2 vols., Garden City, N.Y.: Doubleday, 1930), are the letters of Taft's military aide. They are fascinating to read but need to be checked against the original Butt letters and Taft's own papers. Lawrence F. Abbott, ed., *The Letters of Archie Butt, Military Aide to President Roosevelt* (Garden City, N.Y.: Doubleday, Page, 1924), are valuable for the light they shed on the transition from Roosevelt to Taft. Irwin Hood Hoover, *Forty-Two Years in the White House* (Boston, Mass.: Houghton Mifflin, 1934), the memoirs of a White House usher, have very critical chapters about Taft's performance. Horace Dutton Taft, *Memories and Opinions* (New York: Macmillan, 1942), offers the comments of the president's brother about the White House years. Charles E. Barker, *With President Taft in the White House* (Chicago: A. Kroch and Son, 1947), gives a brief account of Taft's workout regimen and his efforts to keep his weight down. Charles Willis Thompson, *Presidents I've Known and Two Near Presidents* (Indianapolis, Ind.: Bobbs Merrill, 1929), has several insightful chapters on Taft. Joseph P. Lash, ed., *From the Diaries of Felix Frankfurter* (New York: Norton, 1975), has some interesting entries about the Taft administration from his 1911 diary.

Other firsthand accounts of the Taft years are Walter Prescott Webb and Terrell Webb, eds., *Washington Wife: Journal of Ellen Maury Slayden from 1897–1919* (New York: Harper & Row, 1963); Isabel Anderson, *Presidents and Pies: Life in Washington, 1897–1919* (Boston, Mass.: Houghton Mifflin, 1920), and J. C. Levenson et al., eds., *The Letters of Henry Adams, Volume VI: 1906–1918* (Boston, Mass.: Belknap Press of Harvard University Press, 1988). Henry L. Stoddard, *As I Knew Them: Presidents and Politics from Grant to Coolidge* (New York: Harper & Bros., 1927), has much of interest on Taft and Roosevelt. William Allen White, *The Autobiography of William Allen White* (New York: Macmillan, 1946), contains the views on Taft's presidency of an important progressive editor. Victor Rosewater, *Backstage in 1912: The Inside Story of the Split Republican Convention* (Philadelphia: Dorrance, 1932), provides the recollections of a key Taft supporter about the Republican National Convention. William Dudley Foulke, *A Hoosier Autobiography* (New York: Oxford University Press, 1922), publishes some of the correspondence of this civil service reformer with Taft about the Payne–Aldrich tariff and other issues. Oscar King Davis, *Released for Publication: Some Inside Political History of Theodore Roosevelt and His Times, 1898–1918* (Boston, Mass.: Houghton Mifflin, 1925), documents a reporter's disillusionment with Taft's performance.

Taft's relationship with Theodore Roosevelt was at the heart of the outcome of his presidency. Elting E. Morison et al., eds., *The Letters of Theodore Roosevelt* (8 vols., Cambridge, Mass.: Harvard University Press, 1951–1954), are vital for understanding the interaction of the two men. The sixth and seventh volumes, covering 1907–1914, have Roosevelt's letters to Taft and his comments to others about his one-time friend. George E. Mowry, *Theodore Roosevelt and the Progressive Movement* (Madison: University of Wisconsin Press, 1946), etched a negative portrait of Taft into the historiography of the Progressive Era. Mowry did not, however, have access to the Taft Papers, and his account is often slanted against the president. Mowry was a little more balanced toward Taft in *The Era of Theodore Roosevelt* (New York: Harper & Bros., 1958). William Manners, *TR and Will: A Friendship that Split the Republican Party* (New York: Harcourt, 1969) examines the breakup of the friendship from the perspective of the Mowry thesis. An earlier treatment of the Taft–Roosevelt rupture, based on the recollections of some of the participants, is in Mark Sullivan, *Our Times: The United States, 1900–1925 — Volume IV, The War Begins, 1909–1914* (New York: Charles Scribner's Sons, 1932), 289–540. Herbert H. Rosenthal, "The Cruise of the Tarpon," *New York History* 39 (1958): 302, 320, considers the 1910 meeting between the two one-time friends. Patricia O'Toole, *When Trumpets Call: Theodore Roosevelt after the White House* (New York: Simon & Schuster, 2005), is very critical of Taft.

Less attention has been given to the interaction of Woodrow Wilson and Taft, both during the transition of 1912–1913 and during the Wilson presidency. Arthur S. Link et al., eds., *The Papers of Woodrow Wilson, Volume 27: 1913* (Princeton, N.J.: Princeton University Press, 1978), is illuminating on how Taft reached out to his successor about the issues that the new president would confront. Frederick C. Hicks, *William Howard Taft: Yale Professor of Law and New Haven Citizen* (New Haven, Conn.: Yale University Press, 1945), is useful for the transition from the White House to Yale in 1913.

John G. Sotos, "Taft and Pickwick: Sleep Apnea in the White House," *Chest* 124 (2003): 1133–1142, makes the case that the president suffered from a tendency toward sleep apnea that impaired his ability to function as president. The article contains some interesting insights but assumes that Taft was a presidential failure, does not mention letters when Taft expressed pleasure in his good health, and often relies on secondary sources to buttress his argument. Robert Bolt, "William Howard Taft: A Frustrated and Fretful Unitarian in the White House," *Queen City Heritage* 42 (1984): 39–48, examines Taft's religious views.

The members of Taft's cabinet have not received extensive biographical attention. By far the best treatment of these men is Elting E. Morison, *Turmoil and Tradition: A Study of the Life and Times of Henry L. Stimson* (Boston, Mass.: Houghton

Mifflin, 1960). The chapters on Stimson's two years in office are excellent. Wayne A. Wiegand, *Patrician in the Progressive Era: A Biography of George Von Lengerke Meyer* (New York: Garland, 1988), is very insightful on Meyer's handling of the Navy Department. James Clifford German Jr., "Taft's Attorney General: George W. Wickersham" (Ph.D. diss., New York University, 1969), is a superior study of how Taft and his attorney general interacted. Also important for Wickersham as attorney general is Thomas Roger Wessel, "Republican Justice: The Department of Justice under Roosevelt and Taft, 1901–1913" (Ph.D. diss., University of Maryland, 1972).

Taft's administrative style as president comes through in the relevant chapters of Peri E. Arnold, *Making the Managerial Presidency: Comprehensive Reorganization Planning, 1905–1996*, 2nd rev. ed. (Lawrence: University Press of Kansas, 1998); Robert C. Hilderbrand, *Power and the People: Executive Management of Public Opinion in Foreign Affairs, 1897–1921* (Chapel Hill: University of North Carolina Press, 1981); Stephen Ponder, *Managing the Press: Origins of the Media Presidency, 1897–1933* (New York: St. Martin's Press, 1998); Richard J. Ellis, *Presidential Travel: The Journey from George Washington to George W. Bush* (Lawrence: University Press of Kansas, 2008). Older but still useful on Taft's appointments is H. Hahn, "President Taft and the Discipline of Patronage," *Journal of Politics* 18 (May 1966): 368–390.

The key domestic policy of the Taft years was the protective tariff and the controversy about the Payne–Aldrich law of 1909. Richard C. Baker, *The Tariff under Roosevelt and Taft* (Hastings, Neb.: Democratic Printing, 1941), is still very useful. Stanley Solvick, "William Howard Taft and the Payne–Aldrich Tariff," *Mississippi Valley Historical Review* 50 (1963): 424–442; Claude E. Barfield, "'Our Share of the Booty': The Democratic Party, Cannonism, and the Payne–Aldrich Tariff," *Journal of American History* 57 (1970): 308–323; David W. Detzer, "Business, Reformers, and Tariff Revision: The Payne Aldrich Tariff of 1909," *Historian* 38 (1973): 196–204; Lewis L. Gould, "Western Range Senators and the Payne–Aldrich Tariff," *Pacific Northwest Quarterly* 64 (1973): 49–56; and Paul Wolman, *Most Favored Nation: The Republican Revisionists and U.S. Tariff Policy, 1897–1912* (Chapel Hill: University of North Carolina Press, 1992), all explore various phases of this crucial piece of economic legislation. L. Ethan Ellis, *Newsprint: Producers, Publishers, Political Pressures Including the Text of Print Paper Pendulum: Group Pressures and the Price of News Print* (New Brunswick, N.J.: Rutgers University Press, 1948, 1960), is enlightening on a key phase of the tariff issue. A thorough study of Republican protectionism is still badly needed.

Closely related to the Payne–Aldrich measure was Canadian reciprocity. The president made his case in *Canadian Reciprocity: Special Message of the President of the United States Transmitted to the Two Houses of Congress, January 26, 1911*, U.S. Senate, 61st Cong., 3rd Sess., Document 787 (Washington, D.C.: Government Printing Office, 1911). The essential source is still L. Ethan Ellis, *Reciprocity 1911: A Study in Canadian–American Relations* (New Haven, Conn.: Yale University Press, 1939). Stephen Scheinberg, "Invitation to Empire: Tariffs and American Economic Expansion in Canada," *Business History Review* 47 (Summer 1973): 218–238, is good on the context of the Taft proposal. Kendrick A. Clements, "Manifest Destiny and Canadian Reciprocity in 1911," *Pacific Historical Review* 42 (February 1973): 32–52, looks at the controversy from both sides of the border. A good discussion of Taft's legislative strategy in pushing for Canadian reciprocity is in Claude E. Barfield, "The Democratic Party in Congress, 1909–1913" (Ph.D. diss., Northwestern University, 1965). Barfield's study is one of the best accounts of Congress in this period. Elizabeth Sanders, *Roots of Reform: Farmers, Workers, and the American State, 1877–1917* (Chicago: University of Chicago Press, 1999), has less to say on the Payne–Aldrich Tariff and Canadian reciprocity than on other legislative issues in her important book.

Taft faced a rebellious Congress in part because of insurgent Republican opposition. Kenneth W. Hechler, *Insurgency: Personalities and Politics of the Taft Era* (New York: Columbia University Press, 1940), is very much out of date. Stanley D. Solvick, "William Howard Taft and Cannonism" *Wisconsin Magazine of History* 48 (Autumn 1964): 48–58, considers the relationship with Speaker Joseph G. Cannon from Taft's point of view. James Holt, *Congressional Insurgents and the Party System* (Cambridge, Mass.: Harvard University Press, 1967), is more critical of these GOP dissidents. John D. Baker, "The Character of the Congressional Revolution of 1910," *Journal of American History* 60 (1973): 679–691, is helpful on the fight to topple Speaker Joseph G. Cannon. Scott William Rager, "Uncle Joe Cannon: The Brakeman of the House of Representatives, 1903–1911," in Roger H. Davidson, Susan Webb Hammond, and Raymond W. Smock, eds., *Masters of the House: Congressional Leaders over Two Centuries* (Boulder, Colo.: Westview Press, 1998), 64–89, is a more recent treatment of Cannon and his fall in 1910. Robert Harrison, *Congress, Progressive Reform, and the New American State* (New York: Cambridge University Press, 2004), is very informative on several phases of Taft's interaction with Congress, including the Payne–Aldrich tariff and the Mann–Elkins act.

The enactment of the Mann–Elkins act is placed in the context of railroad regulation in Gabriel Kolko, *Railroads and Regulation, 1877–1916* (Princeton, N.J.: Princeton University Press, 1965), which argues that the railroads supported regulation, and Albro Martin, *Enterprise Denied: Origins of the Decline of American Railroads, 1893–1917* (New York: Columbia University Press, 1971), which takes the more persuasive view that the railroads opposed the measure.

The Ballinger–Pinchot controversy became one of the key turning points in the Taft presidency. Gifford Pinchot, *Breaking New Ground* (New York: Harcourt, Brace, 1947), offers his perspective on his difficulties with secretary of the interior Ballinger. Although there is an extensive literature on the dispute, James L. Penick Jr., *Progressive Politics and Conservation: The Ballinger–Pinchot Affair* (Chicago: University of Chicago Press, 1968), has become the standard work on the matter. Penick cuts through the polemics to focus on the bureaucratic dispute over resource policy that drove the public battle between Ballinger and Pinchot. Samuel P. Hays, *Conservation and the Gospel of Efficiency: The Progressive Conservation Movement, 1890–1920* (Cambridge, Mass.: Harvard University Press, 1959), is another important source for the background of the Ballinger–Pinchot tension.

Taft enforced the Sherman Antitrust Act with vigor, with the result that both the business community and Theodore Roosevelt criticized his performance. James C. German Jr., "The Taft Administration and the Sherman Antitrust Act," *Mid-America* 54 (July 1972): 172–186, and German, "Taft, Roosevelt, and United States Steel," *Historian* 34 (1972): 598–613, are two excellent articles on this phase of Taft's record. Bruce Bringhurst, *Antitrust and the Oil Monopoly: The Standard Oil Cases, 1890–1911* (Westport, Conn.: Greenwood Press, 1979), examines one of the important cases of the Taft antitrust policy.

As president, Taft devoted much attention to the issue of race. Richard B. Sherman, *The Republican Party and Black Americans from McKinley to Hoover* (Charlottesville: University Press of Virginia, 1973) has good coverage on Taft. Even more detailed and well researched is David Charles Needham, "William Howard Taft, the Negro, and the White South, 1908–1912" (Ph.D. diss., University of Georgia, 1970). The Booker T. Washington Papers, which are available online, have many primary documents about the increasing disillusion among black Americans about the president's policy.

For other domestic issues that Taft confronted, see Clayton Coppin and Jack High, *The Politics of Purity: Harvey Washington Wiley and the Origins of Federal Food Policy* (Ann Arbor: University of Michigan Press, 1999), Kriste Lindenmeyer, *"A Right to Childhood": The U.S. Children's Bureau and Child Welfare, 1912–1946* (Urbana: University of Illinois Press, 1997), and Hans P. Vought, *The Bully Pulpit and the Melting Pot: American Presidents and the Immigrant, 1897–1933* (Macon, Ga.: Mercer University Press, 2004). Richard T. McCulley, *Banks and Politics during the Progressive Era: The Origins of the Federal Reserve System, 1897–1913* (New York: Garland, 1992), and Elmus Wicker, *The Great Debate on Banking Reform: Nelson Aldrich and the Origins of the Fed* (Columbus: Ohio State University Press, 2005), cover banking issues. David Sarasohn, *The Party of Reform: Democrats in the Progressive Era* (Jackson: University Press of Mississippi, 1989), is very good on the opposition party during Taft's presidency.

The Supreme Court and the state of the federal judiciary were topics that engaged Taft's interest more than any other domestic subject. For the Supreme Court, Alexander M. Bickel, "Mr. Taft Rehabilitates the Court," *Yale Law Journal* 79 (November 1969): 1–45, remains a graceful and well-informed examination of Taft's nominees. Also instructive is Daniel S. McHargue, "President Taft's Appointments to the Supreme Court," *Journal of Politics,* 12 (August 1950): 478–510. David M. Tucker, "Justice Horace Harmon Lurton: The Shaping of a National Progressive," *American Journal of Legal History* 13 (July 1969): 223–232, considers one of Taft's appointments. For the appointment of Edward Douglass White to the court, see Walter F. Pratt Jr., *The Supreme Court under Edward Douglass White, 1910–1921* (Columbia: University of South Carolina Press, 1999).

Because of the role of "dollar diplomacy," Taft's foreign policy problems have received much scrutiny. Ralph Eldin Minger, *William Howard Taft and United States Foreign Policy: The Apprenticeship Years, 1900–1908* (Urbana: University of Illinois Press, 1975), is illuminating on the formative period of Taft and foreign policy. Rene R. Escalante, *The Bearer of Pax Americana: The Philippine Career of William H. Taft, 1900–1903* (Quezon City, Philippines: New Day Publishers, 2007), is an interesting assessment of Taft by a Filipino scholar. Walter V. Scholes and Marie V. Scholes, *The Foreign Policies of the Taft Administration* (Columbia: University of Missouri Press, 1970), begins well with a useful introductory chapter. The rest of the book consists of detailed case studies of various foreign policy questions in which President Taft sometimes does not appear for many pages. Robert E.

Hannigan Jr., "Dollars and Diplomacy: United States Foreign Policy, 1909–1913" (Ph.D. diss., Princeton University, 1978), is a superior study of Taft's diplomatic record. David H. Burton, *William Howard Taft: Confident Peacemaker* (Philadelphia, Pa.: Saint Joseph's University Press, 2004), looks at Taft's entire involvement with foreign policy issues across his life. Frank Ninkovich, *The Wilsonian Century: U.S. Foreign Policy since 1900* (Chicago: University of Chicago Press, 1999) has some interesting insights on the differences between Taft and Roosevelt on foreign policy issues. Richard H. Collin, "Symbiosis versus Hegemony: New Directions in the Foreign Relations Historiography of Theodore Roosevelt and William Howard Taft," *Diplomatic History* 19 (Summer 1995): 473–497, has much more to say about Roosevelt than Taft.

General treatments of various aspects of American foreign policy that cover the Taft years include Richard D. Challener, *Admirals, Generals, and American Foreign Policy, 1898–1914* (Princeton, N.J.: Princeton University Press, 1973), Dana G. Munro, *Intervention and Dollar Diplomacy in the Caribbean, 1900–1921* (Princeton, N.J.: Princeton University Press, 1963), Lars Schoultz, *Beneath the United States: A History of U.S. Policy toward Latin America* (Cambridge, Mass.: Harvard University Press, 1998), and Emily S. Rosenberg, *Financial Missionaries to the World: The Politics and Culture of Dollar Diplomacy, 1900–1930* (Durham, N.C.: Duke University Press, 2003).

Philander Knox was a key player in the foreign policy actions of the Taft years. There is no biography. Paige E. Mulhollan, "Philander C. Knox and Dollar Diplomacy" (Ph.D. diss., University of Texas at Austin, 1966), is a sympathetic survey of Knox's performance. Francis M. Huntington Wilson, *Memoirs of an Ex-Diplomat* (Boston, Mass.: B. Humphries, 1945), provides the recollections of Knox's primary associate at State. They make clear why so many people disliked the irascible Wilson.

Many authors have explored what Taft and Knox did toward China and Far Eastern diplomacy in their four years. Meribeth E. Cameron, "American Recognition Policy toward the Republic of China, 1912–1913," *Pacific Historical Review* 2 (June 1933): 214–230, is an early examination of Taft's response to the Chinese Revolution. Charles Vevier, *The United States and China, 1906–1913: A Study of Finance and Diplomacy* (New Brunswick, N.J.: Rutgers University Press, 1955), is highly critical of the workings of American policy. Jerry Israel, *Progressivism and the Open Door: America and China, 1905–1921* (Pittsburgh, Pa.: Pittsburgh University Press, 1971), puts China policy in its domestic political context. Michael H. Hunt, *Frontier Defense and the Open Door: Manchuria in Chinese–American Relations, 1895–1911* (New Haven, Conn.: Yale University Press, 1973), is a well-informed treatment of Taft's policies. Michael H. Hunt, *The Making of a Special Relationship: The United States and China to 1914* (New York: Columbia University Press, 1983), is also very useful. Daniel M. Crane and Thomas A. Breslin, *An Ordinary Relationship: American Opposition to Republican Revolution in China* (Miami: Florida International University Press, 1986), contends that the United States did not in fact have a special relationship with China during the Taft years.

Charles Chia-hwei Chu, "The China Policy of the Taft–Knox Administration, 1909–1913" (Ph.D. diss., University of Chicago, 1956) and James Randolph

Roebuck Jr., "The United States and East Asia, 1909–1913: A Study of the Far Eastern Diplomacy of William Howard Taft" (Ph.D. diss., University of Virginia, 1977), offer more information on Taft's handling of foreign policy in the Far East. Jacob J. Sulzbach Jr., "Charles R. Crane, Woodrow Wilson, and Progressive Reform: 1909–1921" (Ph.D. diss., Texas A&M University, 1994), provides background and insight into one of the diplomatic controversies of the administration.

Edward H. Zabriskie, *American Russian Rivalry in the Far East: A Study of Diplomacy and Power Politics, 1895–1914* (Philadelphia: University of Pennsylvania Press, 1946), examines the international environment in which Knox and Taft had to operate. William Reynolds Braisted, *The United States Navy in the Pacific, 1909–1922* (Austin: University of Texas Press, 1971), is a superb analysis of the strategic setting for the United States during the Taft years.

For the Taft administration and its attitude toward Nicaragua, see David Healy, *Drive to Hegemony: The United States in the Caribbean, 1898–1917* (Madison: University of Wisconsin Press, 1988), Jurgen Buchenau, "Counter-Intervention against Uncle Sam: Mexico's Support for Nicaraguan Nationalism, 1903–1910," *Americas* 50 (October 1993): 207–232, and Richard Salisbury, "Great Britain, the United States and the 1909–1910 Nicaraguan Crisis," *Americas* 53 (January 1997): 379–394.

Henry Lane Wilson, *Diplomatic Episodes in Mexico, Belgium and Chile* (Garden City, N.Y.: Doubleday, Page, 1927), are the memoirs of Taft's controversial ambassador to Mexico. P. Edward Haley, *Revolution and Intervention: The Diplomacy of Taft and Wilson with Mexico, 1910–1917* (Cambridge, Mass.: MIT Press, 1970), is critical of the record of both Henry Lane Wilson and President Taft.

Seward Livermore, "Battleship Diplomacy in South America, 1905–1925," *Journal of Modern History* 16 (March 1944): 31–48, looks at another episode in Taft's diplomatic record with Latin America. Thomas A. Bailey, "The Lodge Corollary to the Monroe Doctrine," *Political Science Quarterly* 48 (June 1933): 220–239, examines the furor over Magdalena Bay in 1912.

International arbitration was a major initiative of the Taft years. John P. Campbell, "Taft, Roosevelt, and the Arbitration Treaties of 1911," *Journal of American History* 53 (September 1966): 279–298, is very critical of Taft's position. E. James Hindman, "The General Arbitration Treaties of William Howard Taft," *Historian* 36 (1973): 52–65, considers Taft's campaign for the treaties. David S. Patterson, *Toward a Warless World: The Travail of the American Peace Movement, 1887–1914* (Bloomington: Indiana University Press, 1976), places Taft's effort in a larger context. Robert Fischer, "Henry Cabot Lodge and the Taft Arbitration Treaties," *South Atlantic Quarterly* 78 (1979): 244–258, looks at one of the president's critics.

On the presidential election of 1912, Norman Wilensky, *Conservatives in a Progressive Era: The Taft Republicans in 1912* (Gainesville: Florida State University Press, 1965), Francis L. Broderick, *Progressivism at Risk: Electing a President in 1912* (New York: Greenwood Press, 1989), James Chace, *1912: Wilson, Roosevelt, Taft and Debs—The Election that Changed the Country* (New York: Simon & Schuster, 2004), and Lewis L. Gould, *Four Hats in the Ring: The 1912 Election and the Birth of Modern American Politics* (Lawrence: University Press of Kansas, 2008).

For the impact of the Taft presidency on state-level politics, Richard M. Abrams, *Conservatism in the Progressive Era: Massachusetts Politics, 1900–1912* (Cambridge, Mass.: Harvard University Press, 1964), is an older study with many insights about state and national politics. Robert S. La Forte, *Leaders of Reform: Progressive Republicans in Kansas, 1900–1916* (Lawrence: University Press of Kansas, 1974), is a well-researched monograph. James Wright, *The Progressive Yankees: Republican Reformers in New Hampshire, 1906–1916* (Hanover, N.H.: University Press of New England, 1987), comments on the effects of Taft's policies in that New England state. Paul Isaac, *Tennessee Republicans in the Era of William McKinley, Theodore Roosevelt, and William Howard Taft: Factions, Leaders, and Patronage* (Lewiston, N.Y.: Eric Mellen Press, 1998), provides a good sense of the impact of Taft's patronage policies in a key southern state.

Biographies of important congressional figures of the Taft presidency shed light on the president's legislative performance. Nathaniel Wright Stephenson, *Nelson W. Aldrich: A Leader in American Politics* (New York: Charles Scribner's Sons, 1930), is the only biography of the key congressional figure during Taft's first two years. Richard Lowitt, *George W. Norris: The Making of a Progressive, 1861–1912* (Syracuse, New York: Syracuse University Press, 1963), profiles one of the leading House critics of Taft's policies. John Braeman, *Albert J. Beveridge, American Nationalist* (Chicago: University of Chicago Press, 1971), is a perceptive study of a leading Republican insurgent. Thomas R. Ross, *Jonathan Prentice Dolliver: A Study in Political Integrity and Independence* (Iowa City: Iowa Historical Society, 1958), considers the leading Midwestern rebel against Aldrich's dominance. Robert La Follette, *La Follette's Autobiography: A Personal Narrative of Political Experiences* (Madison, Wis.: Robert M. La Follette, 1913), provides the anti-Taft critique of a key Republican reformer in Congress. Nancy C. Unger, *Fighting Bob La Follette: The Righteous Reformer* (Chapel Hill: University of North Carolina Press, 2000), places La Follette's conduct in a larger analytic context. William C. Widenor, *Henry Cabot Lodge and the Search for an American Foreign Policy* (Berkeley: University of California Press, 1980), sheds light on Lodge's ambiguous relationship with Taft. Joel Tarr, *A Study in Boss Politics* (Urbana: University of Illinois Press, 1971), is a superior analysis of a political controversy that clouded Taft's relations with Congress. Herbert F. Margulies, *Senator Lenroot of Wisconsin: A Political Biography, 1900–1929* (Columbia: University of Missouri Press, 1977), is very informative on the legislative actions of the Taft years. Philip C. Jessup, *Elihu Root* (2 vols., New York: Dodd, Mead, 1938), has much to say about a Republican insider who was very close to both Roosevelt and Taft.

The civil–military relations of the Taft years emerge in several informative biographies. Elting E. Morison, *Admiral Sims and the Modern American Navy* (Boston, Mass.: Houghton Mifflin, 1942), is a graceful study that has an interesting chapter on Sims during the Taft presidency. Jack McCallum, *Leonard Wood: Rough Rider, Surgeon, Architect of American Imperialism* (New York: New York University Press, 2006), discusses the most controversial soldier of this period. Edward Coffman, *The Regulars: The American Army, 1898–1941* (Cambridge, Mass.: Belknap Press of Harvard University Press, 2004), is useful for understanding the army during the Taft years.

Biographies of those active either for or against Taft's record in office were very important to understanding his presidential career. Allan Nevins, *Henry White: Thirty Years of American Diplomacy* (New York: Harper & Bros., 1930) touches on Taft's dismissal of White from the diplomatic service in 1909. John A. Garraty, *Right-Hand Man: The Life of George W. Perkins* (New York: Harper & Bros., 1960), traces the political career of a critic of Taft's policies toward the trusts. James N. Giglio, *H. M. Daugherty and the Politics of Expediency* (Kent, Ohio: Kent State University Press, 1978), is important for the controversial pardon case of Charles W. Morse. Stacy Cordery, *Alice: Alice Roosevelt Longworth, from White House Princess to Washington Power Broker* (New York: Viking, 2007), has many insights into the evolution of the Taft–Roosevelt relationship from the point of view of a family member who was friendly with the president.

There is a sense in the literature on Taft that little new remains to be said about this president and his administration. In fact, the Taft years offer scholars a rich field for investigation into the issues and personalities of the age of reform.

INDEX